Robin —
What an
adventure we
are going to
share. I can't
wait.
Love,
Tammy
2022

Women of the Way

Embracing the Camino

Women of the Way

Embracing the Camino

Jane V. Blanchard

Women of the Way

For information, address inquiries to

Jane V. Blanchard
PO Box 18364
Sarasota Florida FL 34276

Unless noted otherwise, all artwork and photography was created by the author.

Published in Sarasota, Florida

Email Contact: jane@janevblanchard.com

Web page: WomenoftheWay2011.com

ISBN-13: 978-1475247411
ISBN-10: 1475247419

Third Edition V4.0
Published: January 15, 2018

First Published: June 25, 2012

Dedication

To all the Women of the Way and also, especially, to Dennis, my partner on this journey through life.

Disclaimer

This book describes the author's experiences on the Camino de Santiago, (the Way of Saint James or, simply, the Way), and reflects her opinion relating to those experiences. The women she interviewed told their stories with the understanding that they were to be published. Each story reflects that individual's opinion, which is not necessarily that of the author. No warranties or guarantees are expressed or implied by the author's choice to include any of the stories in this volume. Neither the author nor the individual narrator shall be liable for any physical, psychological, emotional, financial, or commercial damages, including, but not limited to, special, incidental, consequential or other damages.

To My Readers

"We are pilgrims on a journey,
We are travelers on the road;
We are here to help each other
Walk the mile and bear the load." ~ Richard Gillard

The Camino Francés

Why am I writing about the women who travel the Camino de Santiago de Compostela? In 2011, the year I hiked the Camino, more than forty-four percent of the approximately one hundred and eighty thousand pilgrims who walked the Camino were women, each with a different story. As I walked, I talked with women of various cultures and nationalities. It was inspiring to hear what motivated them to undertake this adventure and what they had learned, if anything, from the Camino. The women spoke to me with candor and honesty. We were comfortable with each other and often shared our innermost thoughts and feelings. We laughed and sometimes cried together, bonding in a unique way: each woman becoming part of my Camino. When I returned home, I reflected on the Camino, and I realized how empowering my bonding with these women was. The Camino is unique. It allows people to let down their barriers and speak frankly, and it opens hearts in such a way that people can acknowledge and validate each other. For me, embracing these women was embracing the Camino.

I am hoping that as you read this book, you too can embrace the Camino, whether it be a physical journey or one of the spirit. I invite you to come on this pilgrimage with me, to walk at my side, to meet unique women and listen to their compelling stories. Come and share my experiences, sorrows, and joys. Join my journey and you will not be alone on the road.

About the Book

"A pilgrimage across northern Spain to the sanctuary at Santiago de Compostela [is] the finest journey in Spain." ~ James Michener, *Iberia*

Spain is divided into seventeen "autonomous communities" (states or regional governments), each with a capital. Each autonomous community is comprised of provinces, of which there are fifty. Each province has its own capital city. Often the capital city has the same name as the province. For example, Burgos is the capital of the province Burgos; on the other hand, Pamplona is the capital of Navarra.

The Camino Francés crosses four Spanish autonomous communities

There are many "Caminos" or routes leading to Santiago de Compostela. Some originate in Portugal, some in France or other European countries, while others start in various places within Spain. The Camino Francés (the French Way), the most popular Camino, extends from the Pyrenees to Santiago, wandering through four of the seventeen autonomous communities: Navarra, La Rioja, Castille and León, and Galicia. In *Women of the Way*, the author describes her journey on the Camino Francés.

In the Pyrenees and the eastern part of Navarra, many towns have multiple names, depending on the language. This book indicates the various names in the following order: Spanish/Basque/Catalan. (Basque is the ancient language of the Basque people spoken in northeastern Spain. Catalan is a Romance language and the official regional language of the western Pyrenees.) This information should make it easier for you to locate a town or village on maps and in guidebooks. Perhaps this will help you understand how easy it is to get lost.

Distance and weight are indicated in metric units with a following conversion into miles, pounds, and so on.

Each woman's story in the book is intact, even if the conversations were gathered over time. Many "conversations" include post-Camino experiences and conclusions expressed by the women in follow-up emails and phone calls. All reflect the women's words. The following symbol indicates the end of a conversation:

In Spanish, *camino* can mean route, way, or lane. In this book, "Camino" always refers to the Camino de Santiago. Likewise, the "Way" is an alternate name for the Camino.

Table of Contents

Preparation

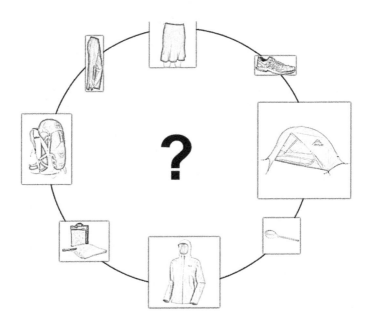

Preparation

"When preparing to travel, lay out all your clothes and all your money. Then take half the clothes and twice the money." ~ Susan Heller

Will I have the stamina to walk day in and out, for weeks on end, in good and bad weather, through high mountain passes and arid lowlands, under a scorching sun? Can my body withstand the pounding? Will boredom be a problem?

I ask myself these questions as I contemplate my first long walk, the Camino de Santiago, a 790 kilometer (500 mile) pilgrimage across northern Spain. I remind myself that countless pilgrims have walked this route, also known as the Way of St. James, for over a millennium. The ancient itinerants faced real dangers: warlords, wolves, thieves, and disease. Today, I tell myself, Spain is a modern, civilized country; the journey will be easier; and I can always find solace in the Spanish wine.

I am not averse to physical challenges. I have climbed Mount Washington, the highest peak in the Northeastern United States at 1,917 meters (6,288 feet) several times and also half of the forty 1220-meter (4,000-foot) mountains in New England. For my thirtieth birthday, I chose to seclude myself in the White Mountains of New Hampshire, climbing five of the tallest peaks. However, that was more than thirty years ago. Could I now, as a sixty-one year old technical writer who spends the day seated at a computer, sustain that level of exertion for such a long distance? Would I have the endurance? Would my body adapt or

3

balk at the sudden change in lifestyle? The only way to find out is to take the first steps.

I do not usually let the universe surprise me. I make plans, set goals, and commit to achieving whatever I set out to do. To assure success on this venture, I start reading, researching, and preparing to become a pilgrim.

The first time I heard of this pilgrimage was in the 1990s, when I read Shirley MacLaine's book *The Camino, A Journey of the Spirit*, in which MacLaine described her adventure and quest for spiritual understanding as she walked for thirty days on the Camino. It amazed me that someone could undertake such a journey and I marveled at her courage. Twenty years later, a friend raved about his Camino de Santiago experiences and this time I felt the calling. This January, when my husband, Dennis asked if I would like to go on an adventure with him, I proposed hiking the Camino to Santiago de Compostela; it would be my first long walk.

As I research, I am surprised to discover that there are many routes known as the Camino, originating all over Europe, Portugal, and Spain. I am interested in the main route, the Camino Francés, which is the one that Shirley MacLaine walked and the one shown in the movie, *The Way*. There are two possible starting places for us on the Camino Francés: St-Jean-Pied-de-Port, France, which requires going over the Pyrenees to Roncesvalles, Spain, or starting in Roncesvalles, as do most Spaniards. If we start in France we can choose to go to Roncesvalles via the Route Napoléon, which goes over the Pyrenees, or via the traditional route used by the medieval pilgrims that goes through the Valcarlos valley. This lower-level route is neither as strenuous nor as isolated as the upper one. We decide to do both routes, descending into St-Jean-Pied-de-Port via the Route Napoléon and then returning to Roncesvalles through the valley. This way, we figure, we will avoid that long, steep climb out of France, see France from the peaks as we descend into St-Jean-Pied-de-Port, and have an easy return to Spain after a strenuous first day.

How long does it take someone to walk that distance? Many younger people walk the Camino Francés in thirty days. I suspect that as a sexagenarian, I will need more time and add ten days. Logistically, I figure six days travel time, including air and ground transport. I add in three "just in case" days for emergencies and another three days upon arrival in Europe for acclimatizing to the time difference. Additionally, after reaching Santiago, many pilgrims hike "to the end of the earth": Cape Finisterre on the Atlantic Coast. This is another four-day hike, eight days round trip. How will I manage to get fifty-two to sixty days off from work to do this? For many companies in the US, asking for this much time off, either for vacation or for religious or personal reasons, is not deemed "sufficiently compelling" to grant a sabbatical.

Wanting to see how other people manage to take the time off, I join several online forums. In one forum, people—mostly Americans—discuss how they plan to get four to six weeks off from work. Some responses are lighthearted: "I lived long enough to accrue the time." Others are more serious, discussing the gravity of potentially losing one's job in these uncertain economic times. One person suggests convincing your boss about the benefits to the company of your going on the Camino: in addition to returning rested and re-energized, the Camino can make you more open-minded, increase your communication skills, and expose you to international cultures. Others propose "paying back" the time off by working holidays or shut downs; "paying it forward" by working overtime and getting compensated for the work in time off instead of money; or walking the Camino in sections, completing it over several years. Someone mentions doing the Camino as a fundraiser and asking the company to donate the time. I am amazed by the number of people who are prepared to quit their jobs to walk the Camino.

The decision to go on the pilgrimage, knowing that I may not have a job when I come back, is difficult to make. I like my work, and not being able to return to it will be a struggle financially. Dennis points out that we are not getting younger and that somehow we will get through it. Our personal history is testimony to the fact that we can overcome challenges; this will not be different.

Eventually, I ask for an eight-week leave of absence from work—four weeks of accumulated vacation time and a month's leave without pay for the months of September and October. My boss is not happy: there is too much work, too many projects, it will be a burden on my coworkers. I understand the rationale, since she is ultimately responsible for the department's output. Before she can approve the request, she must speak with Human Resources and seek guidance/approval from Headquarters. My continued employment is now in their hands; they will let me return to work or they will not.

Pilgrims hike the Camino throughout the year. I do not like the cold, so that easily eliminates choosing to hike during November through April. May and June are warmer, but many people walk the Camino during those months to arrive in Santiago on July 25, St. James' Feast Day, especially during a "holy year," when the 25th falls on a Sunday. During a holy year, pilgrims can receive a plenary indulgence, a full temporal forgiveness of sins for the pilgrim or for the soul of a deceased person. 2010 was the most recent holy year and there was a swell of pilgrims flooding the Camino (more than 272,000 people received a certificate of completion that year). July and August are the hottest and most popular months, when most Europeans take vacations, and the subsequent overcrowding on the roads, in restaurants, and hostels does not appeal to me. That leaves September and October as the optimum time for our Camino; the Way is less crowded then and the temperatures are mild, even though October can be rainy and mornings quite chilly.

After deliberations, we decide to depart on September 2 and return on October 28. I book our tickets with flights arriving in Barcelona and returning from Madrid. This way, I get to see Barcelona, a city I have always wanted to visit, and to show Dennis Madrid, where I lived for a year after college. In my mind, I keep singing "Barcelona" by the rock group Queen and hope that I will not continue to do so until we leave six months from now.

Having decided on the route and the dates, I start training for hiking and backpacking. Even though I routinely walk several miles a day, I am physically unprepared to walk 20 kilometers (12.5 miles) a day as I expect to do on the Camino. To prepare, I walk on the beach, in state parks, on streets and dirt roads—everywhere. On one of my training excursions, I comment to Dennis that I am looking forward to the entire trip, the thrill of discovery, the introspection, the food, the wine, the camping, the heat, the rain. Everything! I am ready to fully embrace the Camino. With a snicker, he promises to remind me of this after a week's walk.

I work out daily with Jillian Michaels *30 Day Shred* in hopes of building strength and endurance for hiking the trail. Even after *ninety* days I am still struggling with the workout. It takes a lot of work to counter the effects of my sedentary life. Having had shin splints in both legs and a torn meniscus in my right knee, I hope that preparatory exercise will prevent mishaps on the trail. Living in Florida offers little opportunity to develop thigh muscles: it is too flat and there are too few stairs. I do squats and thigh exercises until my muscles burn. Slowly, I start to get in shape.

I research hiking clothes and gear. It amazes me how difficult it is for me to decide upon my ideal lightweight clothing and equipment. For each item, I spend hours researching, reading products reviews, deliberating the pros and cons, and then making a decision. Some decisions are simple: a "spork" is a half spoon, half fork utensil and I definitely need one. I choose titanium instead of stainless steel because it is lighter. Others are more complex. Perhaps I am attaching too much significance to each decision, but I want everything to be perfect. I do not want things to go badly on the pilgrimage because I failed to consider something that could prove significant.

For example, I need to decide whether I should hike in pants or in a skirt. There is much debate in the forums about this topic. Some women manage to pull down their pants and urinate without taking off their backpack; others have more difficulty. One woman puts on her poncho for privacy, but that seems like a waste of time and effort. Some wear loose shorts and just pull them aside. There is discussion about female urination funnels, but these devices seem impractical. Wearing a skirt, especially if going "commando" (without underwear), makes it easy to piddle and also provides coolness and prevents chaffing; the ability to urinate without having to remove the pack is another plus. From my research, the area in Spain known as the Meseta is very barren; there are not many trees to hide behind when nature calls. Being able to stand on the side of the road like a guy to urinate without exposing myself is definitely a plus. Cleanliness, practicality, and modesty win and I decide to hike in a skirt.

That decision made, I do research to find the best hiking skirt for me, and at last I order a khaki-colored "Sierra Skirt" from Kuhl. It has front and side pockets and is made with Tufflex, a soft durable stretch fabric that is quick drying, wrinkle resistant, and has a UPF 50 rating. From my research, wearing clothes with a high UPF rating prevents sunburn and enhances protections from harmful UV-related health risks. Clothing with a high UPF rating is better than sunscreen, which needs frequent reapplication.

I am concerned about the effect of repeated washing on the UPF rating, but research eases my worries. Apparently, as long as I don't wash the skirt with soap that contains an optical brightening agent, the UPF ratings should remain unchanged after forty or more washings.[1]

Once the skirt arrives, I realize that the 0.56 meter or 22-inch-long hiking skirt is too short for me, because I feel it comes up too far above my knee. I decide to use it in the evening as "dress up" clothes to visit the town or go out for supper. The second skirt I purchase is a black Royal Robbins "Women's Discovery Skirt" that comes to just above my knees. It too provides a UPF 50+ rating and is quick to dry.

Women of the Way

At the local outfitters, I check out the backpacking gear. I am adamant about selecting the right gear for me. I don't want to spend too much money, yet I want the best I can get. The salesman fits me with the Osprey Talon 33L backpack. It feels comfortable and I like the purple color. In the end, in spite of all the research I have done, the eye appeal is the deciding factor and I purchase it.

After examining and rejecting many sleeping bags, I must decide between two. The Mountain Gear Ultralamina 45 sleeping bag compresses down to about the size of a one-pound coffee can. With the salesman's blessing, I spread the bag out on the floor, and crawl into it. It is a mummy bag, which is narrower at the bottom than at the top, and only zippers halfway. I like to sleep with my feet uncovered and fear that they might get too hot in the bag. More important, I cannot zipper the mummy-style bag with Dennis' bag to create one bag, which would be a bonus when we tent. My other choice is a Eureka dual-temperature-rated bag, depending on which side the bag faces up. I liked its roominess and the zipper extends down both sides, which would allow me to expose my feet or zipper our two bags together, but it takes up more than a third of my backpack. Because I value the compactness and low weight of the mummy bag more than the freedom to air out my legs, I purchase the Mountain Gear bag.

I get increasingly excited with each trip to the outfitters. Shopping for the hike seems to make it more real to me. Each item purchased is one thing less to prepare, and one more reason to smile.

Selecting the correct hiking shoe is very important; a bad fit can cause a lot of pain and possible injury. Anecdotal stories indicate that a long-distance hiker's feet grow and spread, the change often noticeable after only a few hundred miles. Since I have wide feet and since men's shoes are wider than women's shoes, I buy a men's shoe by Gore-Tex with OrthoLite insoles. These shoes are comfortable and light; it should be easy to break them in. I purchase a size larger than normal and three pairs of wool socks—heavy, medium, and lightweight, and plan to switch thicknesses as my feet grow. The first time I wear the shoes on a training walk, I get a hot spot under my sole after only ten miles. I switch to the thicker socks and that resolves the problem.

Other items purchased at the outfitters include a microfiber towel, a titanium spork, several waterproof bags to protect my clothes and my Kindle e-reader, rain gear, and a fleece jacket and pants. My most cherished purchases are a "Rite in the Rain" all-weather travel journal and an all-weather felt pen. I want to be able to chronicle my journey and these will allow me to write when I am moved to do so, no matter the weather.

In my excitement, I stuff my backpack with the hiking paraphernalia to see if I can get all my supplies into it. Though I do not have everything necessary for the trip, I simulate the space with similarly sized, non-hiking gear. Yes! I am able to get everything into the pack, including the Kindle and my laptop, although my packing skills need improvement; there is too much weight on my left. After redistributing the contents to balance the load, I try to figure out a way to attach the sleeping mat and the hiking umbrella on the outside. Without food, water, or medication, the pack weighs 7.8 kilos (17.3 pounds). That is a bit heavy, but acceptable. According to the backpack-weight-to-body-weight guidelines, a healthy woman should carry no more than twenty percent of her body weight. I weigh about 56.7 kilos (125 pounds), so I should be able to carry 11 kilos (25 pounds). Since a bottle of water weighs about 0.5 kilo (1 pound) and my medicine and essential vitamins in the original bottles weigh twice that amount, I figure I should have plenty of leeway for food weight.

In addition to being prepared physically and with the right gear, I want to be culturally prepared. I do not want to be the "Ugly American" or the foolish tourist, easy prey for anyone. For example, I look into the Spanish tipping custom. In Spain, the *propina* (tip) is a reward for extraordinary service and not obligatory. According to Spanish custom:

- It is not required to tip at most restaurants, though leaving the change returned after paying the tab is becoming acceptable. The exception is at formal sit-down restaurants where a one- or two-euro tip is typical. Locals do not tip when eating the "menu of the day," a specially priced menu that includes soup or salad, a main dish, bread (without butter), dessert, and a glass of wine or beer.
- Though taxi drivers do not expect tips for taxi fares, rounding up the fare to the next euro and adding a little something (coins less than a euro) for assistance with luggage is also acceptable.
- In hotels, it is not necessary to tip except in upscale settings. Though it is courteous to tip the bellhop for lugging suitcases to the room, it is not necessary to tip anyone else in the hotel.

The reason for not tipping is that waiters, hoteliers, and taxi drivers earn a decent salary and are not dependent on tips to make a living wage. These workers also get government health benefits and paid vacation time, unlike similar employees in the United States.

In June, we receive the Credencial del Peregrino (Pilgrim Passport) from the Pilgrims on the Camino, a US association dedicated to providing information about and support for the Camino de Santiago. The Credencial del Peregrino is a document issued by the cathedral in Santiago to designate the hiker as a pilgrim, grant access to pilgrim lodging and discounts, and provide a record of the pilgrimage. The Credencial has fifty-six places to collect the stamps that certify our journey along the Camino. Each day, we must get a *sello* (stamp) from the *albergue* (hostel, pronounced al-*burr*-gay), church, town hall, office of tourism, or certain cafés and restaurants in towns along the Way. Since the Pilgrim Passport is made of cardstock, I will protect it in a plastic ziploc bag in my backpack.

Pilgrim Passport Stamps

In the front of the Pilgrim Passport, there is a Pilgrim's Prayer from the Codex Calixtinus (The Book of St. James).

Women of the Way

This twelfth-century manuscript, decorated with gold and silver, was commissioned by Pope Callixtus II and is known as Europe's first travel guide. On July 3, 2011, someone stole the Codex Calixtinus from its security case in the Cathedral de Santiago archives and it has never been recovered.

The Pilgrim's Prayer asks for guidance at the crossroads, strength in weariness, defense in danger, shelter on the path, shade in the heat, light in the dark, and comfort in the discouragement. Walking over five hundred miles will test my intentions and strength. I hope to arrive safely in Santiago de Compostela.

Written to assist pilgrims of the Camino de Santiago, the Codex includes five "books": the history of St. James; miracles attributed to him; the transfer of his body to Santiago de Compostela and how the scallop shell became a symbol of the saint; the history of Charlemagne and Roland; and a guide for the traveler, which describes the route, works of art along the Way, and the customs of the local people. I look forward to seeing these same sights as witnessed by travelers in the twelfth century.

The Credencial del Peregrino also has a page about the Spirit of the Camino. It encourages you to "Share what you have with pilgrims. Live in the moment. Watch for the sign that you are on the path. Welcome all that comes to you. Sense the prayers of those who have gone before you, leave good will behind for those who will come after you, appreciate your companions who walk with you. Care for the *albergue* as if it were your own home. Give thanks at the end of each day. When you arrive in Santiago, embrace the saint on behalf of all those unable to make the pilgrimage." Even as an atheist, I can easily follow the nonreligious aspect of this Spirit of the Camino.

Many of my friends are puzzled why I, a nonbeliever, want to go on a pilgrimage. This long journey for me is not for religious devotion, but for introspection and adventure, providing me with an opportunity to discover languages, customs, and ways of life different from my heritage, as is the case for most people. In 1987, the Council of Europe declared the Way as the first European Cultural Itinerary—one of the great footpaths of Europe, and in 1993, UNESCO designated it a Cultural World Heritage Site.

I am so excited now that there are only two months left before leaving for Barcelona. These few months of planning have been rewarding. Instead of just passing the time, I learn, train, and anticipate. I find myself singing Carly Simon's song "Anticipation," and it reminds me that "these are the good old days." I am happy.

On one forum, I read that many people get the jitters about two months before leaving. One woman expresses her anxiety: "Exactly two months from now I will be standing in St-Jean-Pied-de-Port about to take my first steps towards Santiago. HOLY $#!&. I've been excited for months (in fact years), but now my heart is fluttering fast, my head is spinning, and my feet are cold. For the first time I've thought, 'Can I really do this? Am I crazy? Can my body handle this? Do I have everything I need? Do I have too much? Have I been saving enough money? Will my company be okay without me? Will it be even better without me? Will I be different when I come back? Do I want to be different?' I'm just a bit freaked out." This anxiousness is normal; many people become nervous prior to commencing on a momentous journey or new adventure. So far, I have not had these fears. I think my preparations, my research, my having been to Spain previously, and the fact that I am not going solo, all help build my confidence. Perhaps these self-doubts will come as I get closer to the departure date, but now I simply want to be on my way. I feel like I am at the beginning of a race, waiting for the sound of the start gun, confident that I am trained and ready.

I list the gear I still need for the trip, which merits another visit to the local outfitters. I also list what we need to do before departure. On this list are:

- Arrange ground transport from our home in Sarasota, Florida, to Miami International Airport and back
- Get a tetanus shot (since the Camino goes through farmlands) and discuss with the doctor which supplements are essential and which I can stop for the duration
- Book accommodations in Barcelona and St-Jean-Pied-de-Port
- Arrange for a house sitter
- Prepay utilities and stop the paper
- Check out travelers medical insurance

As I prepare my lists, I ask myself what women did throughout the ages to prepare for their pilgrimage. Most likely, they too made arrangements for maintenance of the home, family, and existing duties. I imagine some, like me, made lists of things to do prior to leaving while others just winged it.

The work I put into planning and arranging for the journey is simplified with the Internet. Medieval pilgrims found most of their information by word of mouth; few could read or write. Many relied on the church for direction and guidance. They walked in groups and hired guides and translators. By the end of the Middle Ages, there was an increase in commercial travel. For those who could afford it, merchants in Venice offered complete tour packages to Jerusalem, which included travel, food, accommodations, and guided tours. Merchants in England offered similar packages for Santiago, which included sailing from various ports to northern Spain.

For centuries, the reasons for venturing to Santiago have been personal and individualistic. I would love to know why women of various centuries set out on this journey. I am sure many of the reasons would reflect the same reasons women are doing so in the twenty-first century, with some being religious and others not. For whatever reason, it takes courage to make that first step, a sense of adventure, and a willingness to test the mettle of one's physical and emotional being. I believe that every woman who is open to the Camino is changed by the venture. I look forward to whatever the journey may bring.

My research reveals that there is little information about women and the Camino, especially about the women themselves. I start thinking about writing a book about the women who, throughout the ages, have endeavored to complete this pilgrimage. Perhaps I could discuss the queens and saints honored along the Way, the evolution of women as pilgrims, or the portrayal of women in the arts along the Camino.

Getting from Sarasota to the Miami airport is a huge hurdle that I leave for Dennis to solve. He checks out buses, planes, and trains without success. It is frustrating that the only bus transport from here to Miami is for cruise ships. To fly from Sarasota to Miami means first flying to

Atlanta. There is no train service between the cities. As a last thought, he checks into renting a car and finds out that it would cost only $80 for the round trip. It is a shame that there is no public transit from Sarasota to Miami, which, after Jacksonville, is the second largest city in Florida.

On July 8, I complete our trip plans. We will fly out of Miami and land in Barcelona. From there, we will take a train to Pamplona and then a bus to Roncesvalles, where we will start to walk. We have reservations at a B&B in Barcelona and at another in St-Jean-Pied-de-Port for the night we climb over the Pyrenees into France. From there, we will officially start the Camino.

I buy an Eagle Creek packable duffel bag to use for the items that we cannot carry on the plane: sleeping mats, umbrellas, sandals, medicine, Swiss Army knife, and Dennis' walking pole. What I like about the tote is that it stuffs into its own small pack-in pocket and weighs merely 223 grams (8 ounces). Without regard to its weight, I blithely plan to stow the bag in my backpack.

After stuffing Dennis' clown-size shoes and everything else into it, the bag is bulging, as are our backpacks, which contain "throw away" clothes for touring in Barcelona. I hope we are able to cram everything from the duffel bag in/on our backpacks when we start hiking.

I prepare and have two hundred *Peregina* (pilgrim) business cards printed, complete with my name, email address, and trail journal URL. This should make it convenient for me to pass on my contact information to people I meet on the Camino.

Camino de Santiago 2011

Jane V. Blanchard

Peregrina

Janevblanchard@yahoo.com

http://www.trailjournals.com/KFun

@JaneVBlanchard

Eight days before the departure date, my boss approves my leave request. I have mixed feelings: I am thankful to know that I have a job (and a paycheck) waiting for me at the end of my journey, but also woeful at having to return to work at all. Two days later, my boss calls me into her office. When I arrive, the head of Human Resources (HR) is there; they both look grim. I have a sick feeling in my stomach. My boss says very little; the HR rep does most of the talking. She tells me that the company is eliminating my position; I am to pack up and leave immediately. She shoves a bunch of forms at me to sign; everything is terse and "professional," almost clinical. I am shocked and don't know what to say— after all, the company had just approved my vacation plans. Once again, I have ambivalent feelings: relief at not having to return to work, but worry about not having insurance, or a job upon my return.

Being terminated saddens me. I enjoy my work, my coworkers and, of course, the compensation. Without a paycheck, I will no longer receive direct deposits into my bank account, so I make alternate arrangements for paying bills while I am away. I resolve not to worry about money and costs on the Camino, but rather to see this turn of events as an opportunity to improve my life and to make changes that will result in increased happiness and fulfillment. The Camino offers time to consider my options and try to figure out what to do in the next phase of my life. That introspection may surprise me; I may discover opportunities that I would never have considered had I not been terminated. Who knows, I may—eventually—thank my boss.

Having made the decision to be positive and focus upon my future eases my sadness at losing my job. I am ready for the change, for the adventure, and for the experience awaiting me.

Finally, it is September 2, departure day. Oddly, I don't feel as excited about leaving as I had the week before. As we complete the hustling of packing and last-minute chores and say goodbye to my parents, the reality sinks in. After eight months of planning, I am off to the Camino, my first long walk.

I set off on this venture with several purposes: the adventure of traveling in the footsteps of so many other pilgrims, finding my path at the crossroads of my life, and meeting pilgrims along the Way. I am particularly curious about the women who undertake this adventure or who live along the Camino and make a living by catering to the pilgrims. I am looking forward to interesting conversations and insights into the lives of these women. I believe that women matter, and that women matters are of utmost interest. For the past nine years I have been an activist for women's rights. For more than two years, I hosted a one-hour weekly radio program, "Women Matters," dedicated to women and issues that affect women. I am curious to see what women of other cultures feel and think, and I look forward to exploring these topics with the women I meet along the Way.

"Here begins the Journey
Now begins the Day.
With one step upon the Road
My soul is on its Way." ~ JS Selfe

Barcelona

Arc de Triomf, Barcelona

Barcelona

"Barcelona – Such a beautiful horizon. Barcelona – Like a jewel in the sun." ~ Freddie Mercury, Queen

At last, it is Friday, September 2—departure day. The signage for the Miami International Airport (MIA) is misleading and we miss a turn and need to backtrack. As we sit in traffic for more than an hour, I grow more anxious by the minute. There is plenty of time to make the flight, but we have to return the car before 5 p.m. to avoid extra fees. I am sweating the delays; I hate paying late charges, especially when it is not my fault. When Dennis pulls into the rental drop-off garage with one minute to spare, I am relieved and thankful for luck and Dennis' good sense of direction.

After a delay, we board the Airbus A340 jet, which is a huge, widebody airplane accommodating 375 passengers. We sit in the tourist section directly below a TV. Although the sound is off, the flashing bright lights make sleep almost impossible. I manage to catnap; Dennis does not.

We land in Barcelona late on Saturday morning. We have no trouble finding our way to baggage claim and from there to customs. I am surprised how easy it is to get into Spain. The amiable passport control agent merely asks us why we are visiting the country and how long we plan to stay. As he stamps our visas, he is the first to wish us a *Buen Camino* (good Camino).

After all those months of planning, it is hard to believe that we are in Spain. Now that we are here, we must learn to navigate in a country with different customs and language. They say that money talks, but first we need the local currency. We find the *Caixa Electronica* (ATM), but it keeps rejecting our card. After a moment of panic, we realize that there is a €500 ($630) daily withdrawal limit. Relieved, we withdraw €200 ($250) and look at the colorful bank notes, so "foreign" to us. Strange, I never thought of researching the European currency prior to leaving. To get change, we buy a soda for Dennis, and then look at the coinage. There are eight euro coins. Unaccustomed to the look, I must read each coin to see the value. The common side of the coin portrays a map of Europe; the obverse differs for each Euroland member country. I notice that the 1, 2, and 5 cent pieces feature the Cathedral of Santiago de Compostela; the 10, 20, and 50 cent coins honor Cervantes; and the euro coins have the face of King Juan Carlos I, the current King of Spain.

After we study the money, we go to the airport tourism office to get maps of the city and directions to the shuttle bus into Barcelona. We have difficulty figuring out how to get the tickets to the city and watch others for a while to see how they do it. We use our credit card, get the tickets, and await the bus. Soon we are heading for the city, gazing out the window at tenement homes, factories, suburbs, and, occasionally, the landscape. As the excitement wears off, I realize how tired I am.

The Aerobus stops at various locations in Barcelona before we disembark a half hour later at Plaça de Catalunya, a large square surrounded by imposing edifices, interesting sculptures, a fountain squirting water high into the air, open-air cafés and restaurants, and pigeons flocking everywhere. We feel like bumpkins in the big city as we take in the vista.

One of the major streets intersecting the square is Passeig de Gràcia. The Nisia B&B where we have reservations is located four blocks down. Exhausted by the flight and lack of sleep, we hardly notice the businesses and storefronts as we trudge to the inn. Once there, Alex, one of the hosts, greets us with a friendly demeanor and in good English. He shows us the B&B, explaining the rules and procedures and tries to engage us in conversation, but we are bone-weary— all we want is to sleep. In short time, we cuddle in bed and nap.

After the nap and with our map in hand, we set out to explore Barcelona. Since the Spanish dinner hour starts around 8 p.m., we plan to have dinner, do some sightseeing and get to bed early, so that we can adjust to the six-hour time difference. To that end, we leave the B&B around 8 p.m. and walk for about an hour. Paseig de Gràcia is one of Barcelona's most important shopping and business areas. We pass stores displaying designer clothes, furs, jewelry, modern or traditional furniture, and linens. Almost every block has at least one bank. There are a plethora of coffee houses and bakeries, their aromas wafting to the street.

Many Spaniards go on a *paseo*, (stroll). As they slowly amble, enjoying the cool evening air, they chat with friends, often arm in arm. This makes it very difficult to walk at a good pace, as is my custom. It does not occur to me that I should learn to shed my rat race mentality and relax a little bit; I am on vacation. Instead, I squeeze past them and hope that Dennis can keep up. We stop at an outdoor restaurant, have a light dinner and an Estrella, the national beer, and watch the crowd.

The dress code in Barcelona is casual. There are plenty of

people clad in jeans and T-shirts while others wear high quality, well-fitting clothes with designer labels. My impression is that these are a proud people, who enjoy looking good in comfortable clothing and shoes.

The Barcelonans have a special love for their dogs. As we sit, we see all sorts of breeds walking with their owners. Most dogs are leashed, while some are not. The dogs are well behaved; there are no territorial fights among them. One retriever waits untethered for its owner by the door of a store. Other small and large canines sit or lie while the owners share a moment with friends in a café or sip coffee while reading the paper. No one minds having the dogs in the open-air restaurants; some proprietors even put out water dishes for the animals. In spite of having all these dogs on the walkways, there is no dog poop; the owners take care of that.

It is strange to be in a non-English speaking city. Although I studied Spanish in college and lived a year in Madrid forty years ago, I am not prepared for in-depth conversations with the locals. Also, there are two official languages in Barcelona: Spanish and Catalan. Catalan is not a Spanish dialect, but an entirely different language. For this reason, I cannot read many signs or posters. Fortunately, the city is very cosmopolitan; menus, placards in museums, and tourist information are written in several languages; the only time we have trouble communicating is when we purchase our first subway ticket.

As we sit in the café, several emergency vehicles speed by. Dennis pales and says, "I don't know what is going on, but there must have been an explosion." After thinking about it, I conclude that he mistook *bomberos,* who are firefighters, for the bomb squad. We laugh at his mistaking the word and wonder what other misinterpretations await us.

On our first full day in Barcelona, Dennis and I walk about seven miles to visit the town and train our legs for trekking. We pass Casa Batlló, a colorful, fairytale-like building juxtaposed between large drab granite structures and decide to skip the tour of this Gaudí masterpiece. As we enter the courtyard to the large old Cathedral de la Ciutat, we see a ring of a hundred and fifty or more people doing a folk dance as a band plays music. Women cannot enter the church with bare shoulders, so vendors sell shawls near the entrance. Instead of going into the church, we tour the nearby Museo de Ciutat, with its ancient Roman ruins of a laundry, fishery, and winery. Later, we enjoy the Museo Picasso, but I am disappointed that it only displays his works from his early and later years; all the really interesting art is scattered in museums around the world. I hope to see more of his art at the Prado in Madrid.

As I see photographs of Picasso's Parisian workshop and read about his early years as a struggling artist, I am reminded of my son, Tom. He, too, is an artist, trying to find his niche in the art world.

That afternoon, we walk along the Ramblas, which are tree-lined esplanades with tourist attractions, sidewalk eateries, and multitudes of pedestrians. The boardwalk, La Rambla de Mar, is a floating gangway to Port Vell, Barcelona's largest leisure area, where we wade in the Mediterranean. I notice that some women are topless and I think it is marvelous; I never understood the conflicting American attitudes towards women's breasts, sexualizing that portion of the female anatomy while publicly expecting that women modestly cover them up, as if showing cleavage were obscene. In 2002, the United States Department of Justice shamelessly spent $8,000 to cover a female statue known as "The Majesty of Justice" because it had an exposed breast. Everywhere in Barcelona there are statues of nude men and bare-breasted women. Unlike in the US, the Spaniards do not relegate nude artwork to museum vaults and niches for fear of offending puritanical sensibilities; they publicly honor the human anatomy. I wish we had more acceptance in the States.

That evening we walk around town and dine at an outdoor restaurant, sharing a *paella marisco*, a seafood rice dish seasoned with saffron. The fare and service are mediocre but the atmosphere is wonderful, especially as Dennis and I share a bottle of *vino tinto* (red wine). The weather today was splendid, 27 to 30° C (81 to 86° F) with sunny skies and a slight breeze off the ocean. As we dine outdoors, I am comfortable, relaxed, and carefree. Barcelona is a great place to start an adventure.

I cannot sleep. Even though I need rest, my mind is active. Is it because of the time shift, the excitement of the adventure, or the late evening meal? At four, I get up to take a Tylenol PM. With that, I manage to get a few hours sleep before awakening at 8:15 the next morning.

Monday is again sunny and pleasant. We walk about nine miles. First, we hoof over to the Renfe train station to get the tickets to Pamplona. The attendant is efficient and helpful as he explains that we will need to board the train in a different station, Barcelona Sants, in the northwest part of the city, and that we can get there via the metro.

From the station, we continue to tour the city on foot. In

the middle of a long promenade, we see the reddish-brown Arc de Triomf. Adorning this triumphal arch is a coat of arms beneath a crown, the official logo of Barcelona. There are also twelve statues of women, representing different aspects of the city. On each side of the promenade are rows of palm trees interspersed with decorative lights. Nothing is small in Barcelona. These lights are as tall as the palm trees, with bases 3 to 4.5 meters (10 to 15 feet) wide. Each base supports a column decorated with four curlicues. Atop of the column is an urn, from which two long decorative poles rise, like the fronds of the palms. At the end of these hang the lights.

We head to the Sagrada Familia by Gaudí. This church is an architectural masterpiece with its spires, three grand facades, and stained-glass windows. Though it will take another thirty years to complete, that which is done is worth seeing. We each rent an audio guide, a device that provides audio commentary for self-guided tours. Throughout the church, there are numbered plaques. All I have to do is punch in the number and listen to the narrative explaining the history, symbolism, and details in the decorations. Sometimes the narrative is accompanied with music or contains dialog. The use of this device greatly enhances my experience and appreciation for the cathedral. On the exterior, my favorite part is the Glory Facade, with its colorful stones and beautiful imagery. I love the interior, with columns that mimic trees and branches. It is hard to believe that one person could imagine and design so grand a structure, with such elaborate details and attention to minutia. We spend hours at this site, trying to absorb all that there is to see. We each have stiff necks from the constant looking up at the cathedral designs and sore feet from standing on the pavement.

Women of the Way

We return to the B&B to take a late afternoon nap. Dennis sleeps, but, once again, I remain awake. I decide that, no matter how much I like it, I have to quit drinking the delicious deep-roasted Spanish coffee. At home I usually drink brewed decaffeinated coffee; in Spain a *descaffeinado* is almost always an unpalatable instant coffee. Though I have not tried it, the *descafeinado de cafetera*, a decaf coffee made in a real Italian-style machine, is said to be tasty.

I wonder if the Spanish decaffeinated coffee has more caffeine than American decaf and that is why I cannot sleep. I find out that, although the US method of calculation differs from the EU way of calculation, it appears that both countries limit the caffeine content to 2 to 4 milligrams of caffeine per cup. For example, a coffee from the same lot decaffeinated in the same vat might be labeled "97.5% Caffeine Removed" in the US, but "99+% Caffeine Free" in the EU. Even though the caffeine levels are relatively the same, I refrain from drinking the brew and end up sleeping peacefully.

That evening we have a light supper at an outdoor café not far from the inn. As we munch on our sandwiches and wash them down with Spanish beer, we enjoy watching the passersby. People watching is a different experience for me, something I never take time to do in the States.

I get about seven hours sleep; my circadian clock is resetting. The next day, our last in Barcelona, we enjoy a lazy morning, and then take the metro out to the Plaza de John Kennedy to hike up the hill about a mile to the base of the funicular, a cog-rail train that takes us to the top of Tibidabo Mountain. From the top, we have a bird's-eye view of the city and Dennis takes a panoramic photo of

Barcelona. There is also an amusement park and the temple of Sagrat Cor at the top. Since we arrive near closing time, we do not visit the church nor take any rides. From here, we walk to Parc Güell, a garden complex designed by Gaudí, and then we stroll back to the B&B to pack and prepare for an early start the next day. To reduce the weight, I combine my medication into two containers; no point in carrying the heavy jars. In my journal, I write, "We have come to the end of our being tourists; tomorrow we become pilgrims."

To make the 9:20 a.m. departure from Barcelona Sants, the train station on the other side of town, we leave the B&B before anyone else is up. Despite confusion in the subway, we arrive at the depot without incident. We board the train not knowing that we have assigned seats and have to change cars, going from the roomier business class to the more crowded tourist class. Four hours later we arrive in Pamplona and then head to the bus station. On our way there, we see pilgrims walking on the Camino de Santiago. Soon, we too will be walking on this pilgrimage.

We find the bus station, which is underground, and buy tickets to Roncesvalles. The bus departs in three hours. With time to spare, we lunch on sandwiches outdoors in the shade of a canopy; the intense sunshine makes us squint, even while wearing sunglasses, so we both keep on our visored hats while we eat. It is siesta time, shops are closed and people are in the eateries. I am impressed with Pamplona, the wide streets, the fountains, the flowers. Does everything seem special because I am on vacation?

At 4 p.m., the overbooked bus pulls out of Pamplona. Even though the bus tickets have assigned seating, people sit where they want; some are in the stairwell, others stand.

Women of the Way

The driver maneuvers the tight turns and narrow country roads, stopping in several villages, and then we arrive in Roncesvalles about an hour and a half later. Roncesvalles is a small Spanish village located about 8 kilometers (5 miles) from the French border. It consists of the abbey, the church, a hotel, two cafés and a tourist office. There are no shops. Since we are too late to make reservations for dinner at the hotel, we eat appetizers and drink beer in the bar.

As we register in the abbey, we have our first opportunity to buy a scallop shell, a symbol of the pilgrim. Pilgrims throughout the Middle Ages identified their destination with a symbol that offered them protection and safe passage—pilgrims to Jerusalem displayed a palm cross; to Rome, a key; to Santiago, a scallop shell. According to legend, James the Greater, apostle and brother of St. John, was martyred in Jerusalem. After his death, his bones were placed in a stone ship, which then transported the body—without crew—to the shores of Galicia, Spain, where a wedding was taking place. As the ship approached, the groom's horse spooked and both the horse and the rider plunged over the cliffs and into the sea. Miraculously, the horse and rider emerged from the water alive, but covered in shells. In addition to this legend, the grooves in the shell, which come together at a single point, represent the various routes traveled to get to Santiago. As a practical matter, the pilgrim could use the shell as an eating implement. When medieval pilgrims asked for food, they were offered as much as they could pick up with one scoop, thus diminishing the burden on the household providing the charity. Nowadays, a yellow scallop shell painted on a blue background is used as a way marker to the cathedral of St. James, as is a yellow arrow.

We hope to camp at the abbey, but the outdoor bathrooms are locked and we must sleep inside the ivy-clad auxiliary building. This is our first *albergue* experience, the first stamp in the Pilgrim Passport, and the first night of interrupted sleep as others in the dormitory cough, snore, or rustle in their sleeping bags. The monk who runs the *albergue* explains the rules: leave the boots and hiking pole at the entrance, be respectful of other pilgrims, do not put the backpack on the bed, and clean up after yourself. He also warns us that the doors lock at curfew; if we are not there in time, we will spend the night outdoors.

In the ladies' room, I am surprised by the European acceptance of one's body. One naked woman brushes her teeth, another sponge bathes, and no one seems to notice or care. I am not particularly shy about my body, just unaccustomed to attending to personal hygiene in front of strangers. In the abbey, the showers have doors; those more modestly inclined can have privacy.

I believe there are two aspects to modesty: how comfortable one is viewing others, and how comfortable one is being seen. Most dormitories on the Camino are non-gendered; the bunk beds are assigned on a first-come basis. People change clothes, sleep in underwear, and are, at times, scantily clad as their clothes dry after laundering. Avoiding seeing someone's body may require blinders. I see someone gawking and realize how uncomfortable he must feel in the presence of this near nudity. I think about alternatives for those who plan to walk the Camino, but are afraid of this sensory overload. They could request a corner bunk and then face the wall, or they could consider private hotels or boarding rooms: the comfort might be worth the extra cost. On the other hand, they could step outside their comfort zone and view this challenge to their sensibilities as a lesson learned on the Camino. By acknowledging the fact that exposure to different ideas and cultures is part of the Camino experience, it might be easier for them to tolerate a lifestyle different from their own.

It is easier for those are who are personally modest to adjust to the unisex dormitories. They can change in the showers or bathrooms, dress comfortably, and not fret about it. If changing from nightwear to hiking clothes is stressful, they can wear the next day's hiking clothes to bed. This can also lighten the load, eliminating the need for night clothing.

At exactly 10 p.m the monk locks the doors and turns the overhead lights off, but leaves a lantern on as a night light. From my position in the cots, this light beams on me. No matter which way I turn, I cannot find relief from the light. Then the snoring starts, and the sonorous sound is amplified in the cavernous room. Between the light and the noise, I get little rest. In a way, I am relieved when the monk turns on the lights at 6 a.m.

Along the Way, pilgrims have several choices of places to sleep. In Roncesvalles, the abbey has two dormitories: the new albergue has a capacity for 183 pilgrims; and the auxiliary (overflow) building can sleep 114. Large dormitories such as this are the exception and may be found in some large cities, Typically, smaller *albergues* and *refugios* (pilgrim shelters) are found in most towns and villages along the Way. For €3 to €10 ($4 to $12), these *albergues* and *refugios* provide the pilgrim with a place to sleep, a shower, a tub for washing clothes, and sometimes a kitchen to prepare meals. They can be simple or elaborate, private, religious, or municipal. Some of these shelters are dormitories with fifty or more bunk beds, while others offer single or double rooms. Some just provide mats on the floor. Most do not provide linens.

Monasteries and convents also provide shelter and are often *donativos*. These are *albergues* where, for a donation or minimum fee, one can get a place to sleep, shower, wash clothes, a communal evening meal preceded by a blessing, and, in the morning, coffee with toast or biscuit and jam for breakfast. This donation is then used to feed the next day's pilgrims. Many are run by trained volunteers who ask the pilgrims to help prepare the meal, set the table, and tidy up after the dinner. Traditionally, these refuges are for pilgrims who cannot afford to walk the Camino if they have to pay for accommodations.

The municipal *albergues* are often large dormitories and often do not have a full kitchen, just a microwave and vending machines. These large *albergues* do not provide as much camaraderie with other pilgrims as do the other *albergues*. In Galicia, the municipal *albergues* do not have doors or curtains on the shower stalls.

Accommodations are usually on a first-come basis and preference is given to pilgrims who walk over those who ride bicycles or come on horseback. All require the Credencial del Peregrino, which they stamp and date with the seal of the *albergue*.

Most shelters have a lights-out time at 10 or 11 p.m., at which time the doors are locked. Some places do not allow the pilgrims to leave before 6 a.m. This is to ensure that the pilgrims get sufficient sleep and to prevent noise by those packing their bags in hopes of leaving at 4 or 5 a.m. This early departure occurs most often in the summer months when there is overcrowding and people believe an early start will guarantee them a bed at their next destination.

Not all pilgrims stay in primitive accommodations. Some stay in *pensiones* (guest rooms), inns, or hotels. *Pensiones* may cost around €24 ($30) per night while inns and hotels may charge €60 ($75) or more. In addition to the monastery dormitories, Roncesvalles has a two-star hotel that is a converted monastery building with stone walls and wood beam ceilings. For those wanting to stay at this sixteen-room hotel, I recommend making reservations.

After washing up the next morning, I check the hiker box. This is a box or location in the *albergue*s where hikers leave items they no longer want for other hikers to use. I am delighted to find a small bottle of body wash. Initially Dennis and I planned to share one bottle, but, after last night, we now realize how inconvenient that is. With a second bottle, we will no longer need to wait for the other to finish before washing up. We use body wash to shower, wash our hair and our clothes. Without much thought to the additional weight, I slip the bottle into the toiletry bag. I would soon appreciate the Spanish proverb, "On a long journey even a straw weighs heavy."

I am not proficient at packing my backpack. It takes several attempts to get everything stuffed into the bag in such a way that it is balanced and comfortable. At last, we are off. Since the hotel does not serve breakfast until much later, we have breakfast in the little café that faces the dormitory where we slept. I start drinking *leche caliente*, (warm milk), instead of coffee. The hot, steamy milk with an added packet of sugar is a delectable accompaniment to the bread and jam. Fortified, we set off over the Pyrenees to St-Jean-Pied-de-Port. Am I ready?

The Pyrenees

Border
Valcarlos "Valley of Charlemagne"
Route Napoléon over Pyrenees

St-Jean-Pied-de-Port

D933

Orisson

FRANCE

Arneguy

Valcarlos

Fontaine de Roland

Col de
Bentarte

Collado Lepoeder

SPAIN

Puerto de Ibañeta

Roncesvalles

Pyrenees

"Every mountain top is within reach if you just keep climbing." ~ Barry Finlay

The Pyrenees are a range of mountains that form the border between France and Spain. According to legend, Pyrene was a virginal princess who was raped by drunken Hercules. She subsequently gave birth to a serpent and ran away to the woods crying. Her sobs attracted wild beasts that then attacked and killed her. When the sobered Hercules found her remains, he mournfully screamed from the mountaintops, "Pyrene!" and the rocky pinnacles echoed back "Pyrene!" Since then, the mountains have retained the wept-over name.

Most Spaniards start the Camino in Roncesvalles, while other nationalities start in St-Jean-Pied-de-Port, France. From France there are two routes: one over the mountain (Route Napoléon) and the other through "The Valley of Charlemagne." Dennis and I decide to see both the Pyrenees and the valley. Since it is a long and steep climb out of France, we decide to climb over the Pyrenees from Roncesvalles, which is already at 900 meters (2952 feet) above sea level, and return through the valley the next day.

Leaving Roncesvalles that morning, we have difficulty finding the trailhead. Our guidebook is unclear about where the trail starts because it is written for pilgrims descending into Roncesvalles, not for those leaving from it. We find a path in the beech woods leading up the mountain, but it does not look well traveled. We ask directions; one pilgrim says he came down that path the previous night. A French pilgrim tells us that the path we are contemplating is the hard way up the mountain and that a much easier access starts behind the abbey. Figuring that "the easier route" is the one through the valley, we proceed to the woods and unceremoniously take our first step on the Camino.

This is our first mistake. Our second mistake is not taking sufficient water and food for that day's ten-hour hike. Our third mistake is not understanding that the towns in this area have different names, depending on the language. The Spanish Roncesvalles is Roncevaux in French and Orreaga in Basque. Since the guidebook names do not match the names on the signposts, we are often unsure of where we are.

Immediately the woodsy path becomes arduous, with a steep ascent. Here and there, it seems as if our noses touch the ground. Dennis estimates that we are climbing at a 35° to 45° angle. He uses his pole to help with the precipitous slope. I find it difficult to maintain a stride with poles and hike without them. Soon I am panting, my chest heaving as I gasp for breath. I place each step with intention, and, at times, use my hands to pull me up the mountain. Under the guise of looking at the view, I stop often to catch my breath. My nonchalant breaks do not fool Dennis; he knows that I cannot continue at the rapid pace I set for myself and encourages me to slow down. At this slower gait, I notice the individual stones, the shape of the leaves, and the clarity of the cerulean sky. The slower I go, the more I notice. I am not thinking of reaching the top or getting to the other side; I am happy doing what I am doing, climbing the Pyrenees on a sunny September day. As I get into my rhythm, the effort diminishes. It is still a difficult climb, but I am no longer gulping air or working as hard. As this transition happens, a peace flows into me. I am actually having fun!

Once above the tree line, we are exposed to the hot September sun. Fortunately a light breeze keeps the perspiration in check. Several hours later, we reach the highest point on the high route, the Collado Lepoeder at 1430 meters (4961 feet). Looking back we can see Roncesvalles below us and realize that there are two ascents from the town: the steep one we have just climbed and a longer one through Puerto de Ibañeta (the Roncevaux Pass), a mountain pass where both the Route Napoléon and the lower route join. According to the signpost, the way we just came is called "*Camino de fuertes pendientes*" (Way of steep slopes). Looking down, we realize that the road behind the abbey would have been an easier climb than the way we came. I am humbled. It is not a matter of misinterpreting the French pilgrim earlier that day, but of second guessing what I thought he meant.

Dennis and I study the signpost, trying to determine which way to go. There are four arms with names that do not match the guidebook. We decide to follow the sign with the scallop shell. Based on the 20.8 kilometers (12.9 miles) distance, we determine that Donibane Garazi must be the Basque name for St-Jean-Pied-de-Port. According to the sign, it is five-and-a-half hours away.

From this high point, the view is breathtaking. The Pyrenees range as far as the horizon and I realize just how immense our planet is, how parochial my life has become, and how much I needed this venture. As I stand upon the mountain with the wind mussing my hair, I do not fret the past or fear the future: I just am.

Women of the Way

Everywhere I look, there is beauty. Peaks poke through the clouds, reminding me of frilly Elizabethan collars. A few mountains are green with forest or pastures; most are bare and rocky. Flocks of sheep and herds of wild horses dot the highland pastures. It is impossible to describe the magnificence and majesty of the Pyrenees.

Apart from signposts at trail crossings and occasional cairns, we see very few markings. Perhaps we miss them because we are hiking the trail in reverse to what is customary. Even without the markings, we do not get lost. Pilgrims walking this path for more than a millennium have etched the Way through the mountains.

It is a hot day; the sun pours down and I consume most of my water. I berate myself for carrying only one bottle, especially since my backpack has a pocket on each side for water containers. I am disappointed when there is no water at the modern stone shelter, Isandorre. I traipse up and down several cols (mountain passes) before arriving parched at the Fontaine de Roland. I guzzle the cold spring water that tastes so fresh, without traces of chemicals or minerals, quenches my thirst, and cools me down.

The pilgrims coming from St-Jean-Pied-de-Port say that there are no other fountains from this point on to France. I see a woman who is walking barefoot. I cannot imagine myself doing that. Sharp cutting rocks, hot asphalt, entangling roots, hay-stubbled fields, animal and human waste are my reasons for not doing so; besides, my feet are too tender. This woman says that she has been walking barefoot for a long time and has developed heavy calluses. She believes that she will have fewer foot problems than those wearing shoes. I wonder if she will be refused admittance to restaurants, stores or churches for not having footwear.

My tank top provides no protection from the cutting backpack straps that have rubbed sores into my upper body. It's too hot to wear a long-sleeve shirt, so I stick a shirt under the straps and across my chest to prevent further abrasion. It looks silly, but is effective. I munch on granola bars, the only food I have, and gulp more water before filling the bottle and continuing the hike.

I know we are on an overall descent, but marvel at how many hills we climb. As I pass the Col de Bentarte, I see a second shelter, Aterbea. This is a low, stony structure built into the mountainside, resembling a sheep shed. I guess it would be inviting to those lost in a storm. On the rocks behind this building is a lammergeier, or bearded vulture. The bearded vulture is Europe's largest and rarest vulture, with a wingspan of up to 2.8 meters (9 feet); we are lucky to see it. I see numerous large birds of prey flying over the mountain: vultures, eagles, and other raptors, but I cannot distinguish one from the other.

Even though there is a cool breeze, I am hot from the exertion. My hair clings to my head, beads of sweat shimmer on my brow. My body is working hard, yet I feel energized, strong, fit. I must be on an endorphin high.

Shortly after this shelter, the mountain path turns into a paved country road. St-Jean-Pied-de-Port is 18 kilometers (11 miles) away. To get there we must descend 1100 meters (3600 feet). Soon we are at the cattle grid (animal barrier) that marks the frontier; I step carefully over the metal grating and into France. Continuing down the road, we walk by the Refuge Auberge Orisson where many hikers end their first day's climb. It does not cross my mind to stop at the inn to ask for water; I am still too new to the pilgrim's ways. From here, the road descends steeply, winding down the mountain and I consider myself lucky to be walking down rather than climbing up to this point. From this height, I see glimpses of our destination below and the road as it zig-zags into the valley.

The last several kilometers are difficult. Not only are we unaccustomed to walking all day with the backpacks, but we have not eaten enough food to fuel us. Our bodies are stalling, or "bonking." Dennis is more affected by this than I am. How could I have put in all the time and effort in planning the trip, and not plan the first and most arduous day? I am an experienced hiker and should have known that climbing the Pyrenees is no walk in the park. In my haste to start the Camino, I was reckless. I should have asked the café where we ate breakfast to make sandwiches for us. What was I thinking! Why wasn't I thinking? I have been too long enamored with the idea of walking the Camino; I must now push aside my infatuation and start being practical.

Then, the Camino provides. We come into a patch of wild blackberries. Many pilgrims have picked over the lower branches, but Dennis uses his walking stick to lower some of the higher branches and we munch on the succulent berries. This unexpected treat helps energize the last hours of our day's walk.

When we arrive at the old town gate to St-Jean-Pied-de-Port, Dennis sits, spent, while I try to locate the *auberge* (French inn). In front of us is a great looming citadel with a large portal. I do not realize that this is the entrance to the city, and proceed to the train station to ask directions. I then walk back to Dennis and we set off, adding what feels like miles to our walk as we enter the Rue de la Citadelle from the back, climbing old granite steps, and walking uphill on a narrow, cobblestone street lined with red sandstone walls. The inn is located in the heart of the medieval old town, just down the street from the Accueil Saint Jacques, which is the pilgrim's office. We are exhausted. At last, we enter the Auberge du Pelerin.

The inn is pristine, with white walls, dark wood beams, and dark tiled floor. A staircase on the right leads to the second floor dormitories. The dining room is bright and overlooks the terrace. As lovely as it sounds, it does not feel homey. The hosts do not greet us and seem too busy to be friendly. Everything is business.

I soothe my aches and wash the road dust from my body in a steamy-hot shower. When I leave the stall, I notice that the shower water flowed into the bathroom. Embarrassed, I check to see what I did to make this mess, but can see no reason for it. I conclude that there must be cracks in the shower tiles that conduct the water into the room. I find a mop and pail in the corner of the room and sponge up my mess. At this time, I do not know that the mop and pail will become ever-present and the swabbing up of spilled water a nightly routine.

We share a room with Trish, a woman from Canada who arrived that day on the train from Paris. Excited about starting her adventure, she wants to chat, but we are too tired. That night we share supper with Trish and other pilgrims from Ireland, Germany, and France. The hostess offers an aperitif, a half shot of sherry. Dennis and I are in a celebratory mood, having crossed the Pyrenees and completed our first day on the Camino. Everyone except

Trish will start their hike in the morning; she will visit the town and await a friend's arrival. Before retiring, I want to check my email, but the French keyboard frustrates me and I go to bed.

The next morning my thigh muscles are screaming and my legs wobble. Trying to get down the stairs to the dining room for breakfast is excruciating. I am hoping that today's "easy" walk will keep the blood flowing and help the thighs recover. I did not drink enough water yesterday to wash out the lactic acid. Today, I promise myself, I will drink more.

Prior to leaving St-Jean-Pied-de-Port, we visit the pilgrim's office to get directions for the lower route. There is information for cycling the lower route, but not much for walking it. Since the Accueil Saint Jacques encourages pilgrims to take the Route Napoleón, they only have a one-page sketch showing the route through the valley. From there, we go to a deli to buy ham-and-cheese sandwiches for a picnic later in the day, then to the local outfitters to buy wool socks for Dennis, because he has forgotten his at home, and then we walk out through the citadel portal and towards the valley route.

We do not get very far. Once outside the gate, there are no markers or signposts indicating the way. We need to ask several people before finding someone who can tell us how to walk to Arnéguy, a small town on the border between France and Spain. Once again, not having a good guidebook or accurate map causes us to walk an extra mile or two.

Camino Waymarkers

We follow the D933, a fast vehicular two-lane road all the way to Arnéguy, missing the path through the beautiful tranquil forest with a bubbling brook. The guidebook explains that there are several footpath options: the Camino, marked with yellow arrows; the French GR 65, one of the European network of long-distance trails, but it does not describe the markings (a blaze consisting of a white stripe over a red stripe); and new blue and yellow posts. How can we go wrong with three different markers? Dennis, having recently hiked the Appalachian Trail in the US, is accustomed to looking for blazes and sees several GR markings, but, without an accurate guidebook, he is unable to interpret their meaning. I do not see any markings, either because I am counting on Dennis to find the path, I am distracted, or because they are not there. Eventually, we would learn to look for a variety of trail markings.

Some, like the yellow arrow, remain constant throughout the Camino; others are specific to a region.

In Arnéguy, I ask a policeman for directions, specifically inquiring about the Camino, which he does not know about. I do not think to ask about the "Chemin de Saint Jacques," the French name for the Camino; perhaps, he would have recognized that name. Eventually we find a trail, but miss a turn and end up climbing about 600 meters (2000 feet) on a switchback road up some mountain peak. Dennis keeps insisting that, according to the sun, we are heading in the right direction. I no longer hear the highway nor see the river; we are too high. The bucolic town across the river with its white houses and tiled rooftops, steepled church, and vibrant green pastures appears smaller with each switchback. At one point, there is a sign in Basque and French stating that the hill is infested with vipers; we walk in the middle of the road. Dennis keeps assuring me that we are heading west and soon will descend into the next town. I am starting to have doubts.

It is getting late and we are out of water. When I hear an old truck whining its way up the mountain, I stop the driver to ask for directions and water. The balding, paunchy Frenchman is wearing a green T-shirt with the saying "Time to make it happen." He tells us that the trail we are following is *très désolé* (very desolate) and that we have to descend about 7 kilometers (4.5 miles) to get back on the Camino. My weariness and disappointment must have touched his heart. He talks with his wife and they agree to turn around and take us to where we missed the turn. We hop into the back of the white Nissan pickup truck and they give us a bottle of cold Perrier. As I swig the delicious water, I can feel my body respond; my temperature lowers and I can speak more clearly with my mouth no longer parched.

At the missed turnoff, we are amazed to see a bare sign the size of a storefront window with a tiny Camino sticker in the upper right-hand corner. The "trail angel" tells us that he used to work on the corner and was constantly whistling to pilgrims to point them in the right direction. Why no one improved the marking is a wonder.

In gratitude, we offer money to pay for the gas and their time, but these two kind Frenchmen refuse to take it. Instead, they ask that we pray for them when we arrive in Santiago. I promise to think of them and their kindness and generosity when I get to the cathedral. Once again, the Camino provides for us.

We cross the border river into Spain and hike uphill to the town we kept seeing from the mountaintop. Valcarlos/Luzaide is a small village with a population of about four hundred inhabitants. We stay at Casa Marcelino, a refurbished historic hotel with modern amenities. Our room has twin beds with a private bath and overlooks the street.

The tub is short, but deep. I fill it with hot water and soak my overworked and painful thighs. Although I cannot extend my legs, the hot water helps alleviate the tightness. Because of the wrong turn, today's gentle walk was more strenuous and steep than I had anticipated, and, once again, without sufficient hydration. My quadriceps are rock hard, my legs wobbly.

I use the handrail to hobble down to the dining room. That

night I feast on hake, a white fish, Dennis has pork tenderloin, and we share a bottle of red wine. After two exhausting days, sleep comes effortlessly.

The next day we leave the hotel at 10 a.m. and have no trouble finding our way out of town; there is only one major street. The trail markings are still inadequate, but we do not get lost. I am spent and my thighs ache from the two previous days' climb; every step uphill is an effort, every step downhill produces a moan as it stresses my thighs.

Determined not to run out of water, we fill our bottles at a natural spring trickling down the mountainside. It is cold and tasty and—I hope—safe to drink.

At Puerto de Ibañeta, the two routes from St-Jean-Pied-de-Port to Roncesvalles merge. There is an upright flagstone slab commemorating Roland's call for help to Charlemagne using an olifant horn, an ivory horn made from an elephant's tusk. I am too tired to find this fascinating, though I vaguely recall reading about it in *The Song of Roland* in college. Instead of checking out the monument, I stretch out on the grass, lean against my backpack, and shut my eyes. Dennis is the history buff; he can tell me all about it later.

From here, it is only 3 kilometers (1.8 miles) to Roncesvalles. I am tired and achy; feeling the toll of the last few days. As we approach the monastery grounds, a large Charolais cow comes clomping down the center of the two-lane road, her cowbell announcing her presence. We let her by—she is bigger than we are. Suddenly she stops, and then looks right, left, and behind. She is apparently lost. She then looks directly at me and moos plaintively, as if to say, "Where am I?" Dennis and I find this hysterically funny—even the cow cannot find her way.

This time the monastery officials allow us to camp and we set up our tent in a field behind the abbey. I make reservations for dinner at the hotel and am lucky to get the first seating. All the walking has given me an appetite, and I can hardly wait until dinner. Finally, the doors to the *comedor* (dining room) open and hundreds of pilgrims scurry to tables. Dinner is served family style, with piles of pasta for the first course and a choice of chicken or fish for the second. We talk about our getting lost with those seated with us at the table. Everyone says that the Camino is better marked in Spain.

Sated, we return to the campsite. It is quiet. This silence is very different from the bustling abbey experience a few nights back. Since we are sheltered from the abbey lights, the starry sky is extraordinarily brilliant, the clarity of the twinkling Milky Way takes my breath away; I am in awe. No wonder the Camino is sometimes called the "Way of the Stars."

I use my headlamp to finish reading about Margery Kempe, a medieval pilgrim. I had started reading her autobiographical account before leaving home in hopes of better understanding the medieval pilgrim's travails. Her mystical antics have been a source of merriment to me, even though it was seriously written.

Just before I fall into a deep sleep, I think about how easy it must have been for pilgrims in Margery Kempe's time to got lost; they had few guidebooks.

Margery Kempe

"Sir, you will one day wish that you had wept as surely as I do." ~ Margery Kempe

Medieval representation of
female pilgrim taken from a wall
decoration near Frómista

One of the earliest English autobiographical writings is that of Margery Kempe, who is known for being the first woman to dictate her biography, *The Book of Margery Kempe*. This book chronicles her life and pilgrimages to various holy sites in Europe and Asia, including her visit to Santiago. In the book, Margery calls herself "the creature" and speaks as if talking about someone else.

Margery, an English woman, was born around 1373. At the age of twenty, she married John Kempe and had fourteen children with him. After the birth of her first child, Margery became depressed and was kept in a storeroom for six months, where she started having mystical conversations with God. Afterward, she was a businesswoman for several years before dedicating herself to the spiritual calling. In 1413, Margery started making pilgrimages within England to visit the holy places or talk with other mystics and spiritually minded persons. She later traveled to Jerusalem, Norway, Assisi, Rome, and Santiago de Compostela.

Margery had to get permission to go on these pilgrimages, first from her husband and then from the bishop. She found protectors and benefactors who helped finance her journeys. At times, she had nothing and relied on the goodness of others to feed and shelter her.

In her writing, Margery does not spend a lot of time discussing the hardships of the pilgrimages. She talks more about the spiritual side, and about the hardships that she endured because of her spirituality. She does mention difficulties of being a woman in a foreign country, with little or no money, and no understanding of the foreign language.

Margery recounts that the Lord commanded her to go on pilgrimages two years before she went to visit Rome, Jerusalem and Santiago. When she asked Him where she would get the money to go to these places, Margery wrote, "Our Lord replied to her, 'I shall send you enough friends in different parts of England to help you. And, daughter, I shall go with you in every country and provide for you. I shall lead you there and bring you back again in safety, and no Englishman shall die in the ship that you are in. I shall keep you from all wicked men's power. And daughter, I say to you that I want you to wear white clothes and no other color, for you shall dress according to my will.'"

In her mystical communications with the Lord, Margery would wail and cry out like a woman in labor, sometimes falling to the ground. She could not look on an image of Christ's passion without endless weeping. She would receive communion "with plentiful tears and violent sobbings, with loud and shrill shriekings." In addition to the snoring and body sounds, pilgrims had to endure Margery's nightly wailings, which sometimes lasted for hours. Some people thought that she was mad or possessed by devils, or feigning the fit for attention. She was an oddity, wearing white (reserved for virgins), because the Lord commanded her to do so, and she was criticized for it. Other pilgrims were disturbed by her actions and constant talk of the Lord. For all these reasons, Margery was expelled from or ostracized by the group, or forced to eat by herself. She saw this alienation from the other pilgrims as a persecution to be endured for the sake of the Lord.

About July 7, 1417 Margery set sail from Bristol, England, for Santiago de Compostela in Galicia. Though Margery talks little of the pilgrimage, she does talk about the preparations for the journey and how she solicited money for the trip. "She was summoned to appear before the Bishop of Worcester, who was staying three miles outside of Bristol. The bishop welcomed her into his home and she stayed there until God sent wind, so that she could sail."

People were wary of sailing with Margery and told her that if "They had any storm, they would throw her into the sea, for they said it would be because of her; and they said the ship was far worse for her being on it."

She beseeched the Lord to save her and, "She sailed forth with her companions, whom God sent fair wind and weather, so that they reached Santiago on the seventh day.

"And then those who were against her when they were in Bristol were now very nice to her. And so they stayed there for fourteen days in that country, and there she had great happiness, both bodily and spiritually, high devotion, and many loud cryings at the memory of our Lord's Passion, with abundant tears of compassion.

"And afterwards they came home again to Bristol in five days."

In all, her pilgrimage to Santiago took twenty-six days.

During the later-Middle Ages, solo women pilgrims were looked upon with disfavor and often mistrust. It was believed that an unsupervised female traveler would end in sin and shame. To allay this mistrust, some women would justify the pilgrimage by seeking the intercession of saints to heal maladies for themselves or others. They had to appear to be passive, or be understood as passive, in order to do something active, and, given the negative assumptions often made about female pilgrims, they had to display both that passivity and that activity to the satisfaction of others.[2]

Those females who went to Jerusalem, Rome, or Santiago out of devotion or to visit places described in the Bible were looked upon with less tolerance than the woman who made the trek in search for a miracle on behalf of her child or other person. At that time, the belief was that a woman should be in her home, not traveling for months or years or taking the money from the household to finance the trip. Because of these perceived social roles, male pilgrims did not welcome women as fellow pilgrims.

In spite of this intolerance, women went on pilgrimages. Enough women traveled to Jerusalem that a separate women's hostel was built around 1050 AD.

Women pilgrims had the same legal status in canon law as did the male pilgrims. They could seek hospitality and protection from religious institutions and religious leaders along the route. Yet, women had to endure the same social patriarchy that existed at home. Unmarried women needed permission to travel from their father, married women needed permission from their husbands, and a widow needed the permission of her parish priest. Since pilgrims were to be celibate during the pilgrimage, women accompanied by their husbands were not looked upon favorably either.

In the mid-1400s some shrines, such as the Sancta Santorum in Rome, were closed to women for fear that they would mark the shrine with their menstruation.[3] Other times, the shrines were closed to protect women from the press of the crowd, because women were believed to be prideful, or because women were meant to be silent and invisible. For whatever reason, women of this time were excluded from many holy places.

Just as Margery Kempe was forced from her group, women

had to fear abandonment if they did not confirm to the modest and invisible nature expected of women at that time. Female pilgrims often traveled together, not so much for propriety as for security.

Nowadays, women do not need to fear walking alone. It is safe. I encountered many solo female hikers and none talked about fear. During the Middle Ages, there were thieves, wolves, epidemic diseases and few pilgrims. For these reasons, it was necessary to band together. Last year, there were 180,000 pilgrims who completed the journey, according to the pilgrim office in Santiago. One is never alone for long along the Way.

I did hear about a non-English speaking woman who had started to walk with a male pilgrim. She enjoyed his company until another pilgrim warned her about her companion. She then ran from him to another group, afraid and looking for protection. She told the group that she was walking with a murderer. Alarmed, members of the group checked into her statement and learned that she had been told to beware of the man because he was a lady-killer, the meaning lost in translation.

Navarra

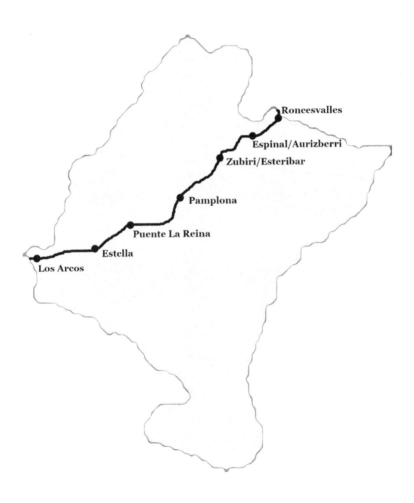

Roncesvalles

Espinal/Aurizberri

Zubiri/Esteribar

Pamplona

Puente La Reina

Estella

Los Arcos

Navarra

"Find a place inside where there's joy, and the joy will burn out the pain." ~ Joseph Campbell

As we leave Roncesvalles, we stop for a photo shoot at the road marking, Santiago de Compostela 790 kilometers (490 miles). We are smiling and eager to travel the road unknown and discover what awaits us on our Camino.

The elevation map we pass indicates that overall we will walk downhill for the next 20 kilometers (12.5 miles). This is a relief after the previous three days. Every time I try to stand, my thighs protest. Someone mentioned drinking more water to help alleviate the pain, another suggested stretching. I know from experience that the ache will last for several days and then dissipate. I figure that today's easy downhill walk will help stretch the muscles and work out the pain. I hope my predictions today are more accurate than those of two days ago.

We walk 7 kilometers (4 miles) to Espinal/Aurizberri, and then another 2 kilometers uphill on the side of a busy roadway to Camping Urrobi. At the top of the hill, we cross the highway and enter a well-manicured campground that features boating, swimming, tennis, racket ball, and promises sightings of deer, wild boars, badgers, and other wildlife. We pitch our tent under beech and oak trees, have a hot shower, and relax. I read while Dennis sets up his ham radio to contact amateur radio operators, hopefully from the United States. After the last three grueling days, my body is ready for this break. My muscles are rigid and tight, just lying on them hurts; my sleeping mat does not seem cushiony enough for comfort.

At 8 o'clock, we stagger over to the restaurant for dinner with rumbling stomachs and thoughts of local cuisine. With all this exercise and fresh air, I can eat a mountain of food and Dennis can probably eat twice as much. We are disappointed to find out that on Sundays they serve dinner earlier and that the restaurant is getting ready to close. The sympathetic bartender agrees to make us ham and cheese sandwiches. In Spain, the *bocadillos* are sandwiches consisting of a meat, omelet, or tuna on a baguette, a hard crusty bread. You can request cheese with it. Customarily, there are no condiments, no lettuce and tomatoes, no butter. Even though this is our third dry-cured, thinly sliced Serrano ham-and-cheese *bocadillo* in three days, we are happy to have food, and wash down the dry sandwich with a draft of cold Spanish beer.

The next morning, we shake the dew off the tent and leave for Espinal via a trail through the beech trees that parallels the high-trafficked road we trekked on the previous day.

My body is adjusting to the daily mileage. My muscular aches and pains are diminishing; I and other pilgrims can now stand up from sitting without groaning or holding onto the table. Unfortunately, many pilgrims are starting to experience blisters and foot problems; luckily, I am not.

The soft soil and the slightly downward grade is infinitely nicer than yesterday's walk. In town, we stop at an outdoor café for breakfast and meet a French couple, Jean-François and Josette Lafarie. We tell them about our lost adventures in France and they assure us that the markings in Spain are well indicated and that we should no longer get lost. This is the second time that we are told that the trail markings are better in Spain and I am relieved; I am tired of getting lost. They leave before us.

Several kilometers later, I am surprised to hear someone calling our names. It is Jean-François and Josette, who missed a turn and had to backtrack. We all share a laugh. As we walk together, Josette and I converse in French about life, sons, politics, differences in culture, and the aches and pains resulting from the first few days of walking. I tell her about losing my job and my fear that I will not be able to find another because of my age. We discuss retirement and how fortunate she was to be able to retire at age sixty, French law having recently changed to age sixty-two. I delight in practicing French, and Josette is most accommodating and patient.

Just before entering Biskarretta, the stony dirt path becomes a level, flagstone one, edged with tall bushes. It is as if we are entering the Land of Oz. We stop in town for a drink and snack and continue to the next town. The trail becomes rockier, but is not difficult. In all, we walk 15 kilometers (9.3 miles) before stopping.

Jane (left) and Josette LaFarie (right)

That evening we stay in an elaborate and modern *albergue* in Zubiri/Esteríbar named El Palo de Avellano, the Hazel Stick. We share a generous dinner of salad, potato soup, pasta, fish or pork, dessert, bread and wine with Josette and Jean-François and another couple from France. We eat family style, serving ourselves from large bowls or platters on the table. Everyone reuses his or her plate, wiping it clean with a morsel of bread between each serving. I had never experienced such acceptance and inclusiveness; everyone is speaking French and giving me time to translate and keep Dennis in the loop. Before sleep, I write, "Everyone is accepting of the other in the moment. It makes no difference what are one's past or future expectations. I feel that, for the first time, I am experiencing the camaraderie of the Camino and what it means to be a pilgrim."

I reflect on the conversations I shared that day with Josette. As we walked, we shared the reasons we were on the Camino and what the Camino meant to us. Hers is a unique, moving, and interesting story, one that matters to me and is now part of my Camino. From memory that evening, I cannot capture in words her feelings and those shared moments; my voice keeps coming through, not hers.

I then realize the direction of my book. As I meet women along the Way, I will record the conversations I have with them. Unlike the books I researched that give very little insight into why women walk the Camino, I want my book to be a testimonial to the women, to their feelings and motives, and to the lessons learned or not learned. I want each woman to share her story, so others can better understand why she undertook such an arduous venture. To remain true to each woman's story, I decide to digitally record the conversations and transcribe them later.

Farther down the trail, I meet Josette again in a café and she agrees to an interview. The recorder batteries are dead; again, I fail to capture her story. What is it with me and gadgets?

The next day I am eager to try out the recorder and test my interview skills. I see women sitting in the shade, taking a break. To date, they are the most senior women I have seen hiking with a full pack. Curious, I stop to speak with them. The two are friends from New Zealand. Virginia is sixty-five and Jill is seventy-two years old. As we talk, I ask permission to interview them; this is my first official interview using the digital voice recorder. I start by asking them how they heard about the Camino.

Virginia Graham and Jill Tucker

Virginia Graham on left; Jill Tucker on right

Virginia: "I once read a book about a woman who walked the Camino barefoot for penance. Later on, a friend at school where I worked went on the Camino. When he returned we talked about it in the staff room. He said that it was a life-changing experience and that I had to do it. Afterward, every time he saw me he said, 'Virginia, when are you doing it?'"

Jill: "Interestingly, I know that man's wife. She finished doing the Camino from Le Puy to St-Jean-Pied-de-Port about 650 kilometers (403 miles) this past July. She had previously done the Camino to Santiago three times. Also, there is a man on my street, which is a very short street I must add, who did the Camino in 2001. 'Oh!' I said, 'I want to do that.' Now, every time he sees me, he asks, 'When are you going?' It took a bit of organization, especially coming from New Zealand.

"It was difficult with the luggage. I knew I had to carry everything for eight weeks. I flew into Paris. Virginia came across from England on the train. We then took the train to Poitier, where we picked up a rental car. The logistics were formidable. I am flying out of Barcelona, as is Virginia, but she is first going on to England to see her daughter and new little granddaughter. I am fluent in French, having lived in France for more than a year studying and traveling; Virginia speaks a little Italian."

Virginia's post-Camino comments:

"One of the issues I wanted to think about on the journey was coping with loss. I needed time to think about my mother, my aunt, and my stepfather who had all died in the previous four years and about how I would deal with the inevitable loss of family and friends as I grow older. So many of my more recent memories of my elderly family are of the demands of their care or of them as they had never wanted to be. I wanted to remember them as well and happy people. Walking the Camino gave me that time, and time for me to count my blessings.

"I was greatly thankful that my body allowed me to accomplish the walk. Daily walking told me I needed to nurture my body; I did and it did not let me down. I may have been weary and sore on many occasions, but there was a growing sense of well-being, of purpose, which I think I have maintained.

"In St-Jean-Pied-de-Port, Jill and I stayed at the Auberge L'Esprit du Chemin, where we were given a small card with a poem by Antonio Machado, which I read often. I find the line 'walking makes the road' to be very empowering:

> Wanderer, it is your tracks which are the road, and nothing else; Wanderer, there is no road, walking makes the road. By walking, the road is made and when glancing back you contemplate the trail which you will trample no more. Wanderer there is no road, only the wakes upon the sea.

"There is much to absorb on the Camino. I have found it helpful since coming home to reread the books I read before starting out and to ask myself: 'Was my experience like the others, what did I miss, and does it matter?' As a keen genealogist for many years, Linda Hogan's quote in John Brierley's book, *A Pilgrim's Guide to the Camino de Santiago,* really spoke to me as well: 'Walking I am listening to a deeper way. Suddenly all my ancestors are behind me. "Be still," they say. "Watch and listen. You are the result of the love of thousands." What a legacy that is.'

"At times, I wanted to connect with others; yet, there was a strong need for solitude. Sorting out the balance between the need to connect and the solitude was sometimes difficult.

"The opulence and splendor of the many churches along the Way did not always move me spiritually as did others, although the skill of the craftsmen was breathtaking and I loved the stained glass windows in the León Cathedral. The sky above and the landscapes around me became my cathedral, my place of worship; the walking was my ritual prayer. Each day the beauty of this earth and the kindness of fellow pilgrims kept challenging me—how can I leave this world a tiny bit better by my actions and interactions?

"Would I do it again? Maybe not the Camino, but who knows? The pilgrimages of St. Oswald and St. Cuthbert in Northumberland, England, are calling me and, while it is not a pilgrim way, the coast-to-coast walk across Britain in 2013 is a definite. Susan from Florida, whom Jill and I met on the Camino, suggested that Jill and I join her for that walk, so the Camino spirit is alive and well in me still."

Jill's post-Camino comments:

"As for the Camino, I found it a wonderful experience, especially as I reflect on it, despite inevitable fatigue. I was sometimes irritated by the commercialization, which is unavoidable. It was often the detours being made by the path that annoyed me, I guess. And why shouldn't poor communities do all they can to profit from the presence of so many pilgrims? Obviously, a good part of the money has clearly been invested in improvement of facilities and previously decaying villages.

"I did enjoy the physical challenge. Step by step, and day by day. One does quickly get into a routine. At the end I thought 'thank goodness, that's over,' but two or three days later I would have been prepared to do it again. We were very lucky to have had no more rain than approximately two hours of fine drizzle on our second to last day, and that must have made a big difference. A good part of the path would have been unpleasant with one's boots heavy with mud.

"We met some lovely people and it was good to have a close friend to walk with and talk to. However, to really get the best out of the experience as a pilgrimage, I feel it would be best to walk alone. Although I am a committed Protestant, I found attendance at Mass, where possible, helped to focus me on the spiritual aspect of the experience."

After we leave Virginia and Jill, we cross many Roman stone bridges and go through several towns with old buildings interspersed with newer ones, with cobblestone or paved streets. Most towns have a fountain with potable water; some have a café or a market. I love the old buildings with the cobalt blue or forest green doors, the flower boxes filled with petunias or geraniums, the brilliant colors contrasting with the golden-ocher fieldstones. The terrain is gentle hills; the weather is warm and dry. Large red squirrels chatter at us.

At one point, we have to cross a washed-out path on the side of a 90-meter (300-foot) precipice. If we slip, we can cause a landslide down the steep hill. By habit, I walk in front of Dennis, but this time he goes first to help me cross the deteriorated section. After getting across, I notice an alternate path that is a lot safer. Leave it to us to do things the hard way!

We are on our way to Pamplona, the first large city that we go through on the Camino. The medieval walled city has a star fort, a fortification style that developed in the mid-fifteenth century to counteract cannonball damage. As the city expanded, it successfully incorporated the medieval ambiance with modern life. Pamplona, the capital of Navarra, is known for the Fiesta de San Fermín, the Running of the Bulls, which Ernest Hemingway made famous in his book, *The Sun Also Rises*. This internationally known Spanish festival attracts more than a million people to the city for the week-long celebration that starts at midnight on July 6. During these festivities, the *albergues* in Pamplona close and accommodation rates triple. Pilgrims who do not have reservations at hotels should not plan to stay in the city during the festival.

As we walk, we befriend Eric and Cheryl. He is a birder and is delighted to be in Spain seeing various bird species for the first time. Cheryl is a minister with the United Church of Canada. When we arrive in Pamplona, Cheryl and Eric stay with us at the Albergue Jesus Maria. We get side-by-side bunk beds. Dennis and I take the upper bunks and then discover that there is an electrical outlet nearby for charging our electronics. This is a piece of luck; otherwise we must find an outlet and sit nearby while the electronics charge, a process that can take several hours.

After an early supper, Dennis and I run across town to Intersport Irabia, a sports retail store. It is late and the store closes at 8 p.m. As we rush, we dodge people and fight traffic. We each buy a hiking shirt. Now I no longer need to place cotton socks, which replaced the shirt, beneath the backpack straps to prevent chaffing.

This compact urbanized city is rated as one of the cities with the highest standard of living in Spain. Concurrent with the high standard of living is a high cost of living; things cost more in Pamplona than in other places.

We return to the *albergue* at a much more leisurely pace. First, we stop at the Hemingway Bar, but the people we planned to meet there have already left, so we return to the *albergue.* It is difficult to sleep. In addition to the nearby cathedral bells, the acoustics in this open three-floor, one hundred-bed *albergue* are all wrong and amplify the snoring. I cannot get the foam earplugs I brought from home to stay in my ears, even with a bandana wrapped around my head. If I do another Camino, I will go to an audiologist to get fitted earplugs.

We leave the *albergue* around 8:20 a.m. The historic part of the city is still quiet. As we pass a *pastelería* (bakery), the aroma of fresh-baked pastries and brewed coffee lures us into the shop. A dark-hair, middle-aged proprietress works the tables, the bar, and the oven. She makes all the irresistible delights herself, getting up at 4 a.m. to do so. Seeing that we are pilgrims, she comments, "We each have our own Camino. This is mine. We all struggle to find our way."

Café Proprietress in Pamplona

After eating our breakfast treats, we follow the marking through a city park to the outskirts of Pamplona. I am glad to be out of the city. I missed the crunching of the stones beneath my footsteps. On the distant hilltops, there are wind turbines that provide electricity. Since it is windy, they are all in full spin. As I get closer to them, I am surprised by how quiet they are. From all the hullabaloo in the papers at home, I had anticipated a loud whirring noise and a steady breeze from the blades. From the distance of a football field, the sound is still almost imperceptible.

We pass a memorial to Frans Koks of Belgium, who died of a heart attack on the Camino. All along the Way, there are markers and memorials dedicated to pilgrims who perished on the pilgrimage. According the Archdiocese of Santiago, ten people, all male, died in 2010: one from drowning, two from being hit by vehicles, and the rest from heart problems. During the remembrance Mass, the archdiocese honored these "eternal pilgrims" who walked straight to heaven. Upon seeing these memorials, I think about how fortunate I would be to die while doing something I liked rather than after a prolonged sickness.

The long, winding climb to the top of Alto de Perdón is not as steep as the Pyrenees, but the terrain is difficult. At the windy summit, I am surprised to see a large cast-iron sculpture of pilgrims on foot and on horseback crossing the mountain on their way to Santiago. Energía Hidroeléctrica de Navarra, S.A., the company that owns all the windmills, commissioned Vicente Galbete to represent the evolution of the Camino in history. He successfully achieves this with the placement of twelve pilgrims. According to Galbete, heading the line of pilgrims is a single character who appears to be sniffing the air, seeking the route, the beginning of interest in the Camino. Then a group of three figures represent the rise in popularity for the Camino. These three are followed by a group of traders and equestrians, which depict the interest in the Camino during the medieval times. Spaced away from these merchants are solitary figures that symbolize the decline of the Camino during the eighteenth century. At the end, two modern figures indicate the renewed interest of today. I am happy to see both male and female characters. In the sculpture, Galbete depicts four of the twelve figures—a third of the group—as female. In more recent times, the statistics on Camino pilgrims show more than forty percent female.

The inscription on the sculpture reads: "Donde se cruza el camino del viento con el de las estrellas," which in English means, "Where the path of the wind crosses that of the stars." True to the inscription, it is very windy at the top of Alto de Perdón.

Alto de Perdón sculpture by Vicente Galbete

Even though the panoramic view is spectacular, I am happy to start down the mountain to get out of the chilly wind. The loose pebble path leads through vineyards and almond groves. It becomes very hot, and I use my umbrella for shade. When we stop at a park about three miles from Puente la Reina where we hope to camp for the evening, I take my shoes off and rest in the shade of a tree. Dennis cracks a few almonds that he picked off the ground.

Someone takes our picture as we walk, moved by our holding hands. In the past week, Dennis and I have had many conversations and shared many laughs. In spite of getting lost, the heat, the aches and pains, we are never short with each other. That is why I am floored when he reveals something about me that irks him: my indecisiveness when he is indecisive. He wants me to make decisions when he does not care or is too tired to do so. I promise to make choices when he does not have a preference. Such a revelation after thirty-seven years! We both laugh.

The amount of the laughter we share on the Camino surprises me. When the pilgrims get together, they joke about their aches and pains, funny occurrences along the Way, or surprising insights they may have had. Some aspects of the Camino are difficult: the heat, the long arduous climbs and steep descents, the blisters, the bedbugs, the snoring, and the getting lost. Yet, I hear very little complaining and a lot of appreciation for the kindness of others. Perhaps the pilgrims put their best foot forward as they walk, and walk, and walk.

We camp in the courtyard of the Albergue Padres Reparadores in Puente la Reina/Gares. This attractive town gets its Spanish name from the Romanesque six-arched bridge over the Río Argo. Doña Mayor, wife of King Sancho III, built the bridge in the eleventh century for the pilgrims on their way to Santiago.

Too tired that night to buy groceries and then cook supper, we eat at a local restaurant. Navarra is famous for its tender lamb, suckling pig, and fresh vegetable preparations. Some local Spanish dishes to sample are trout, cod with garlic, and partridge with chocolate sauce. We order from the pilgrim's menu and await our meal.

For €8 to €12 ($10 to $15), the pilgrim's menu is a reasonably priced three-course meal for pilgrims walking the Camino. It typically includes two entrees, bread and butter, a bottle of water or wine, and dessert. Often, *El Primero* (the first plate) includes a choice of salad, soup, pasta or vegetable. *El Secundo* (the second plate) options are fish, meat or pasta. Dessert is usually fruit, plain yogurt, ice cream, or a local sweet.

We see a young lady sitting by herself in the restaurant eating a vegan meal and drinking cider, a specialty of the region. She declines our invitation to sit with us because she is writing in her journal, but joins us after completing her entries.

Morgan Crowley

"My name is Morgan Crowley. I am writing about the internal and external experiences along the Camino. I am writing an autobiography that is about how my internal experience is impacted by the landscape and whether there is a preferred kind of landscape in the context of pilgrimage experiences. I have been walking for five days and I definitely have had that experience. In Pamplona I was disoriented and confused and I couldn't make any decisions and I didn't know what I was doing. I asked myself, 'What is going on here?' I was trying to stay there an extra day because I was really tired and my hip was bothering me and I just needed to rest. I had come from Toronto and had just immediately started walking. I did not acclimatize at all. I meant to, but at 6:30 a.m. the woman at the *albergue* knocked on the door and I said, 'Okay' and I decided to go, even though I was exhausted. Consequently, I hurt myself on that first day. So, in Pamplona, I stayed in bed until noon. Since I had to mail something, I went out and wandered around really confused and disoriented, trying to decide what to do. Eventually I decided to go to Cizur Minor [4.8 kilometers (about 3 miles) from Pamplona]. It was the best decision, because I now feel considerably better.

"I am not trying to interpret what I liked best about the landscapes until I get back. I am writing into three different journals. My personal diary includes my thoughts, my experiences, and the feelings for the day. On the maps, I make notes about the landscape. In my last journal, I describe the various stages of a place, what it was like, the topography, vegetation, and those types of things. Actually, I am surprised by how much vegetation I can identify. It's similar enough to what we have in Ontario, the species, the genus. I was excited to see almond trees and olive groves and vineyards. Since I grew up in Colorado, I can identify a lot of the leaves. When I walk, I can't help but look at the vegetation. I cannot always identify the species, but I can tell what is an oak, a poplar, or a thistle.

"I definitely prefer the landscapes to the cities, which I found disorientating and chaotic. After I left Pamplona, I realized that the change in pace was so erratic. I had not noticed that I had acclimatized to the walking pace, but when I got into the city I realized how much it had impacted me and I could not really handle being in the city.

"My hypothesis for the thesis is that the natural landscapes are important to the experience of being on the Camino. Anecdotally, that was clear from reading other people's accounts, but no one has ever really spoken about it specifically. My ultimate goal as an environmentalist is to describe how important the natural landscape is to the experience of the Camino, and thus recommend that there be more protections put in place.

"I think the difficulty is that the landscape has always been inhabited. People have been walking this way for almost a thousand years and it has been inhabited for almost all that time. It is inherently a cultural landscape. Using the word 'natural' is problematic. To the average person, this rural area feels like 'nature.' But, what is nature? Is it open space? For example, much of the landscape today is edible. This is evidence enough that it is inhabited.

"I heard about the Camino in the past. It was in the back of my mind that it was something I was interested in doing at some point. I was able to convince the school that I could walk the Camino as part of my thesis. One of my professors who became my adviser suggested that I write a mock proposal. In my program, we have two years of intense course work. Basically, it is a four-year undergraduate landscape architecture program condensed into two. The third year, which I am in now, is for writing the thesis. However, there really is not a lot of time to think about it. In fact, for the first two years, they do not encourage us to do so; they want us to focus on the course work, not the thesis, which will come later. So, when we had to do this mock proposal, I was really thinking about my thesis. I proposed a study on the pilgrimage, the esthetic experience. I had read about how the wilderness can produce momentous, almost religious, spiritual experiences in nature. No one has written about this in regards to the pilgrimage. There have been accounts of the Appalachian Trail in the States or the Bruce Trail in Ontario, long recreational trails that people walk and have these kinds of internal experiences. I believe the experience on the pilgrimage is very similar, but in a cultural landscape versus a wilderness one.

"I feel the landscape of the pilgrimage is inherently supportive, having a community feel. Nature too is supportive, providing food such as blackberries and almonds. Even the landscape provides. It definitely pays to be savvy about wild plants.

"I have received some funding for this pilgrimage. Some is out of my pocket, but I spent all summer applying for various grants and did some fund-raising. I am attending the University of Guelph in Ontario. I did my undergraduate degree in anthropology; this is much more an ethnographic study, even though it is landscape architecture. There is a lot of fluidity in landscape architecture.

"At this point in time, my aspiration is to create intentional communities."

Morgan wrote two post-Camino comments, one about the thesis, and the other about herself.

About the thesis: "Initially I wrote in several journals. This did not remain true for long. I continued annotating the maps from Brierly's guidebook, but only recorded experiences in one journal. I recorded my emotional experience and psychological experience (insofar as I had insight into it) and also the landscapes I passed through each day with the aim of then looking back to determine if certain kinds of landscapes (like trails along the roadside) impacted my experience in reliably specific ways.

"My hypothesis that the natural landscape is important to the experience of the Camino absolutely remained true for me and, based on conversations with other pilgrims, I would say it was true for others as well. Many people, myself included, found walking into the modern edges of cities, or alongside highways and freeways to be unpleasant and not in a 'Oh well I'm a pilgrim, it's not supposed to be easy, this is part of the challenge' sort of way. I found that people were almost more inclined to skip sections like this because these areas did not feel like the Camino at all, but rather places you had to pass through in order to get back to it.

"I'm only just getting into the analysis of all my observations at this point, but one initial point I would make is that having landscapes that are quiet, undeveloped and more conducive to contemplation are supportive of a positive pilgrimage experience."

On a more personal note: "I completed the journey to Santiago in the space of thirty-three days. It had always been my intention though to walk all the way to the sea (of which I am enamored, having grown up in landlocked Ontario and Colorado). The day after arriving in Santiago I set out early once again and made it to Finisterre in another four days. So thirty-seven days walking all in all.

"On the evening of arriving in Santiago, someone whom I had seen many times, but only spoken to once or twice, proposed to me! That was certainly unanticipated. It took probably two hours trying to convince him that it wouldn't work out, but he was drunk and insistent; eventually I had to just slip away. He was really very sweet, but it was a little over the top to arrive in Santiago and experience all of these feelings of accomplishment, while also feeling unfinished, nervous a little about my research, wondering how I'd changed or if I had changed and, on top of it all, trying to deal with a strangely infatuated drunk man! I was pretty flustered then, but in hindsight it's all very hilarious.

"Something I've realized about this journey in contrast to others I've taken in my life is that the Camino was a consecutive series of events and experiences, each one building upon the last. When people have asked me to tell them what my favorite part was or what was most important, I find myself at a loss for where to begin. It seems to me that while many trips we take in our lives have highlights that we can relate like little short stories, telling the Camino would be like trying to relate a novel to someone. Most people don't have the time or patience to listen to that. I am fortunate really to be writing my thesis about it now, because my computer has all the time in the world to receive my ramblings!

"Nevertheless, while it wasn't something that 'happened' to me *per se*, but more like a thought I happened upon, I'd say the most important thing that emerged for me was the sense of freedom I felt in walking. From day one, though I was at times exhausted and cranky, I never lost the center of strength that I felt from knowing that I was doing this with all my own power. There was such freedom in knowing I had no schedule to keep, no train to catch or reservation to hold. I walked at my own pace and ended up where I felt like stopping. It made me realize just how much we can enslave ourselves to schedules in our quest to be more free.

"What are my thoughts on the Camino? There's a question! I could probably cut and paste my entire thesis under this heading.

"I'd say that like meditation, which the Camino could be

said to be a physical form, benefiting spiritually from the experience is made easier in a conducive environment. Perhaps in meditation you create the quiet space you need within your mind and transform it into a conducive environment for personal growth. On the Camino, the moments that were most powerful for me and that really allowed me to feel like I could grow were quiet ones too. This is important, because if you imagine the Camino as a series of places that are getting more and more crowded as more and more people travel this path, then those quiet places, which are the sources of spiritual growth on a long journey, are going to get less quiet over time. I believe that the landscapes on the Camino are threatened by the potential for overuse and insensitive development. Currently, apart from the World Heritage Status and European Cultural Itinerary designations, the landscape itself has no formal protections. This to me is evident in some of the ways the Camino is managed. I could go on and on, but I won't. I would suggest to future pilgrims that stewardship begins with each individual taking responsibility for his or her impact. While the landscapes of the Camino are decidedly cultural and far removed from the wilderness debate, I think pilgrims would be doing themselves and future generations a favor if they approached the Camino with more of a 'leave no trace' attitude. In a world with a population now exceeding seven billion, we need to consider just how much we as a species need quiet places for contemplation and what our individual responsibility is with regard to saving them from our own neglect.

"I would recommend the Camino to a person who seemed like they needed it, but not to just anyone, partly for my reasons stated above and partly because, at its heart, I feel the Camino is a deeply personal journey and commitment that should be arrived at on one's own. For me, my decision to go was a result of a seed that had been germinating in the back of my mind for some time when finally the conditions were right—I could apply for funding —for it to sprout. Had I just gone because someone had recommended it as a beautiful and inexpensive vacation, I don't think I'd have learned as much from the experience. At the risk of veering into the occult, I found the Camino to be populated with mystery and synchronicity—those are the traits that most drew me there and I'd suggest it might be best kept that way for others as well.

"I would summarize the Camino with 'Ultreia et suseia.' The phrase itself is a bit of a mystery, what exactly it signifies is unclear: 'onward and upward.' That works for me because I feel my Camino is yet unfinished. 'Hallelujah' works too, as I often found myself singing or humming Leonard Cohen's rendition of the term, or is it a sort of medieval 'Buen Camino'? I don't really know, nor do I know how to summarize an experience that is ongoing. I suppose I might say it was beautiful, though not all the time, it was spiritual in moments and sometimes it was the hardest thing I've ever done. I think the only way to put it in a nutshell would be to say that I would do it again in a heartbeat, and that is true."

The next day we hike in heat and sun over stony roads. Stopping to rest near the fountain on the town green in Mañeru, I remove my shoes and socks to cool my feet. When I put my shoes back on, my toes are crowded and it takes several minutes for the toes to reposition for comfort. I have been walking the Camino for only a week and my feet are already growing.

We pass vineyards with row after row of deep purple grapes amidst contrasting greenery, a huge stork nest built high on the church bell tower, and ancient hilltop villages. It seems as if all the towns in this area are on hilltops. We start to see olive groves, hay bales stacked four times my height, and *ristras* (strings) of cayenne and red peppers hanging from windows and porch railings.

In the first week, Dennis has lost enough weight that he has to tighten the belt to the belly bag and readjust his backpack. Consequently, I start to carry more food to eat at breaks or as we walk. My favorite treats are Principe cookies, which are delightful chocolate-filled cookie sandwiches. I also carry jars of blackberry or strawberry jam, olives, sardines, cheese, and bread. The extra weight does not bother my back nor slow me down, so I think nothing of it.

We look forward to camping in Estella. When we get to that beautiful medieval town, rich in monuments, we discover that the campground is 2 kilometers (1.5 miles) outside of town. Having already walked 22 kilometers (13.5 miles), we decide to stay at the parochial *albergue* instead of walking to the campground. This is our first *donativo* experience. Many people who stay at these shelters have very little money. Dennis and I "contribute" a fair amount for our room and board. "There's no such thing as a free lunch," as the saying goes.

Hiking the next morning is peaceful. The only noise is the crunching of the clay-chalk soil as we walk, the quiet interrupted by an occasional bird call. My mind is silent. I have no worries, no need or desire to "plug into" the modern world, no concerns. I feel connected to the nature around me, to my body, and to Dennis. I am overwhelmed with an unfamiliar emotion, a feeling of giddiness, contentment, and peace combined. Could this possibly be joy? We walk hand-in-hand, silent, each introspective.

We are both in our quiet place when we first see the Benedictine monastery, Santa María la Real in Irache, which was the first hospital for pilgrims in Spain. The imposing buildings that comprise the monastery include a twelfth-century Romanesque church, two cloisters, a tower, and, most importantly, a winery, called Bodegas Irache. In 1991, the winery built a fountain for pilgrims: one tap for water, the other for wine. We arrive too early for the wine tap, which is turned on about 8 a.m., but I manage to coax a drop out to sample the delicious red wine.

A little way from the monastery, someone calls my name. I do not recognize the man and woman. "Rocky" and "Swamp Fox" are two people from Orlando, Florida, who read my trail journal and recognized me from the pictures posted there. These monikers are Appalachian Trail names for Sandra and Vincent. They have been on the lookout for me—what a compliment. We chat for a while and then depart, each couple walking at their own pace.

Not far from the monastery is a crossroad. The signage indicates that Los Arcos is straight ahead 17.4 kilometers and that the road to the right also goes to Los Arcos, also 17.4 kilometers. I'm glad we have not consumed the wine at the bodega fountain; we would have been doubly confused! We take a guess and go right, hoping that it is the better choice.

The walk that day is beauteous. There are vineyards, peaceful fields, and an inviting cool forest with trees planted in straight rows. The sky is deep blue with wispy cirrus clouds. It is hot, and I sweat as I tread down the dirt path. I am glad to reach Los Arcos, located at the foot of a gypsum hill and on the banks of Odrón river. There are several *albergues* in town and we choose the Casa de Austria, where the hosts speak German. Dennis, at last, has an advantage, knowing the language. I will remember this *albergue* for two reasons. First, it has an old-fashioned clothes wringer for squeezing the water out of our laundered clothes; watching Dennis operate the wringer reminds me of stories my dad has told of his childhood, and I miss my father. Secondly, the *hospitalera* (a volunteer who has walked the Camino and who has taken training to be the host at an *albergue*), upset with the wet shower room floors, gives lessons to those who leave it wet in the proper way to mop the floor after taking a shower; I find her antics very funny. Why not just fix the showers so they don't leak?

That evening we visit the town. As we enter the Plaza de Coso, lightning flashes and it pours like a Florida downfall. We duck into a restaurant, El Museo Del Peregrino, which turns out to be one of the best unexpected treats. Pilgrim memorabilia decorate the walls. There are black iron crosses from various epochs and countries, an assortment of Camino way markers, statuary, pilgrim's garb, gourds, a walking staff, and a wonderful mural of the cathedral in Santiago. The pilgrim's menu is superior to those I have sampled to date. I choose a potato soup for first course and *paella marísco* for the second, and am not disappointed. Sated, we leave under starry skies. What a delightful way to sit out the storm!

Women of the Way

Leaving Los Arcos, the Camino wanders up and down hills with vistas of clouds pouring over the distant mountains and passes an old hermitage that looks like a kiln or a huge beehive. In the midst of a vineyard, the ruins of a stone building contrast strikingly with the green leaves and purple fruity berries. Almond trees are dropping their nuts, and it is fun to pick and crack them open with rocks. We stop for tea at a café in Sansol and are distracted from the tranquil setting by a clanking, motorized din. A Spaniard is using a machine to separate the almonds from the debris; the clamor is the almonds and pebbles banging around in the separator.

Our destination that day is Viana, a small town where Cesare Borgia, a fifteenth-century politician and son of Pope Alexander VI, is buried. While walking towards Viana, I meet Lydie, a French woman who speaks a bit of English and German, but no Spanish. She is walking with Henri, her partner. He speaks English. Henri and Dennis walk together while Lydie and I speak in French. I think it is ironic that for the first week on the Camino I have been speaking more French than Spanish.

Lydie was a secretary who became involved with the city council for twelve years and then was mayor for seven years. She retired at the age of sixty-one to spend more time with Henri, who is older than she is. His rationale is very similar to Dennis': there is only so much time left before our vitality and health diminish. We need to enjoy this period and each other before it is too late.

Lydie teaches me how to descend steep slopes by traversing back and forth across the slope as one does when skiing. This technique makes it a lot easier on the knees and shins, and I immediately feel the difference.

Lydie Sipp

"I am walking for health reasons. I have diabetes and the exercise helps to keep me in balance. Back in France, I did a *cure thermale* (thermal treatment) for diabetes, going for a three-week treatment. The French Camino passes near the clinic where I received the cure and I saw pilgrims walking on it. Three years ago, Henri asked me when we would do the Camino. I said nothing and thought about it for several weeks, and then decided to try it for eight days. After the eight days, I regretted returning to my routine. We then did two more treks, completing 840 kilometers (520 miles). Our goal is to make it to Santiago this year.

"I first heard about the Camino about twenty years ago when I read the book *The Pilgrimage,* by Paulo Coelho. For me it was something unreal, almost like a dream. After that, I heard very little about the Camino. Now, when people ask me what is the Camino, I tell them I cannot tell them about the Camino, they must live the Camino. Everyone who walks the Camino does so in his own fashion and has his own experiences."

Lydie and Henri decide to stop for a picnic lunch and we continue towards Viana, a smaller town with Renaissance and Baroque-style houses. Unlike entering other historic city centers, Viana is festive, with banners, music, and a jubilant atmosphere. The Spaniards are celebrating the wine harvest; it is the Fiesta de San Mateo (the Saint Matthew Festival). As a result, the city is filled with celebrators in colorful costumes, music performances, and young people drinking wine and beer. There is even a largely attended wedding, adding guests to the crowded city.

Because of the fiesta and since one of the *albergues* is closed for three days for fumigation of bedbugs, there is no place to stay. We have to trudge on to the next town, Logroño, 11 kilometers (7 miles) farther. On our way, we cross provinces, leaving Navarra and entering La Rioja, a region known for its wine.

Today's walk seems endless. As we plod on and on, I wonder if it is really the Camino that walks the pilgrim. I ask myself if there is a purpose or a lesson in our having to walk these additional two or three hours. I cannot think of one. I do not have a plan or schedule; I am fit and healthy. I came to the Camino to walk, so I resign myself to doing just that. Maybe that is the lesson.

La Rioja

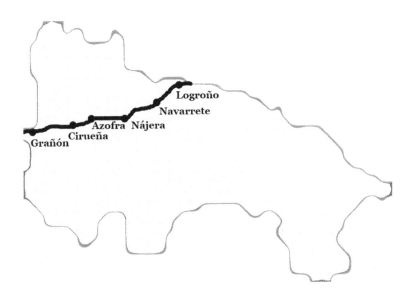

La Rioja

"The greatest gift you can give yourself is joy, not only because of the feeling that goes with it at the moment, but because of the magnificent experience it will draw to you. It will produce wonders in your life" ~ Jack Boland

The traditional scallop shell design changes shape as we cross into La Rioja, the smallest region of mainland Spain. I cannot figure why there are two posts: a taller one with the emblem and a shorter, unadorned one. I like the La Rioja design and think it would make a good tattoo, a permanent remembrance of the Camino.

Everywhere there are vineyards. Clusters of large, almost-black grapes hang behind dark green leaves. The most common grape grown in La Rioja is the *tempranillo*, a grape native to Spain. Throughout the Camino, the local wines I sample are very good wines, but I like the *vino tinto* from Rioja the best. Wine in Spain is considered a food and is not taxed as alcohol. For this reason, a liter of good wine is often cheaper than a liter of Coke. After tasting wine from La Rioja, I can understand the saying, "Las mujeres el vino, todo divino." (Women and wine, completely divine.)

From a distance we see a large black silhouette of a bull. It is about 14 meters (46 feet) tall. El toro de Osborne (the

95

Osbourne bull) was initially an advertisement for a brandy and is now a cultural Spanish symbol.

Logroño is the capital of the La Rioja region. To get into this modern city, the Camino parallels the highway through an industrial area. After being out in open countryside for more than a week, it feels strange to be in a large city with bustling traffic. We are tired as we approach the city, having walked 28 kilometers (17.4 miles).

We arrive at Logroño late in the afternoon. It too is celebrating the Fiesta de San Mateo, but we are fortunate enough to get two mats on the floor at the parish *albergue*, across from the Santiago el Real church, a sixteenth-century edifice. The Camino leads us to the center of the festivities. Getting through the crowd is chaotic, in a Mardi Gras fashion. Thousands of youths are dancing, drinking, kissing, and some falling down drunk. The streets are sticky with spilled drinks, vomit, and urine. There is a police presence, but they do not hassle the partygoers. I can't imagine having such a hassle-free public display of debauchery in the US. Instead of arresting and hauling off the drunks, the police are tolerant. I believe they are there just to ensure safety and to look out for pickpockets and thieves.

That night the *albergue* is overflowing with pilgrims coming in from Viana. Somehow, we squeeze into the dining hall for salad and pasta. As is customary in the parochial *albergues*, the priest announces that the pilgrim's blessing will occur after the meal, adding that those interested can follow him through a secret passage to the church across the·street. The thought of exploring this secret passageway is tantalizing, but exhaustion wins, and Dennis and I go to bed, tired from the long day.

Before bedding, we chat with a roommate. Since he wants to lighten his load, he offers us the Michelin map guide. Until now, we have been using only the guidebook from the Confraternity of St. James, which discusses *albergues*, the towns, and alternate routes along the Way. The Michelin book includes elevation and road maps. With the two guides, we hope to no longer lose our way.

Sleep is impossible. The fiesta continues all night, with the steady thump of loud music, cheering, shouting, even cannon fire. Exhausted, the next morning we decide to take a rest day and head to La Playa, a campground, one kilometer from the city center and on the other side of the river. As we leave the *albergue*, a fire department is hosing down the streets, removing evidence of the fiesta.

In the center of Logroño is a wonderful park with flowers, trees, and fountains. In it we see a strange black and white bird with a long tail. We stop a Spaniard to ask for directions. She is out for a morning walk and changes her course to take us to La Playa. She says she will enjoy the company and doesn't care where she walks—she is out for exercise. I ask her about the curious bird. She tells me it is a magpie, one of the most intelligent birds in the world, being able to recognize itself in a mirror. We walk together, chatting, until we arrive at the campground. She is very pleasant and I thank her for helping us. I had not expected such friendliness and a desire to help in an urban setting. Perhaps the Spirit of the Camino affects more than the pilgrims or perhaps this congeniality is just part of the Spanish culture. Whatever the reason, I am grateful.

After setting up our tent, we both nap; we are exhausted from yesterday's long walk and lack of sleep. That afternoon the fiesta restarts. Even though we are more than a kilometer away, we can still hear the music and occasional shouting. The distance muffles the noise and I get a good night's sleep.

That evening I write, "Dennis and I feel close. Now that I am 'retired' and have lots of time to share with him, I feel that our friendship and love are deepening and changing. I am looking forward to this new stage, but I am a bit trepidatious about the end of life. As Lydie said yesterday, we have to take every opportunity to enjoy our life together."

Along with this acceptance comes peace. Even though I had mentally adjusted to losing my job, I had not, until tonight, acknowledged it emotionally. I am no longer restricted by a workday, by my job description, or by someone else's standard. I can still be productive, but on my terms.

Getting to Santiago is a slow process; it takes time to walk from one town to the next. So, too, is my journey to the next phase of my life. Like on the Camino, I do not want to rush it; I want to take my time and enjoy the progression. But, unlike the Camino, I do not have waymarkers indicating the direction or, as in the early stages of the Camino, I have not yet learned to recognize the markers. At least now I know to look for them.

It is cold and windy in the morning and I wear my fleece pants and jacket. We cross the Rio Ebro on a modern pedestrian suspension bridge. The river meanders through the north side of the city, separating the La Playa part of town where we camped from the center of the city. I admire the Spanish culture's high regard for pedestrians and for keeping nature accessible to the city dwellers.

People are out jogging, walking their dogs, and enjoying the glorious early morning sun.

Before starting back on the Camino, we run errands to the post office, to the pharmacy to buy antibiotics for the blisters I have developed, and then to a café. I am glad I brought hiking sandals instead of shower thongs to the Camino; today I can walk comfortably in the open shoes without fear of damaging my feet.

We follow the Camino arrows through the modern part of the city and then through another park in the western part of town. The day is warming up and I stop to remove my warm clothes. As Grace walks by, she hears us speaking English and stops to chat.

Grace Cameron

Jane on left, Grace on right

"I was afraid of getting bedbugs, so before I left, I sprayed my sleeping bag and knapsack with the chemical that the US Army uses, Permethrin. The spray is good for forty-two days.

"I am originally from Prince Edward Island (PEI), Canada, and I currently live in Halifax, Nova Scotia, after moving there recently from Ottawa. I work for the federal government and have been doing so for about twenty-six years. I work for Health Canada, in finance, as regional director; I have worked in finance for about fifteen years. I am very much looking forward to retirement in about five or six years.

"I have family, all in the Maritimes: two sisters and a niece who live in Halifax, and the rest of the family lives on PEI. One of the reasons I wanted to move back from Ottawa is that, as I get older, I am finding that family is becoming more important. My mom and dad are in exceptionally good health, but they are both eighty-four years old. It is just nice to come back and spend time with family.

"I have not yet entirely figured out why I am doing the Camino. I turned fifty this year; that might be the primary reason, but, I think, there is more than that, even though I haven't yet had any grand epiphanies. But, there are still four weeks left. Patience, the Camino is teaching me patience for many different things and I think that is important, too.

"I am absolutely learning the importance of language as I hear the pilgrims speak in different languages. I did buy a Berlitz DVD before I left, but I never really had time to listen to it or to study it. I would really like to study more

French to get that up to scratch again. Spanish and German seem to be two popular languages on the Camino. I studied German at the university and loved it. It was relatively easy to learn and I think that it would be fun to study again. Since I only remember '*Bitte*' and how to count to five, I have not spoken German on the Camino; university was many, many years ago.

"I find that there are many cognate words in Spanish. The other day I went into the *farmacia*. The pharmacist did not speak English, but understood what I needed. She said a bunch of words and then '*antiinflamatorios*.' I think that there are enough similar words and, if the Spaniards know even only a few words in English, I can order food and get around.

"While on the Camino, I have enjoyed meeting a lot of people from both Canada and around the world. The thing I appreciate the most is the personal challenge. Even though I did not hike over the Pyrenees, just going from Roncesvalles to Biskarreta that very first day, only ten kilometers, but man, oh, man, that was ten kilometers like I have never done in my life. Just the fact that I was able to do it amazed me. Then, climbing up to Alto de Perdón at 770 meters (over 2500 feet) was challenging. I thought, 'Holy frig, I did it.' I cheered, 'Eureka, I am here!'

"Never in my life have I done something like this. When I was in Ottawa, I was with a search and rescue group, but I was the treasurer. I did the financing. I was repeatedly asked to take the basic course, but going out and slogging through the bush looking for somebody was not my bag. I never did take the course. I think if I were still in Ottawa, I could go back now and take that course. If I can do the Camino, I can do anything.

101

"I am hiking with my friend who is currently taking the bus to Navarrete because of foot problems. We had started talking about hiking the Camino when I still lived in Ottawa. To prepare for the Camino, I worked out with a personal trainer and walked to work. Once I moved to Halifax, I did some hikes of fifteen or twenty kilometers, but always pretty much on the level. In PEI, we can't train for the hills because we don't have the kinds of hills we have here on the Camino. I suppose I could have gone to Cape Breton to hike the hills, but one can't just pick up and go there in twenty minutes. Working full time also made it hard to go for a four-hour hike. Admittedly, I did not train enough.

"For this reason, this first week has definitely been a training week. We started slowly, doing only 10 kilometers the first day, fifteen and then twenty. Today I will hike twenty-two-and-a-half kilometers and I feel I can do that comfortably. Since my friend has foot problems, I am looking at the possibility that she may not be able to continue. I am definitely going to continue, even if it is by myself because this is something I have to finish.

"My friend and I attended a few sessions at the St. Nicholas Adult High School in Ottawa. There was a gentleman there who has done the Camino twice and who has written a planning guide that is great. One session was about the Camino, how safe it was and the topography; the other was about preparation, the pack and what it should include, and the training. We used his information and checklist as part of our preparation. I have to admit that I depended a lot on my friend, who followed the forum and looked up Web sites. When she told me something, I would think it a good idea and do it. Without her, I am sure there are things I would not have done, like spraying for the bedbugs, but I would have survived.

"I would have to say that doing the Camino alone has certain advantages. I am very much a loner anyway and I am finding it challenging to keep my mouth shut. Walking alone today has been a break, and probably what we needed.

"The Camino always provides. When I moved from Ottawa, I sold my condo at a profit. I put some away for investments and kept the rest for fun, including this adventure, and a couple of new sticks of furniture for my home. I was very fortunate, as I have been for most of my life.

"I have had no problems with safety and I have not at all felt threatened. I have to admit, stripping down to one's skivvies in front of perfect strangers is an interesting concept. European people seem a lot less shy about this than North Americans are. We stayed at a youth hostel the other night. When it was time for bed, a guy from the Netherlands who was very tall, perhaps six-foot-six, stripped down to his underpants and I thought, 'Okay, I have to get used to this.'"

Grace's post-Camino comments:

"It took me thirty-four days to complete the Camino, starting on the 12th of September and reaching Santiago on the 15th of October. I did cheat a little bit (it did feel like cheating!!) when I took a bus into Burgos and again into León, but I had to make up a little bit of time in order to go to Finisterre that last week. Took the bus there too, but I figured I actually walked six hundred kilometers. I ended up not finishing the walk with the person I had started with. Too much negativity and dark aura and I just didn't feel that I was getting as much out of the experience as I could. When we reached Rabanal del Camino (Day 22), I went ahead to Foncebadón and then carried on alone from there. Alone, yet not alone. There were people that I met after parting ways with my friend and people I had met before; I walked with one or more of them for a day, or two, or more and walked some by myself too. It was nice just to be responsible for myself and no one else. If I had to do this again (and at this point I wouldn't, although I may feel differently when I am sixty), I would go alone and then I alone would be responsible for my level of enjoyment. I also felt more physically challenged when I was on my own as I could go the distance I felt was comfortable. The main thing is I DID IT!!

"I think one does need a better reason than 'I just turned fifty' to do the Camino. Surrounded by all this beauty, nature, and spirituality, it seems a lame reason. I found myself thinking (often) 'What the *&^%$ am I doing here? I don't need to do this, I chose to do it, but why in God's name?' The main thing is I DID IT!

"By the way, the bug spray that the Army uses didn't work! Got bitten on three different occasions, really bitten, but I'm ninety-nine percent sure I didn't bring any bedbugs home. That would be the gift that keeps on giving!

"If I were going to tell anyone about the Camino, I would put more emphasis on the physical challenge of it and show them some pictures of the really high hills and the tough goat paths. I'd tell them about getting the absolute right boots and wearing wool socks and changing them halfway through the day. It worked for me; I didn't get any blisters at all and had zero trouble with my feet. Knees? Well, I had to get elastic wraps for the knees, but they are fine now. I lost ten pounds and am in better shape now than when I started. Therefore, all and all, it was a good idea to do the Camino. And maybe it's like they say about having a baby (not that I'd know), but the pain of it all does seem to be fading as the weeks pass!! Hmmm, will I do it again???"

After leaving Grace, I wonder if I would have the courage to start off on the Camino on my own. After graduating from college, I naively set off alone to live in Spain with only $100, determined to find a job, live on the economy, and practice Spanish. I found a job the day after arriving and lived in Madrid for almost a year. After returning home, I met Dennis and we eloped eight months later. But, after nearly forty years of sharing our lives, being supportive of each other, and growing comfortable with the status quo, would I have the courage to set out solo on such an adventure? Dennis did so when he walked the Appalachian Trail, but would I? Am I still that spontaneous, independent person I was so many years ago? If Dennis died, would I have the courage and self-reliance to try something this adventuresome alone at this stage of my life? I can only hope that the answer is yes.

We make our way to the medieval village of Navarrete, 11 kilometers (6.8 miles) from Logroño. We pass a golf course with its greens that seems incongruous to the dry, parched surroundings. We see the stone ruins of a twelfth-century pilgrims' hospital and *albergue*, Hospital de San Juan de Arce, which was founded by María Teresa

Ramírez. In medieval times, *hospitals* were hostels for travelers as well as clinics, surgeries and homes for the blind, lame, elderly, and mentally ill. All that remains of Hospital de San Juan de Arce is a slab and about eighty percent of the stone foundation.

The Camino runs along the main street of Navarrete, where many houses have coats of arms on their doors. Since the *albergue* where we plan to stay the night has a kitchen, Dennis and I shop for groceries, first buying a bottle of *vino tinto* and cookies at a *supermercado*. We chuckle because this is unlike any supermarket we know. This *supermercado* is a small room with shelves on the sides, no aisles. From there, we go to a vegetable store to purchase salad ingredients and potatoes, and to the meat store for *chorizo* (sausage). I pick up a few tomatoes from the counter and get reprimanded by the woman minding the vegetables. Unlike in American stores, I learn, I must first tell the grocer what I want and then she selects it for me to approve. Perhaps this prevents bruising as people handle the veggies.

This is the first time that we cook a meal in an *albergue*. We share the salad and keep the potatoes and sausage for a picnic lunch.

At the table with us are two Canadians—Diane and Sylvain, and two French women—Chantal and Michelle. Michelle tells us that this is her second time on the Camino. The first time she did the Camino through France, and now she is completing the journey to Santiago. One night on that first journey, a woman found out that her father died. That evening, she and fellow pilgrims went to the parish church and asked the priest for a prayer for her dead father's soul. When the priest announced that the Mass was dedicated to her father, she started to cry. Her Camino friends surrounded her with love and compassion. I am moved by the story and become teary-eyed. After that, we are more jovial and share many laughs.

Though we all communicate in French, I can distinguish between the French women's intonations and Diane's Canadian accent. Having Canadian roots (my father was born in Canada) helps me understand the vocabulary and expressions unique to Quebec. I feel at home with Diane, perhaps because I am more familiar with her informal phraseology, perhaps because of her honest and engaging sincerity.

Diane Rodrigue

"My name is Diane Rodrigue and I am from Quebec. I am walking with Sylvain [Cyr] from Montreal and with a Korean woman named Rosa, who is having problems with cellulitis in her legs. That is an infection and inflammation of the tissues beneath the skin. On a doctor's advice, she will have to stop walking for several days. She is very tired from having walked over thirty kilometers today. I like how everyone is sharing their food with her. This is a good moment for me because it shows the sharing along the Way, the solidarity of the pilgrims, it's great. On the Camino, I have seen many humane moments like this.

"Why am I doing the Camino? Last October (2010), I wondered what to do for my fiftieth birthday in 2011, something special and just for me. I met a friend who did the Camino and I decided to train [for it]. Those who have done the Camino have a nice star in their eyes; their eyes shine when they talk about the Camino. I was curious and I wanted to get that star.

"Many people told me I had courage to make such a long journey on foot. I answered, 'It is not courage, the real courage was telling my family about my decision to walk the Camino.' I had no problem with my spouse and my children, but it took courage to tell my father, mother, brother, and sister. It was very difficult because I knew how they would respond. My father asked 'Why in Europe? You can walk in Quebec.' My mother said not a word, my brother does not understand, and my sister still wonders why I left.

"And I answered, 'Just for me, a gift for my fiftieth birthday, a break from family and job, and that's it. I want to cross the Atlantic once in my life and meet people.'

"I started alone on August 10 in Puy-en-Velay and am going to Finisterre and will return home on October 25."

I saw Diane and Sylvain again in Santiago at the Mundoalbergue. She summed up her journey:

"What a wonderful trip! I can tell you that I have that star in my eyes. I can define myself as Diane, the pilgrim. I loved the sharing, the exchanging, the way time stopped. Wow! I looked at my life and did considerable self-reflection. And when I got to the ocean [Finisterre], the road stopped. It was over. But as I watched the ocean, I found that the path continues with ME."

Back in the dormitory, Dennis tends to the blisters on my feet because they are difficult for me to reach. When Michelle sees what Dennis is doing, she gives me packages of ointment to help heal the blisters. She also mentions using Compeed blister patches that are available at the pharmacy to relieve pain and pressure. My blisters are small, so I stick with using just the antibiotic cream. Though I have seen this caring spirit and generosity among the pilgrims, it is the first time that someone extends it me. I am appreciative and humbled by her simple acts of kindness. Earlier that day I had spoken with a woman who was doing her second Camino, the first being seven years back. She had said that she found this Camino more touristic, more about the money than the spirit of the trail. With all the love and acceptance that I see among the pilgrims, it is difficult for me to imagine a more "spiritual" way. I guess it boils down to one's point of view, and proving that each person has his or her own Camino and that each Camino is different. People who do multiple Caminos should not expect the same revelations and sentiments as from previous journeys, but should be open to new insights and feelings that only living in the moment can provide. Comparing this moment with past ones may prevent someone from enjoying the present, as it did for this woman. Had she lived in the moment, she may have found this Camino more joyful and more meaningful.

In the morning it is 11° C (51.8° F) and I dress warmly. We walk over undulating hills of patchwork acreage, vineyards, wheat fields, and bare earth. Our shadows are getting longer, indicating that autumn is near. We stop for breakfast and to warm up in Ventosa, a village with one hundred and seventy inhabitants.

I have a new pain in the front of my legs and the downhill walk to Nájera aggravates the condition. In town, the pharmacist recommends ibuprofen cream and pills for the apparent tendinitis (shin splint). I guess my body was not prepared for the last week's constant pounding, especially as I recklessly added food and toiletries to the backpack. In hopes of relieving the stress on my legs, Dennis takes about 2 kilos (4.4 pounds)— the toiletries, medicine, and food.

We arrive at the *albergue* around 1 p.m. Stopping early gives us time to upload pictures, write in the online trail journal, and call home. I try to call home via Skype each day. My parents are in their mid-eighties and keeping in touch is important. Mom's voice quivers as we say goodbye.

Before dinner, I have an interesting conversation with Ná Áak. I first saw her in Zubiri eight days ago in the presence of two Irish women who said that Ná Áak was responsible for their being on the Camino. I was attracted to her because she projects a very palpable sense of calmness and peace. I thought, "What an interesting person, I hope to get a chance to speak with her." Since she is staying in the *albergue* with us, I get that opportunity.

Ná Áak **Paola Ambrosi**

"My father's family comes from Italy, some of my mother's family comes from Spain, and I was born in Mexico City. I can speak Spanish, Italian and English. I met the Irish women in Ireland where I work as a healer. They were in the healing apprenticeship and meditation programs that I run. We have been working for peace since the beginning of the year and decided to walk for peace. We searched for a starting date that would be energetically convenient and we chose the eleventh of September.

"This year, in the spiritual work that I do, I have put a lot of attention to working with peace, teaching others how to find a place of inner peace within themselves and to become the living archetype of peace and, thus, have a better society. In other words, rather than looking for peace on the outside, looking for peace on the inside and letting that peace manifest naturally and organically into our society. That has been the focus of the work that I have been doing this year, particularly with the way things are going worldwide.

"With that, I have always had it in mind to do the pilgrimage. I could not think of a better living expression of peace than doing a pilgrimage. By using our own stories, our own footsteps, struggles and experiences, and by praying for peace and becoming the experience of peace as we are walking, and then using that as our intention.

"I have experienced peace within myself. I am not looking for peace. I believe peace is an experience within. I understand that it comes and goes in waves. The pilgrimage is an analogy for life. Sometimes it gets really tough and I am in a lot of pain. Those moments of pain are times when the internal peace shakes, and anger comes up and when frustration, tiredness, the demons, and the mother of demons come to sit inside. These are moments when the peace gets lost. These are also the moments when the gift comes or the learning comes because you have to find again a place of tranquility and calmness, in spite of the tough experience you are going through. That is the challenge I see about life. I don't think that to live in peace means to live without pain or trouble or frustration. I think to live in peace is that, even though the circumstances are tough, one is able to keep a still mind and embrace the circumstances in the best possible way.

"In the bigger picture, I hope that if there are enough people who can find that place of peace within themselves, they can become the leaders that will promote that peace. I don't know how this can manifest itself in the outside world. It is not that I don't have hope for humanity, but it makes me very sad to see what we have created. I am not sure that we will be able to pull together the strength in order to break through the vicious cycle of violence that we live in and that we have created. But I feel that even if we cannot and if, for whatever strange reason, let's say, humanity ends up destroying itself, I believe it is still worth the effort to find and hold that place of peace. I believe that when we die consciousness remains.

"So whatever experiences we are able to give to the consciousness will remain in our consciousness, and we will be able to give birth to a new era, somewhere else, in a different world, a different dimension, or wherever it is, that we will have that information and a way of living without violence.

"The objective is not necessarily simply to live or to die. For me, it is to be able to choose what experience I want my consciousness to live in. I think that is enough.

"My work is hands-on healing, but I don't believe that is where healing is. I believe that the healing is in helping people to find themselves, and in helping people to connect with the willingness to choose and embrace their own life and their own individuality in order to break free from any of the behaviors or patterns that are making them unhappy or that are making them suffer. They can then create the circumstances in their lives that bring them peace or love or compassion or whatever it is that they are seeking. Although I have learned from indigenous healers and shamans and I have done that work, it is not what I do for the most part. For example, if someone comes to me and says, 'Can you just fix this on me?' I would normally refuse because it would be no different from the person going to the drug store and getting an aspirin. The healing would have the same effect as an aspirin. The permanent effect comes when the person is willing to find himself. Then I am willing to work with that person to help him find himself.

"I have always had that sense of self, that awareness. I project it onto different things. I was born into a middle-class family, and baptized Catholic. I was not born in an indigenous community and I did not have access to that when I was young, but I did have access to religion. I remember from very early on, perhaps three or four years old, that I was very spiritual and prayed a lot. I was always involved in missionary work with the church, and I had considered signing on to be a nun, but for strange circumstances I did not do it. When I was a teenager, I started to have access to indigenous wisdom and to the communities from my own country. As I looked into it, it made so much sense. Very quickly it became clear to me that religion was a narrow container for spirituality and that my experience of 'God' had so far been limited by the confines of my religion. It did not fit in the dogma that I had learned. Indigenous wisdom gave me a lot of the answers that I was seeking. I studied medicine because I thought it was important to understand the Western brain and the logical rational mind. I then studied transpersonal psychology and other forms of healing. I became really, really interested in the mystical traditions of the different religions that I had studied, particularly Tibetan Buddhism and other forms of mysticism. After all of that, I believe that there is one consciousness behind it all. We can give it whatever name or shape, it is all the same.

"I am not inclined towards any particular way of practicing

spirituality. I do believe in faith, in love and compassion. I feel at the core that we can become compassionate by truly understanding our nature and who we are. To me, this understanding is the path to freedom from suffering because we learn patience with ourselves, we stop blaming and feeling guilty. Once we are able to free ourselves from those states of consciousness, we leave room for states of consciousness like love and peace.

"In Ireland, I work most of the time in seeing people one-on-one on a donation or barter basis, so everyone has access to healing. Most of the people I see have suffered trauma. More than half of the women who come to see me have suffered sexual or psychological abuse. The next large group of people who comes to see me are those diagnosed as mentally ill: depressed, bipolar, suicidal. It is demanding work, but I am drawn to those on the edge of society and to seeing who lives at the edge because this is where people are forgotten. It seems that whoever does not fit into little, tidy Western boxes are put into prisons or psychiatric hospitals. As an analogy, these people on the edge are the rubbish of Western society. Governments and health care services don't care about these people. In the way that the world has been going, I have found that those populations are increasing exponentially in the last years. This 'disease' of society is increasing because society has reached a point of disharmony. I like to work with these people because they are very sensitive to everything. I feel that as the water of society boils and the temperature rises, the people who are sensitive are the weakest links. Their minds cannot cope and explode into what people call psychosis. I feel that they are simply exploding because there is too much pressure in society. There is no balance and this is not healthy. When I speak with them and hear about the hell they are experiencing, what I am really hearing is what society has created. I find it vital to give them a voice, and let them tell us 'Stop. Just stop. What are you doing?'"

My lower legs ache all night. I debate having my bag taxied ahead. All along the Way, there are transfer services available; for a nominal fee, I can send the heavy backpack ahead and then carry just what I need for the day. The trouble with using the porter service is that I still have to make it to the bag; misjudging the ability to walk the distance can leave me without my belongings. I decide to trudge on with my pack. I am thankful that Dennis does not mind slowing down, even though it is my fault for previously pushing too hard. I must realize that I am not Superwoman. I need to take care of my body and not exert it to extremes. I was too aggressive with the pace and the weight. Now I am paying the price.

We walk over the bridge leaving town; the riverbed is dry, another indication that this area is in a drought. In Nájera, I start seeing public bathrooms without toilet seats. I am not talking about a squat toilet, a porcelain pan on the floor with places for feet; I am talking about bowl toilets. I never find a definitive reason for this bizarre custom, though someone mentions that the Spanish law requires that the toilet seats be clean. To avoid a possible fine, café and restaurant owners remove the seat. Apparently, according to the law, only the seat needs to be clean, not the rim or the bowl.

To date I have encountered only one squat toilet on the Camino, but I have squatted in the outdoors. When nature calls, I leave my backpack near the trail and take toilet paper with me. A pack on the side of the road indicates that someone is attending to nature and in need of privacy; most hikers just walk by without a glance. I try to find a tree or bush to conceal me, as have many other pilgrims before me, which means taking care not to walk in someone else's mess. If I am lucky, I can bury the results. When the dry and sun-baked ground is impenetrable, I use rocks to cover the "landmine." All along the Camino, there is human waste; to expect otherwise is unrealistic since there is no place else to go. But courteous hikers should carry away the toilet paper or at least use biodegradable paper, which decomposes quickly.

After Nájera, the terrain changes to rolling hills with red dirt. The next town, Azofra, is 5.8 kilometers (3.3 miles). Halfway there, I can no longer walk, the pain in my shins is excruciating. Dennis takes my pack, carrying it over his own. With the two packs, he is carrying over 20 kilos (46 pounds). He does not complain about the load and is more concerned with my being able to make it to the next town. Using his walking stick, I wince and hobble down a relatively flat, paved path into the municipal *albergue* in Azofra. It is too early in the morning to register, but they allow me to sit in the courtyard and cool my legs in the ice cold natural spring pool. We are out of money and Dennis walks to Alesano, a nearby town that is not on the Camino to get to an ATM.

We could not have stopped at a better *albergue*. This one has semiprivate rooms, a large kitchen, washing machines (€3 or $3.75 per load), the spring pool, Wi-Fi, and a foot masseuse. Everyone tells me I have to stop walking for two days minimum. The *albergue* permits me to stay until the doctor says I can continue walking and tells me the *médico* (doctor) will be in town in three days.

I have A-type personality tendencies. I am competitive, and achievement oriented. I walk quickly with a sense of urgency. For me, time is precious and should not be wasted. For these reasons, stopping to heal is difficult. At first, I am guilt-ridden; it is my fault that we have to hole up in Azofra for three days; because of me, we may not have time to walk to the Atlantic or, perhaps, complete the pilgrimage. Dennis is easy-going and counters my reasoning with a kinder logic. This is a beautiful *albergue* and a great place to rest and heal. We have plenty of time to reach Santiago. We can take the bus to Cape Finisterre, it really isn't the end of the world if we ride there instead of walking there. He makes me realize that this hiatus in walking is happening for a purpose: I need to learn to slow down, the goal is self-imposed and may not be realistic, life is too short to fret about such inconsequential matters. At the end of these "lessons" I unconsciously hear, "Because I am getting older." Am I really looking at my mortality? What is going on here? In my mind, I am still in my twenties. Because I am fit and relatively healthy, I do not feel sixty-one (whatever that is suppose to feel like); nor do I think that someone in their sixties is old. As I look around, I see pilgrims younger than I limping and dealing with injuries, others older than I who are doing just fine, and conclude that the problem is not about age, but about pushing to the limits. I just have to learn what my new set of limits are, given my age, health, and physical abilities. Realizing this eases my anxiety: the clock is not winding down for me just yet.

That afternoon while I soak my legs in the pool, a pilgrim who runs marathons and knows about shin splints suggests that I get a foot massage to help the tendinitis. She has just had a massage from Manuel, the *hospitalero*, and recommends him. He is a trained masseuse who offers his services for a donation. I ask her what would be a reasonable donation and she tells me she gave him what she would have paid in the states for a similar treatment, about €30 ($40.00).

Manuel wears a free-flowing, colorful tunic over a kurta, cotton pants gathered at the ankle, and has a Sikha, a lock of braided hair on the back of his shaven head. He reminds me of Gandhi. In Switzerland, he had been a dentist before learning message therapy from a Chinese practitioner about twenty-five years ago. In summertime, he works in this *albergue* and in the winter, he works at one in Portugal. People like him for his caring and gentle demeanor, and so do I.

He takes me into a semidark room. I lay on a mat on the floor and he covers me with a woolen tartan blanket. He lights incense and massages my feet. As he uses a thin, carved wooden implement that resembles a thick chopstick to prod various pressure points on my feet and toes, my eyes fill with tears from the pain. He suggests deep breathing, which helps a little. After the massage, he recommends drinking lots of water and staying off my feet for several days. The next day, Manuel offers to treat me again, this time gratis. His massages make me more comfortable and seems to help promote healing, along with rest, ibuprofen, and sports cream.

As I soak my ankles in the fresh water pool, I delight in seeing Rosa enter the courtyard; I met this Korean woman from Orlando, Florida, in Navarrete, four days ago. She had been to the doctor's because of a rash on her feet that was darkening and excruciating. The doctor told her she had cellulitis, a severe inflammation of the skin. He prescribed antibiotics and suggested she take a day off to see if the antibiotics were going to work. Now, the cellulitis was better, but she had developed tendinitis in her knees. We talk as we soak our feet.

Jung-Hye Lee (Rosa)

"I was born in South Korea and immigrated to America where I have been living for almost twenty years. I first heard about the Camino from a book by Paulo Coelho called *The Pilgrimage*. After I read that book, I was very interested in the Camino; then last year I was fortunate to come with a group to walk the one hundred kilometers from Sarria to Santiago. I was very impressed, even though I was not prepared. This year I am walking from St-Jean-Pied-de-Port to Santiago. I have two days missing that I need to make up. I had cellulitis and tendinitis and the doctor in the clinic said I had to stay in bed for two days. It was very hard for me to stay in bed. Everyone was leaving in the early morning, and I had to stay alone. I am glad I am walking again today.

"I am walking alone. I was supposed to walk with my

husband, but he could not find the time. I love the walking. It reminds me a lot of Korea: the mountains, the rivers, the barnyards, the rich abundance of fruit and food. When I started walking my pack was very heavy, about 10 kilos (about 22 pounds). Since I weigh about 55.5 kilos (120 pounds), people have told me that my pack was too heavy. I threw out some old clothes, toilet paper, and other items I did not absolutely need. Now it weighs about 8 kilos (about 17.5 pounds). Next time, when I return, I will more wisely pick out what I can carry.

"I like meeting people. I never am alone even though I came alone. I am a little lonely and think a lot about myself and my family. Most of my time in reality, back in America, I am busy working every day. I forgot what was important in my life. I just ignored it and didn't admit it. Now when I walk, I think a lot about what are the important things in my life. I think about my parents, my brother and other relatives; some are in America, others are in Korea. And I think a lot about my husband. I don't feel lonely for them, just more alive. Though I am not religious, I pray for them and I think that they are praying for me because they know I am on the Camino."

When the doctor is in town, I go to the clinic where there are posters on the wall concerning the benefits of breastfeeding, immunizations, AIDS prevention, and birth control. First I interpret for a Scotsman, who fell in the *albergue* the previous night and gashed his head, and then the doctor sees me. I leave the clinic with permission to walk at a slow pace and without a load. As an American pilgrim, there was no charge for the visit; the Scotsman showed his European Health Insurance Card. The free EHIC simplifies accessing healthcare services for those EU travelers who fall ill or suffer an injury while traveling.

Along the Camino, I see many feral cats begging for food at *albergues* and cafés. I feed them chips, crackers, cookies, and other substances not considered cat food; they are hungry and fight over each morsel. While in Azofra, a stray calico befriends us. Each morning our furry friend sits on our laps, purring softly, more interested in the contact than the food. She is not welcomed in the *albergue* and is shooed away. Dennis comments, "It is a bitch to be born poor, even for a cat."

Throughout my last afternoon in Azofra, I sit by the pool and speak with women pilgrims who arrive at the *albergue*. Though most conversations are short, I find several interesting.

Sara, from Cocoa Beach, Florida, needed a break from fourteen-hour work days. Since starting the Camino, she has not thought about her business, just about where she is going, where to get water and food, and where to sleep. She finds this time of living in the moment very therapeutic and is now contemplating whether to continue with her business or start something else.

Ellen and Carol are sisters from Denmark who started at St-Jean-Pied-de-Port and will end at Burgos, having competed the Burgos-to-Santiago stretch several years ago. Though the sisters live in the same town, they do not see each other daily or even weekly and are, therefore, enjoying this time together, discussing things they never told each other before. Earlier that day, they stopped to take pictures of a flock of sheep. The one-toothed shepherd then came over for a kiss as payment for photographing his animals, but not the European peck on the cheek. I laugh as Ellen explains how she had to move quickly to prevent him from making full lip contact.

At last, after three days of rest, I am walking again. I taxi my bags 9 kilometers (5.5 miles) to the Albergue La Virgen de Guadalupe in Cirueña. Step by step, I make my way uphill, following a trail that weaves and winds around pastures and hillocks. Pink and purple thistle contrasts with the golden hay stubble, and green shrubbery separates the trail from the fields. Monica, a tall, blond Lithuanian economist, passes me. Since she has written "In the name of love" on her backpack, I ask her if she is looking for love. She replies, "I want to love more and to feel more. I want to slow down, see what there is to see, and feel the love."

On the hilltop before Cirueña is the Rioja Alta Golf Club. The dark green fairway with its four fabricated "lakes" appears incongruous among the parched, agricultural fields. To me, this golf course just seems wrong, out of place, representing opulence and worldliness and runs contrary to my concept of the Camino. I am happy to get past it.

In contrast to the modern, verdant golf course, Cirueña is a dying town, with dilapidated buildings, a single café, and no store. We arrive at the blue stucco *albergue* with its window boxes of red geraniums about two hours before it opens. Dennis explores the town while I sit on a bench near the *albergue*. As I sit there swatting at flies, a van pulls up and honks its horn. I am curious. Old women clad in black shuffle to the van from several houses to buy their daily bread. This is the first time I see this form of local commerce. One woman arrives too late, and the van is gone; her disappointment evident even from my distance. I wonder if she will have anything to eat today.

Upon entering the building, there is a dank, musty odor from the dimly-lit sitting room on the right. I hope the bedrooms will not smell; I really do not want to walk another 5.5 k (3.5 mi) with my pack today. On the left are two toilets and showers. We climb dark wood stairs to the bedrooms and kitchen, which I am happy to find are free from mildew.

At first, I think the apron-clad *hospitalero* is angry, yelling at the pilgrims. Then I realize that he is trying to communicate with someone who doesn't understand Spanish. This IF-I-YELL-IT-LOUD-ENOUGH-THEY-WILL-UNDERSTAND phenomenon seems universal; people everywhere increase the volume in hopes of overcoming their language deficiency.

We are sharing our room with four people. One is Kim, a thin, quiet Korean woman who is a social worker for mentally ill patients. She is homesick, missing her banker husband, and is looking forward to reaching Santiago and then returning home. Even though modern technology makes it easy to stay in touch with loved ones, the physical separation can make being apart very difficult. I imagine that being alone in a different culture with a foreign language exacerbates the loneliness. When I lived in Spain after college graduation, I became homesick when I learned my mother was ill. It was a palpable pain that left me with a raw spot in my emotions that is, to this day, sensitive to another's loneliness. Hearing Kim speak about her longing for home and her loved ones rekindles that emotion; I feel her pain, but do not know what to say to help her.

From my observations, there are many more solo walkers than couples. Only a few have spoken to me about homesickness. Perhaps because we have been walking for only about two weeks and the newness of the adventure is buoying people's spirits, perhaps after two weeks people have passed through the homesickness, or perhaps people are too shy to speak about something this personal. I wonder if through homesickness the Camino is teaching a lesson to be more appreciative of loved ones, to be more flexible in adapting to new situations, or to live in "the now" and not the past, even if the past is just a few weeks ago.

Since I am curious, I ask other pilgrims if they get homesick and, if so, what triggers it. One person says that kind gestures remind her of the kindness of loved ones, which set off the homesickness; humor and the company of others helped alleviate it. Other unexpected triggers include scenery or smells that remind people of home. One person who was reminded of home by the smell of the eucalyptus trees belted out Australia's anthem in the forest. Many people wish to have loved ones with them, not primarily because they miss them but to be able to share a certain experience. Most say they accept the occasional homesickness as part of the Camino and this acceptance helps get them through the ordeal.

After my conversation with Kim, I lie on my bed to let my legs recuperate, reading *The Canterbury Tales*. This quote from the Knight's Tale seems relevant: "The world is but a throughway full of woe, and we be pilgrims passing to and fro."

The next morning we breakfast in Santo Domingo de la Calzada, an industrial town with many government buildings, a large square, and a monastery run by Cistercian nuns. Santo Domingo de la Calzada's Gothic cathedral is famous for the live white cock and hen kept in a cage to commemorate St. James' miraculous intervention in resurrecting a young pilgrim hung on the gallows. According to legend, during the fourteenth century a young male pilgrim rejected the sexual advances of a Spanish girl. Dejected, she hid a silver cup among his belongings and then accused him of thievery. He was hung. When his parents took down his body, he miraculously came back to life, telling his startled parents that St. James had saved him. They reported the incident to the magistrate, who was dining at the time. He remarked that the son was as alive as the rooster and chicken that he had been feasting on. Upon his saying that, the birds jumped from the plate, and then clucked and crowed.

The fountain in the square is unusual. It is a bronze sculpture of a bicycle, staff, backpack, and scallop shell. Very simple, but artistic. Across from it, there is a photo cutout board of a medieval pilgrim; we stick our head into the cutout and take pictures of each other. Dennis makes a great pilgrim; my face is smaller than the cutout and it looks hokey.

Very often, from a distance we can see where we want to go, but then the road will veer around a field, adding a kilometer or more. This time the crop is mowed and there is a marked shortcut through the field. As we traipse across the tract, careful not to trip on short hay stalks or stones, I remark to Dennis that the stones remind me of the weights I had used during my Jillian Michaels training. Laughing, I pick up the stones to demonstrate, but the tendinitis prevents me from getting into a full squat. Jillian would be disappointed in me.

Grañón is the last town in La Rioja. We stay at the Hospital de Peregrinos San Juan Bautista, which turns out to be one of my favorite *albergues*; the dormitory is in the bell tower of the church. At this well-liked *donativo* we meet many pilgrims with whom we continue to leapfrog all the way to Santiago.

Gemma, one of these pilgrims, is visually impaired and is walking the Camino alone. When she cannot find the markings, she waits for someone to come along and show her the way. She became ill and is spending a second night at the *albergue*. As some of the pilgrims are helping to prepare supper, Gemma entertains us by playing the guitar and then the piano. She plays classics, boogie woogie, folk songs, and Australian songs—all from memory. It is such a pleasure and everyone is in a good mood. She plays Fur Elise, a song that my daughter, Áine played as child, and I become teary-eyed and homesick for her. I remember reading Proust. For him, the smell of a *madeleine* (a small sponge cake) brings back vivid childhood memories; for me the trigger is auditory; she is once again that little girl who sits on my knee.

Gemma Ryan

"I am a student, studying music and anthropology. I came to Europe for three months. Before the Camino, I went to the World Youth Day in Madrid [WYD or Jornada Mundial de la Juventud in Spanish], which was a huge gathering of youth from all over the world (2.5 million at the final Mass). I then wanted to stay around for a bit. Some friends of mine back in Australia have already done the Camino and their stories intrigued me. Since I am Catholic, the Catholicity of the journey was quite interesting. Other than that I didn't know much about the Camino and just came to experience it. I started on the fifteenth of September. Last night I became ill with vomiting and the *hospitaleras* were worried about me and wanted to call the doctor. I was lucky to be in this *albergue*, because it is the nicest place I have stayed to date.

"I was staying in the bell tower for the first two hours. Because I was vomiting, they moved me into the little dormitory that you have to go through to get to the choir loft in the church. This was good because it has a toilet next to it.

"So far the Camino has offered me the opportunity to pray, which has been wonderful. Even though I have met people along the Way, I have had a lot of time to be by myself to think and pray. I was talking to a man a few days ago and we were talking about our faith. Since he was older than I am, he had had more time to think about his faith; he gave me things to think about for the next couple of days such as the Eucharist, which is something I don't usually think about. I have been visiting the churches, but keep missing Mass. They say it is at one time and it is not. When I go into some of the really old churches, like the one in Cirauqui [Church of San Román, built in the twelfth century], which has a twelfth-century crucifix in a glass casing and I think, 'Wow!' I have found the churches along the Way to be incredible, with a lot of nice gold and stonework. I have spoken with a few priests as well. After the pilgrim's blessing or at the end of Mass, the priest often asks where the pilgrims come from. When I say Australia, they are amazed.

"I have a visual impairment. I had been using a monocular to find the arrows and markings. Unfortunately, this broke a few days ago. But, that is okay because there is always someone behind me. I just wait a few minutes and they can show me the right way. Sometimes someone in the village will call out, 'No. You don't go that way, you go this way.' So, my impairment has not been a problem.

"I don't feel particularly brave for journeying with the eye impairment. I feel that each person has his or her own problems. Everyone has something that can hold them back a bit, but they still go on. There is a guy in this *albergue* that has broken his foot and is planning on

129

moving on in a few days. I had to take a few days off, but I now plan to go on to Santiago."

Gemma's post-Camino comments:

"I finished the Camino on October 16 with my cousin Gen, who joined me in Astorga on the 6th. Afterword, I went via Lourdes to Paris, where I spent a week with some of my family (also on holiday) before flying back to Perth, Australia (home), on the 27th.

"The whole Camino was an amazing experience for me that I hope to repeat one day. My favorite part was probably the time I spent in Grañón. I got sick on my first night there and, therefore, spent three nights there altogether. I loved the sense of community, the amazing *hospitaleros* who looked after me, and the piano!"

Margherita is one of two *hospitaleras* at this *albergue*. Her presence enriched my stay there: she is very kind and caring with a bright smile and a readiness to help.

Margherita Parlavecchio

"My name is Margherita. I am from Palermo, Italy, but I live and work in Milan. I hiked the Camino last year. After this experience, I wanted to have another point of view of the Camino. I then found an association to volunteer as *hospitalera* and now I am a volunteer Camino de Santiago hostel keeper for the Spanish Federation of the Association of Friends of the Camino de Santiago. It was great for me and I decided to do this experience. I did not have to learn how to cook since cooking is one of my specialties. I have cooked a lot and been part of cooking groups. Cooking for a large group is like a party each day. Sometimes people disagree with what I cook, but most times people like it.

"I arrived on September 15 and I have six days to go; it is a two-week commitment.

"As *hospitalera*, I feel the Camino inside, just as when I was walking. I recognized in pilgrims that arrive very tired, the days that I was very tired and I like to help them. When I go around this city, I follow the arrows and I feel as if I am on the Camino again.

Women of the Way

"As *hospitalera*, I have a chance to discover many stories because each day more than forty pilgrims come here and many of them give me the gift of what they think. I love the hugs I receive from the pilgrims before they leave in the morning as they thank me. For me, this is proof that I have been a good hostess. Yesterday there was a woman who asked me if she could rest an additional day because she was very tired. This morning she told me, 'I slept like a baby, ate in a great way, and spent a very good night with the other pilgrims. I am renewed and ready to go again.' It was a good experience for me to be able to help her restore like she did.

"Each day there is something remarkable that I think about. There are only a few moments that are not good; there are many more moments that are great. I remember a Canadian couple who put their mats on the floor, set their backpacks down, and then put a glass of flowers between the mats. It was very sweet.

"I am spiritual, as opposed to religious. Many pilgrims are not religious or Catholic. For this reason, I do not think the Camino is just a religious pilgrimage. It is a place to experience spirituality and 'groupness.'

After completing her volunteer work, Margherita said, "Grañón is a place where the energy of humanity can be shared, and I am happy to have lived my first [volunteer] experience there. Now I can't wait to go back somewhere as *hospitalera* again, and to walk the Camino again."

The dormitory is on the third landing. Since we arrive

early, we are lucky to spread our mats on the floor in the corner of the room. Later, it becomes crowded, the mats almost touching each other. There is a washtub for laundry one floor up, just below the belfry. As we wash our clothes, we stand on the stones that support the tower; very primitive. We have to walk two blocks to get to the communal town clotheslines; the steady breeze and direct sun dry the clothes quickly.

Our chores complete, Dennis and I go to a nearby café for a drink and munchies. A Spanish woman returning from the *panadería* shows us where the bakery is; there is no sign advertising its location. Although it is siesta time, it is open. I do not understand the Spanish customs; when posted, store hours are only approximate and advertising is by word of mouth. This bakery is on the Camino, but who would know? Imagine how many pilgrims would stop if they only knew.

Just before supper, a large group of Koreans arrives. Everyone scrambles to add additional seating. Since supper was already prepared, we share what there is. This is the only time that I am hungry after a meal, which consists of salad, tortilla, bread, wine, and apples for dessert. I do not feel cheated, but part of the community, happy to share what I have with others. Focusing on how good things are instead of griping about not having enough creates a positive energy amongst us. As we go about with the after-dinner chores, there is laughter and happiness, and I feel joyful, a state of mind that is becoming more and more familiar to me as I experience the Camino.

Women of the Way

Castille and León

Castille and León

"Joy is a sustained sense of well-being and internal peace—a connection to what matters." ~ Oprah

Knowing that from Grañón to Belorado there are no open markets, we stop at a bakery before leaving town. Since the owner is busy in the back and does not come out to greet us, we leave without buying anything, rationalizing that we need a cup of tea to enhance the flavor of the pastries and that it will be awhile before the cafés open.

Soon after Grañón, we leave La Rioja and enter the autonomous region of Castille and León. This region consists of nine provinces; the Camino Francés crosses three: Burgos, Palencia, and León. The terrain consists of the Meseta, a dry but fertile plain of clay soil, surrounded by mountainous regions. Castille and León is known as "the granary of Spain" for its production of wheat, barley, rye, and oats. In addition to the grains, this area cultivates sunflowers; there are vast fields of these withering plants with drooping brown heads picked over by the birds. Why this is so is still unclear, but Dennis and I surmise that there must be a glut of sunflowers and the government has subsidized the farmers not to pick the crop.

The local cuisine is famous for its roasted suckling pig and lamb, as well as its hearty stews, and I look forward to sampling the local cuisine. I recall eating suckling pig when I lived in Madrid and how delicious it was.

The sun rises over the mountains and my world is rosy. I love the Meseta, particularly at dawn when the expansive wheat fields take on a golden hue and all the colors intensify. A sense of joy and calmness overwhelms me; I feel connected with the earth and the sun. I sing "I'm Alive," by Celine Dion, my feet pounding to the rhythm. I am full of energy, glad to be alive, joyous.

Once again, we chase our shadows down pebbly roads. My legs remind me not to go too far, too fast, and I limit the distance that day to 16 kilometers (10 miles). I am glad to stop in the provincial village of Belorado. Since it is too early to register at the *albergue* next to the church of Santa María, we explore the town and have a leisurely lunch in the Plaza Mayor. The large square has a gazebo in the center surrounded by pollarded plane trees, which are sycamore trees pruned close to the trunk to produce a thick mass of branches. I snack on a Spanish tortilla and Dennis has two *pinchos*, skewered kabobs, one meat and one cheese.

It is market day and vendor stalls fill the square. We sit under the restaurant's striped white and gray canopy and watch the villagers buy bras, underwear, watches, dresses, vegetables, hardware, toys, and various sundries. To the villagers, shopping day is a gala event, and they talk and joke as they make their purchases. Though Belorado is said to have Spain's oldest market-fair, this portable "market" apparently moves from town to town, bringing its wares to villages without stores.

In the foyer of the *albergue* hangs a poster that describes bedbugs and the bedbug cycle. That poster puts me on alert. Staying in a place with bedbugs is a worry for many pilgrims. I have seen the symptomatic line of three red welts, referred to as the parasite's "breakfast, lunch, and dinner," on unfortunate pilgrims. To prevent this, at each *albergue* I check the mattress seams and bed frames for black "dots," which are fecal matter left by the bugs and for the bugs' exoskeletons as they molt and shed their outer shell. Until now, I have not seen any signs of the little bloodsuckers nor been bitten by them. Nevertheless, the fear of sleeping with the bugs persists, and often I imagine the critters crawling on me before falling asleep.

At the registration table, there are glasses of room-temperature chamomile tea and biscuits. I gobble a few as we wait our turn to check in. The *hospitaleras* are discussing bumps on a young hiker's shoulders and, deciding that these are not signs of bedbugs, let her register. She and her walking companion were Willing Workers On Organic Farms volunteers—WWOOF-ers—who work on a farm in exchange for room and board (vegetarian or vegan) while learning the theory of sustainable agriculture. They heard about the Camino from other volunteers and decided to hike it before returning home. WWOOF, a loose network of international organizations, teaches organic and ecologically sound growing practices through hands-on experience.

Dennis and I talk with them about our history with farming and living off the grid. We tell them about living in a tent in Massachusetts while building a log cabin with hand tools; surviving without running water or electricity for more than a year; and being self-sufficient on a "gentleman's farm," where we raised pigs, goats, chickens, sheep, and a steer, and grew vegetables for eating and storing. We tell them how we admire their ideology and active participation in changing the world.

This *albergue* is in an old theater. The lower floor has the dining room and two bathrooms with showers; the stage is the communal kitchen; and the balcony, accessed by steep, narrow, and winding steps, is the sleeping area. Our room sleeps ten. A single, low-watt bulb is the only illumination; there is no window. As is his custom, Dennis graciously yields the bottom bunk to me.

This small town has two churches, one used in summer and the other in the winter. We visit the fifteenth-century summer church next to the *albergue*. Huge marble columns support the domed ceiling. The main and side altars are gold-leafed, while the worn pews and kneelers are wooden. There are two statues to St. James, one as the Moor slayer and the other as a pilgrim. The amount of gold and wealth in the churches is an astounding contrast to the small, poor, rural towns they reside in.

Behind the church are remnants of a citadel, which was a wedding present to El Cid, "the lord-master of military arts." He is a legendary Spanish hero and an inspiration for Spanish patriotism. His remains are buried in the cathedral in Burgos.

The church bell tower is a nesting colony for the white stork, which are large carnivorous birds that eat small prey from the ground and shallow water. They are monogamous, pairing to mate and raise offspring, but do not pair for life. Since the white storks migrate to Africa in the summer, these nests are now empty. Later this year, the male birds will arrive first, choose a nest and wait for the female. The pair will then raise a single brood, typically four chicks.

Even though for the past twenty years more storks are remaining in Spain year-round instead of migrating, I have not seen any. The storks are not leaving due to the availability of food; birds are now eating out of the garbage dumps, the improved water quality in the wetlands ensures more prey, and many towns that take pride in their stork population feed the birds.

According to European legend, the stork brings babies to parents in a basket or on its back. Those wanting a baby merely have to put a sweet on the windowsill. I cannot imagine how many unexpected babies arrived because the cook put a pie on the windowsill to cool.

I sit in the *albergue* courtyard writing in my journal. From here I can see the caves where the hermits once lived. As I sit in the last rays of the evening sun, Antonia, a *hospitalera* from Switzerland, joins me.

Antonia from Switzerland

I ask her about the bedbug problem. She explains that the

albergue has not had an infestation in three years because they are vigilant and look for signs of bedbugs on the pilgrims. For example, several weeks prior a pilgrim came with the telltale welts. The *hospitaleras* disinfected his sleeping bag and washed his clothes in hot water to remove the bedbugs and their eggs. As a precaution, they did not allow him to sleep in the bunk beds, but offered a mat on the floor of the main room. The *hospitaleras* also vacuum the beds each day and disinfect the bedrooms every six weeks. I wish all the *albergues* were as attentive as this one.

Antonia hiked the Camino several years back and belongs to the Swiss Friends of the Camino, who support this *albergue*. Each volunteer comes for fifteen days. They, along with the curator, sleep at the parish house.

With all the vegetables we see growing in communal gardens, we cannot understand the lack of fresh vegetables served in local restaurants. I wonder if this is so because we are eating on the cheap or if it is simply the custom. Most inexpensive pilgrim's menus offer fried or roasted potatoes, green beans, asparagus, and the ubiquitous "Ensalada Mixta" (iceberg lettuce, frozen carrots, peas or corn, hard boiled egg, and tuna tossed with olive oil). Since we miss eating a variety of fresh vegetables, that evening we make sandwiches of roasted onions, peppers, and zucchini on a baguette and toss a salad with olives and cheese. Delightful! We donate the leftovers to the other pilgrims, several of whom have little money and are out of food, or who arrived at the *albergue* late and are too tired to cook.

Later, I awake with cramps and diarrhea. I lie on the cold floor in the bathroom, so as not to disturb the other pilgrims. Before leaving in the morning, Antonia gives me homeopathic medicine that she brought from Switzerland. It does not work. As I walk to Villafranca Montes de Oca, 12 kilometers (7.2 miles), "Montezuma's revenge" has me running to the trees about every kilometer. We now believe that I have food poisoning, most likely from the Spanish tortilla I ate the day before. The first three villages that we go through do not have a *farmacia*, so we continue forward. In the small town of Espinosa del Camino, I am very weak and I lay on a bench while Dennis has a Coke. A pilgrim from Australia gives me two Imodium tablets and something similar to an Alka-Seltzer. I love the way that pilgrims help each other! I muster my strength and continue climbing to Villafranca de Montes de Oca. I am in such misery that I do not notice my surroundings. As we enter the village, I see there is a three-star hotel, Hotel San Anton Abad. At this point, I do not care what it costs; I want a bed in a private room with a private bath. As I shower, Dennis goes in search of a pharmacy or doctor, neither of which is available. In the smaller, rural towns in Spain, the doctor and pharmacy open for a few hours once or twice a week.

The kind hotel owner gives Dennis Fortasec, an antidiarrhea medication; Sueroral Casen, an electrolytic powder; and bottled water to mix with the powder. Showered and medicated, I sleep for 17 hours, getting up once to luxuriate in the oversized tub.

The next morning, the cramping and diarrhea are gone, but I feel drained. Though the concerned owner recommends that we stay an extra day, I decide to go forward. As a precaution, he gives me more medication and electrolytic powder and suggests that I eat only dry toast for twenty-four hours. I take his advice and thank him for his assistance and genuine concern for my welfare.

To leave town we climb up through an oak and pine woodland for about 6.5 kilometers (4 miles) until reaching Alto de Valbuena, where we start our descent. My legs are better, but I am still careful on the downhills, using very tiny steps and the traversing technique that Lydie taught me. Dennis is a fast downhill hiker, so he goes ahead, enjoying his downward cadence, and then waits for me at the bottom.

We pass the church in San Juan de Ortego to which childless women make pilgrimages in hopes of conceiving. The barren Queen Isabel la Católica visited the church in 1477 and subsequently had three children. I don't stop here —just in case.

We arrive at the newly opened municipal *albergue* in Agés. I take a long, hot shower in the men's room, not realizing that there is one for women. In my bed, I use my shirt to cover the pillow since there are no pillowcases. Our destination for the next day is Burgos and the guidebooks list several alternate routes to the city. We consult with other pilgrims and plan our itinerary, deciding to follow the southern route, which is slightly longer, because it goes around the airport, but which is off the main road and, therefore, quieter.

Here, I meet Phil from Oregon. He uses our Skype connection to call home. Though I give him privacy, I can see in his demeanor how much he misses his wife. I am lucky to be sharing this adventure with Dennis; I would be lonely without him.

Phil and other pilgrims take a tour to Atapuerca, which is several kilometers from the *albergue*. In 1964, archeologists found hominid and human remains in the area that were more than a million years old. For this reason, the village is now designated a UNESCO World Heritage site. Since I am still recovering from the food poisoning, I do not want to go, and Dennis forgoes the tour as well to keep me company.

We leave Agés just before dawn, around 8:15. About forty-five minutes later, Dennis realizes he left his hiking pole at the *albergue* and returns to fetch it. I continue forward, since he is a faster hiker than I. At the top of Matagrande, a hill west of Atapuerca, stands a large wooden cross that surprises me because the guidebook did not mention it. From this crest, I can see the valley below and, in the distance, Burgos. Someone has left hiking poles near the cross. I debate taking them with me in hopes of meeting up with the person who forgot them. I decide to leave them and start descending when I meet Elodie (rhymes with Melody), who is returning to retrieve the poles. After she picks them up, we walk together. Since she has a painful knee, she needs her poles, especially when going downhill. She also has an infection in her mouth from something she ate or drank. She says that these sores are a sign from God to stop talking so much, which she cannot do.

I sip chamomile tea in the next town's café, waiting for Dennis. Once he arrives and rests, we continue to Burgos, following the alternate route around the airport. In the distance, we can see a large building with a mural of a knight on a horse and we wonder what it is. Later we learn that it is the San Miguel brewery and that visitors can take tours of the brewery and receive free beer. On that steamy, sunny day, we would have enjoyed a cold beer and an air-conditioned tour. Why did our guidebooks not tell us about it?

In Burgos, because we are following an alternate route, the Camino arrows are sparse and confusing. As we sit on a bench trying to determine if we should backtrack or continue forward, a gray-haired Spaniard pushing a wheelbarrow approaches and volunteers to show us the way to the park, where we can walk in the shade to the cathedral. This unexpected kindness touches me and I recall a quote by Catherine Pulsifer, an inspirational author: "Never underestimate what a simple gesture can do. It is the little things that you do that make a big difference in other people's lives."

The park flanks the Arlanzón River. Shade from the tree-lined paths provides a welcome relief from the late September heat. I change into my sandals to walk through the park, Fuentes Blancas, to the old city. Burgos, the capital of Castile as well as the capital of the province of Burgos, is a huge metropolis. It takes us about two hours to walk to the cathedral, passing many bridges, fountains, playgrounds, a campground, and even an artificial beach on the riverbank. It is a delight to see the populace enjoying the park, especially midday and midweek. There are bikers, joggers, and people out for a walk, many with their dogs.

We leave the park via a bridge over the river, and then enter the medieval quarters through the Arco de Santa María, which reminds me of entering Fantasy Land at Disney World. The Gothic-style cathedral in Burgos is immense, with flamboyant spires reaching 88 meters (289 feet), a three-story facade, and large squares. Construction started on the site of the former Romanesque cathedral on July 20, 1221, beginning at the chevet (east end of the church), which was completed in nine years. The high altar was first consecrated in 1260, then there was a lengthy break of almost 200 years before construction was recommenced. The cathedral was completed in 1567.

We walk around the monstrous cathedral where El Cid is buried and climb three separate stairways to get to the street where the municipal *albergue* is located. This is a modern six-floor facility with an elevator. Unlike the smaller *albergues,* where we leave shoes and poles at the door, this large hostel has boot shelves that slide out from the wall. I hope I remember behind which door we store our boots.

After settling in, we find a barber to trim Dennis' beard, a process that takes about forty-five minutes of meticulous snipping with scissors. Dennis now looks *muy guapo* (very handsome), a well-groomed pilgrim.

Burgos has many historic landmarks and archeological treasures. One of these treasures is the Paseo del Espolón. This street that runs along the River Arlanzón is lined with plane trees that are elegantly interwoven. The city preserved many medieval churches, palaces, and other buildings. There is an abundance of statues—some fun, others more traditional. The historic area is colorful, with buildings painted in many bright hues that contrast with the gray-colored stonework.

Because the city center is free of cars, and because it has a free bicycle loan system and one hundred percent "clean" public transport, the city has received two Nobel awards for sustainability. Even though there is much urbanization, there are many parks, known as the "lungs" of the city, and one tree for every three inhabitants.

Unaware that parks have both walkways and bikeways, I almost collide with an oncoming bicyclist. I then realize that the bicycle path has two lanes with a dotted line; the walk path is not divided.

Plaza Mayor offers a choice of international eateries, opening at eight for dinner. Tired from the day's exertion, we choose to eat early at an outdoor pizzeria/creperia. Massive four-story stone buildings with gold, green or yellow facades surround the plaza, which is approximately the size of three football fields. The cathedral towers over these buildings. I sip a beer and watch people enjoying the evening, children playing, friends meeting for a drink and tapas. I can't help comparing this convivial lifestyle with the one back home. I would love to have open plazas such as this in the States, where I could sit and reflect or share a moment with friends!

I love Burgos. Even though is it a large metropolitan area, it is not menacing. Its large squares, parks, and landscaping are inviting. The people appear relaxed, going about their daily rituals in a less frantic way than is commonly associated with large cities. I wonder if this friendliness is a result of the city's ecological efforts, the resulting air quality, the openness and grandeur, or what. It would be interesting to discuss this with Morgan Crowley.

We see Phil in the plaza and he joins us. After dinner, while he and Dennis catch up on what has been happening in each other's lives, I return to the *albergue* to speak with

Elodie, the twenty-nine-year-old Frenchwoman I met on the hilltop near Atapuerca.

Elodie Pitrey

"I am from Normandy, France. I have had this idea of doing the Camino for a long time. Recently and in a very short time, I have had many changes in my life.

"First, I finished my studies in June and received my diploma to be a social worker. At the beginning of my studies, I met an Egyptian guy and we fell in love. We met in France, but he had to go back to Egypt. Even though I was still studying, I made many trips to see him there. At one point, we decided to get married. It was really nice, really beautiful, like a dream. But, when he managed to come to France with a visa, it became a disaster.

"While I was studying, I was going through many changes. To be a social worker, you get training in knowing yourself and are taught to analyze everything, including the people that you have in your life. I realized that each person affects my story. There were many things going on in my life and, after some time, I found the key. I found the key even while many bad things were happening at once. It is really strange.

"On July 9 this year, my husband who was in Egypt asked me for a divorce. He waited until I got my diploma to ask me for it. It was a bad time for me. I felt sad and decided to go out with friends and not stay at home. I drank just two glasses over the legal limit. France is very strict, as I think it is the same in America and everywhere now. I was not drunk, but the police stopped me one hundred meters from my house and I lost my driver's license. Then I lost my job. After getting my diploma I had a job, but I needed to get my driver's license for it because I worked with handicapped people and I had to drive them. I had three bad things happen to me all at the same time: I lost my husband, my license, and my job.

"It is strange, because the day after I lost my job I found a new one. Since I did not have my license, I could not be a social worker, so I worked as a waitress. I worked every day and rode my bike to get to work. I felt free. The only thing I wanted was to be at peace with myself and I found it, little by little, day after day.

"Then I decided to do the Camino. It is to take time for me. Before, in each relationship that I had, I was always searching myself, as if I had the feeling that something was missing. Now, on the Camino, I realize that I have everything in front of me. I just started to live in the present without thinking about the past or without thinking about the future. It is not as if I did not know this before, it is just that at this moment I feel it inside me very strongly. I feel very, very good on the Camino. Day after day, I am discovering myself. Day after day, I am finding some answers, though I don't have them all. I don't want to think about the future, just about the present. I feel peace inside of me.

"Though this is the first time I am on the Camino, it is not the first time that I traveled alone. The road, the languages, and the meeting of people have always attracted me. I am very curious. For me, this trip is very different. It is more spiritual. Before, it was a way to search myself when I traveled, but I did not feel well inside. When I decided to do the Camino, so many things changed in my life, with my parents, and with my family. I was not fleeing, not looking behind me, but going forward. I am not running away, but living in the present. I am not trying to escape. Now as I live in the present, I realize that I have had a very rich life; I have traveled and met many people. For this reason, on the Camino I can speak with everybody because I know French, Italian, English, and little German. To me, Spanish is a mixture of French and Italian. Therefore, I can understand the language.

"I am realizing that I am a good person. I am not saying that because I am proud of myself, but just that I am now realizing it, which I didn't before. I feel better.

"On the Camino, I am trying to determine the priorities of my life. What do I want for me? Before, I did not do this. I was doing many things, but for my parents, for others, not for myself. The Camino is helping me find many answers. I still do not have all the answers and will continue to look for them.

"I love singing. I have been thinking that I might like to do this every day, to have concerts. I also love writing, so maybe one day I will write a book. I am not sure if I will do social work all my life, because I have other things within me. I am composing my story."

Elodie's post-Camino comments:

"I had some problems on the Camino after León, but I managed to arrive in Santiago. Life for me is hard now because I cannot find a job as a social worker. I don't feel ready to go to Paris. I think it would be hard for me after the Camino. It was such a great experience! Now, I am leaving Normandy to go to Savoy, in the mountains, to start work as waitress. After, I may travel awhile and then try to start life in Switzerland, where I hope to make a better living."

I saw Elodie two weeks later in Ponferrada where she updated me on her adventure. When she got to Cruz de Ferro, she left her wedding ring and a picture of her husband. As she did this, she felt a special moment, when her spirits lifted and her burdens were gone.

Later when she was in pain and out of money, she met a pilgrim who was going to see the doctor. He took her in the taxi with him to the hospital in León and then paid the fare. She called him an angel. This is another example that the Camino provides and of the kindness of fellow pilgrims. The doctor told her she had lost too much weight and had to stay off the Camino for three days.

Elodie stayed in Ponferrada to visit the medieval Templar castle and then, because of her injuries and general weakness, jumped ahead to avoid the climbs.

That night, after speaking with Elodie, I am unable to sleep. Although my bunk is near the bathrooms and people turn on lights, bang doors, and flush toilets, what really is keeping me awake is the revelry in town. The Communist Party is having a rally and there are chants, whistles, clapping, and sound systems amplifying speeches and music. The clamorous disturbance continues until 4 a.m. My earplugs do not muffle the din and, unlike the soundest sleepers, I cannot manage to rest.

Burgos is a large city. I pair up with Elodie to walk on paved streets through housing developments and industrial areas to the outskirts. She confides that she stopped smoking when starting the Camino and is now eleven days tobacco-free. She has an iPod and we sing along with the song "Hallelujah," by Leonard Cohen. The joy and calmness that this song brings stays with me throughout the day.

I like Burgos, but am happy to walk once again over undulating and picturesque hills. I am amazed that most books about the Camino never talk about its stunning beauty. It is pure eye-candy.

My legs are getting stronger and I feel great. Since my stride has returned to normal, I add weight to my pack, happy to relieve Dennis of it. We pass through the enchanting village of Rabé de las Calzadas. The old, well-kept town square has blooming flowers and bushes, window boxes overflowing with color, coats of arms on doors, and other signs that welcome the pilgrim and show pride in the town. Leaving town, a colorful Camino de Santiago graffito bids us farewell.

From the mountain rise, there is a beckoning panorama of variegated fields separated by a meandering pathway leading to Hornillos del Camino, a small village with about seventy inhabitants. The town, more than a mile in the distance, is picturesque and many people stop to photograph the beauty. From the Meseta, a narrow dirt path with stone walls on either side leads down to the center of the village.

After 20 kilometers (12 miles) of painless walking, we are lucky to get the last two beds in the old stone *albergue* in Hornillos del Camino; others have to sleep on mats on the gym floor. After the sleepless night, I am looking forward to a quiet rest. There are six bunk beds in our room— twelve potential snorers. Four of the roommates are American, all friends from Virginia. One couple is walking for religious reasons; it is their second Camino and they are finding it more moving than their first. The other couple is walking as tourists, having decided to hike the Camino after hearing about it from their friends; they are debating whether to hike the Meseta or jump ahead.

Do the Spaniards ever sleep? It is after 10 p.m. I have been in bed for almost two hours and children are still playing outdoors, dogs are barking, and someone is playing loud "oompah" music. Thank goodness, no one is snoring.

I dress in fleece the next morning. It is 4° C (40° F) as we leave in the dark around 7:15 a.m. I am grateful that Dennis has good night vision, because even with the headlamp I cannot find the arrows indicating the Way. The terrain climbs a little and then levels off. The sunrise is again gorgeous, but the variations in the colors are less noticeable.

We pass San Bol, which has a population of three. The only building is an *albergue*, without hot water, electricity, or bathrooms. Two Rastafarian Italians manage this hostel, which has a reputation for good food and music playing until late into the night. The spring here is said to have curative power; pilgrims who wash their feet in it are supposedly cured of foot problems. A sign welcomes pilgrims for coffee, but the building is a distance from the Camino and we do not stop.

We do stop in Hontanas for breakfast. The town is down in a bowl, barely visible from the Meseta. When we leave, we climb back up to the plateau. The town features a municipal swimming pool, the first that I see on the Meseta.

A solitary tree is the sole distraction from the arid, stony fields surrounding it. The parched land makes me think of Death Valley, and I am curious as to how the farmers can succeed with their crops without apparent irrigation. What vegetation is there is sere: withering thistle, brown crackling grasses, dried lavender. An occasional evergreen appears as an incongruity.

We pitch our tent under pine trees in a campground on the outskirts of Castrojeríz, a Roman town possibly founded by Julius Caesar. I can see the ruins of a ninth-century castle, with its quadrangular tower resting on a Roman basement, on the hill overlooking the campground. In contrast to the ancient surroundings, there are modern solar water heaters on the premises and I luxuriate without guilt in the steamy shower. I machine launder our clothes and then hang them out to dry in the breezy sunshine. I enjoy the afternoon off, away from the crowd. While Dennis is doing his ham radio thing, I nap, write in my journal, and read. This is a splendid respite from our customary noisy sleeping quarters. I am alone for several hours and enjoy the solitude.

That night a dog barks until 4 a.m. Then the birds and roosters start, waking up the cows. I can hear their bells jangling as they walk in the fields. It seems I cannot get away from noise!

I arise in the morning to discover that I have an infection in my gums which aches and throbs. Several days ago, a piece of crusty bread punctured my gum; I now think this puncture is infected. I swish mouthwash and hope that will kill the infection.

It takes about twenty minutes to walk out of the city. Soon after entering the province of Palencia, I huff up a steep ascent (an 18% rise) to Alto de Mostelares, glad that I am not doing the Camino by mountain bike. The descent is also steep, but short, and then the terrain levels. It is hot. There are no clouds or trees to provide shade. To the amusement of fellow pilgrims, I use a hiking umbrella as a parasol.

The *albergue* at Boadilla del Camino is an oasis with green grass, flowers, even a swimming pool. As we enjoy a cool drink on the patio, Phil enters. His sunburn clashes with his orange shirt. Since I had purchased a pilgrim's hat in Burgos, I offer him my spare cap. Hopefully, it will keep the sun off his face. Many pilgrims decide to stop here, relax in the courtyard, and enjoy the greenery, but we continue to Frómista.

For about 6 kilometers (3.5 miles), we follow the Canal de Castilla, an eighteenth-century waterway constructed for use in marketing the wheat grown in the Meseta. Today, the canals are for irrigation, recreation, and tourism. Along the canals are shade trees that provide a welcome relief from the blaring sun and a change of colors. After days in the arid Meseta, my eyes feast on the green leaves and blue water. There are poplar trees planted along the road leading into town, but they are too young to provide substantial shade.

As we arrive in Frómista, a busload of tourists disembarks to visit St. Martin, a Romanesque church built in the eleventh century. Like the tourists, we circle the church to look at the three hundred and fifteen modillion figures (figures carved at the end of structural supports) beneath the cornice of the roof. Among the carvings are animals, humans, monsters, acrobats, flowers, and a harp-playing ass, a symbol of ignorance that dates back to ancient Sumeria.

From the window in our room, I can see the pollarded trees in the square, their bare limbs resembling menorahs. Exhausted, I insert my earplugs, wrap a bandana over my eyes, and go to bed at 8 p.m. I am finally able to catch up on my sleep. The next morning I awake refreshed and eager to go.

Women of the Way

We walk on a gravel path that runs parallel to a two-lane roadway. Bollards (short posts) decorated with scallop shells exclude motor vehicles from the walkway. At one point there is an alternate route away from the traffic, but we continue on the current path. I hear an occasional trill from a songbird, stones crunching beneath my sandals, the whooshing of cars. The rhythmic stride is soothing, the sun warms me in the cool morning air, and I feel at peace. I am happy.

Helen Keller said: "Many persons have a wrong idea of what constitutes happiness. It is not attained through self-gratification, but through fidelity to a worthy purpose." I think it is both. The Camino is demanding, sometimes painful. Yet, I continue forward towards Santiago not just because that is my goal but because the journey itself is gratifying.

One of the most rewarding and unexpected pleasures is the time spent with Dennis. We discuss our life, our future, and what we are experiencing on the Camino. We laugh a lot. We hold hands. We are reconnecting in all the little ways that life has unraveled without our even noticing.

A placard at a bird sanctuary describes the endangered bird the bustard, which is a large, chiefly flightless and ground-running bird related to the crane. Dennis and I are convulsing with laughter when Ana arrives and asks us what is funny. We point to the sign written in Spanish and Braille that describes the bird's size, coloring, wingspan, and other physical characteristics. It takes her a few seconds to understand the absurdity of describing the bird in Braille. How can a visually impaired person recognize the bird by its description? Perhaps, some blind people would be able to identify the bird by its song, but there is no mechanism on the placard by which to listen to the bird's sound.

Ana Ossenbach

Ana hiked the Camino Primativo in 2003. This interior route is 370 kilometers (about 230 miles) long, starting from Valleviciosa, a town on the northeastern coastline, to Santiago. She found this route daunting, perhaps a little scary, not because she feared for her personal safety, but because the scarcity of stores, buildings, and homes required that she walk long distances without resupply, on average 34 kilometers (21 miles) per day. In spite of this challenge, she loved it, and it became her dream to do the Camino Francés.

Ana is a Costa Rican of German descent who lived in Spain

for 18 years. She returned to Costa Rica eight years ago. She has written a children's book and a historical novel based on her German aunt who, over a period of twenty years, developed a friendship with a Jewish woman. The novel, *Our Father, You're Not in Heaven*, is told from the perspective of these women, who remained in Germany during the World War II, armed with their solidarity, while their men fought on the battlefield

Before embarking on the Camino this year, Ana read a book about ultralight backpacking. One night she went to bed worried about her 8-kilo (17.5-pounds) pack. She awoke in the middle of the night to reduce the weight by a kilo. She is also carrying a front pack for her iPad that her sister made and embroidered with the scallop shell.

The philosophy behind ultralight backpacking is to pack only essential equipment and multipurpose gear that are used each day. Thinking about my load and all the unused "just in case" clothes and items in the bottom of my pack, I realized that I could have easily reduced my load by a kilo or more. Now, halfway through the trip, I decide not to purge my bag. Next time, I will substitute safety pins for clothespins, leave street clothes behind (I can buy non-hiking clothes at the end of the trip), and not carry a return bag, even it only weighs several ounces. Had I done this initially, I might have prevented the tendinitis.

Farther down the path, we encounter a shepherd with a flock of a hundred sheep. One comes up to sniff me and then continues. Having raised sheep, I am not as enthralled as Ana is as she videos the incident using her iPad.

In Carrión de los Condes, the *albergue* where we stay is a thirteenth-century monastery. Large 9-meter (thirty-foot) pillars that hold up the ceiling have signs warning people not to lean on them for fear that they may collapse. There are four cots to each room and the doors to the dormitory lock at 10 p.m., though a key is hidden for those who wish to stay out later.

The host has memorized in several languages what he needs to tell the pilgrim. If interrupted, he starts from the beginning, not really understanding what he is saying. In my rustic Spanish, I tell him that I need a doctor or dentist for the brewing infection in my mouth and he hands me directions to the town's clinic. According to the hours listed, I need to get there soon.

Carrión has all the facilities of a modern town. We hustle to the clinic before it closes at 1 p.m. There, I am told to go to the emergency room at 6 p.m., when the doctor will be available. Since our guidebook suggests that we buy food and plenty of water before leaving Carrión, warning that for the next 43 kilometers (27 miles) there are few bars, shops, or accommodations, we go to the *supermercado*. It is large and well-supplied; so different from the ones in the smaller villages. I stop at a dentist's office, hoping that he can help me; the staff also tells me to visit the ER that night.

Owner posing beneath her picture in a Dewar's
White Label advertisement

In the interim, we order *hamburguesas* at a local café and
are surprised when the proprietress who works the bar and
waits on the tables delivers us American-style beefburgers
with lettuce, tomato, onion, and mayonnaise and ketchup
on the side. This is such a treat! That evening I return to the
clinic/ER to have the doctor look at my infected gum. He
asks if I have allergies to medication and then prescribes
Amoxicillin, which cost €2.29 (about $3.00). This is the
second time I need medical assistance and the doctor does
not charge me. This kindness by the doctors towards
pilgrims affirms the belief that "The Camino provides."
Though both doctors waived my offer of payment, this is
not the norm and may depend on the province or the
generosity of the doctor. To have peace of mind, I
recommend buying traveler's health insurance.

Last March, on his fourth day on the Camino, a cyclist fell

on slick cobblestones dislocating his knee. On the Camino de Santiago Forum, this cyclist is known as "DesertRain." He posted the following:

"Purchasing travel medical insurance turned out to be one of the best decisions of my life. Although my normal health insurance at home would have eventually reimbursed me for most of the hospitalization, I would have had to pay out of pocket. More importantly, no home insurance would have paid for the many non-medical costs or helped me with the logistics of getting home in a hip-to-toe cast. My $80 investment in the travel insurance saved me more than $10,000 in expenses. Upon giving the nurse my insurance information in the emergency room, I had absolutely no further paperwork or out-of-pocket costs. My medical travel insurance both paid for and helped me arrange the following:

- 100% of the cost of hospitalization for three days.

- 100% of the cost of a four-hour ambulance ride from Logroño to the airport in Madrid.

- 100% of the cost of a Business Class flight from Madrid to my home in Arizona—purchased the day before the flight. (With my cast, I couldn't even fit into a coach seat and this plane ticket alone would have cost me $4000!)

- More than just paying for these things, the insurance company worked directly with the hospital social worker to make all of the arrangements for my return journey. Imagine trying to arrange for a four-hour ambulance ride without this help: not only would the logistics be a nightmare (even if you speak Spanish fluently), but you would have to arrange for payment, all from your hospital bed, while drugged out on pain meds! Instead, all I had to do was concentrate on getting better.

"Please, please, please! Spend the small amount of money needed to obtain travel medical insurance. If nothing else, it will give you peace of mind. That alone is worth $3 per day!"

Additionally, travel insurance (which may be offered to you when you purchase your ticket or which may be purchased separately) will cover the cost of transporting your body back to the States or arranging for a burial or cremation in Spain, should the worst happen. The American Citizens Services Unit (ACSU) at the American Embassy can assist your family in making arrangements. It seems prudent to leave contact information to the ACSU and directives about your final wishes with your family or friends, or to carry a copy of your directives in your backpack.

During the night I am awakened by someone's violent vomiting. This poor person heaves all night. Could it be food poisoning or the effects of too much wine? For whatever reason, he is apparently very sick.

We walk on a paved road for one-and-half hours. The road, lined with poplars, tamaracks, cornfields, and alfalfa, resembles a New England country road. Birds are singing. Very few cars pass by. In spite of the guidebook's warning about the lack of supplies in this section, an enterprising Spaniard offers drinks and sandwiches at a roadside kiosk. We drink lukewarm tea served in plastic throwaway cups. Dennis eats a chocolate-covered donut that we purchased the day before. It is tranquil sitting on picnic chairs, enjoying the morning and talking with pilgrims, many of whom speak passable English. They tell us about a virus that is spreading among the pilgrims. Apparently, more than one person was sick in the *albergue* last night.

The terrain is changing It is surprisingly beautiful, no longer arid. At times, it reminds me of the Midwestern prairies; at other times of eastern Canada. We cross the halfway mark—only 395 kilometers (245 miles) to go! It has taken us twenty-five days to get this far.

Dennis becomes ill. After vomiting, he feels better and we forge ahead. He continues to be sick and to weaken and I am concerned that he will not make the last 3 kilometers (2 miles) to the *albergue* in Terradillos de los Templarios. When we arrive, he can barely stand, remaining outdoors until the arrangements are complete. This modern hostel resembles a chalet, with knotty pine walls and shiny wooden floors. I pay for a semiprivate room and the *hospitalera* provides me with a laundry bucket for a vomit pan. While Dennis sleeps, I do the chores and then lounge on the terrace, chatting with several young women that I have not previously met. One woman is completing her journey tomorrow and she exchanges contact information with her Camino friends. Claire is staying at another *albergue* but has come to wish her friend farewell. She agrees to an interview.

Claire Payne

"My name is Claire and I am twenty-one years old. I am from Melbourne, Australia. I first heard about the Camino about a year-and-a-half ago. I was reading the paper and some guy was talking about his experiences on the Camino. At the time, I thought it was just about some guy walking across Spain. I thought he must be crazy. After thinking about it, I started reading articles about the Camino. Most recently, I read articles about the preparations for the film *The Way* with Martin Sheen, though I did not see the movie.

"I came into this without having a real knowledge of the Camino. I decided to do it only two or three weeks before I came here to do it. I got the basic information about what I needed to carry. This way I had no expectations; I could have my own experiences without influence.

"All my clothing was lost into the midst of nowhere when Air France lost my luggage. I was scheduled to fly from

Melbourne to Bangkok, from Bangkok to Paris, and then from Paris to Biarritz. The first flight was delayed by three hours, and then rerouted from Melbourne to Singapore. I called Air France and told them that my luggage was checked into Bangkok, but that I was going to Singapore. I was on hold with Air France when they announced that I had to board for Singapore, the plane was leaving in ten minutes. I managed to make the flight, but no one knows where my luggage went. I spent an hour at the Air France counter in Singapore looking for my luggage. Since the first leg was with an Australian company and not with Air France, they told me it wasn't their problem and that I should be talking with the other company, but there was no one there. I had been wearing my hiking shoes, thick socks, pants, and shirt. I had to buy a backpack, underwear, a quick-dry towel, and additional clothes.

"I don't know Spanish. I crammed for a week before coming and can say really useful things like, 'I don't have any children' and 'Can I have a beer, please?' I have been learning more as I listen to it, and I have decided that I would like to stay on and go to a Spanish school. We'll see how that goes.

"I decided to do the Camino to get away from a lot of stuff. I thought that being by myself I could sort out things. Sometimes in a difficult situation, you have the strength in yourself to sort things out; at the same time, the situation itself makes it difficult to deal with things, so you need to get out of the situation. Even though I am not a spiritual person, there is an active faith in me that says that at the end of the Camino I will have figured out some things about myself. I am hoping to have sorted out who I am and then can go back to the situation and be better prepared. I don't really have an expectation, but more a hope and belief that this will happen.

"This is the first time that I traveled by myself for such a long distance. From my readings and from what I have seen, I feel safe.

"My mom died five years ago and my dad actually left us. Financially he was there, but HE wasn't there. I have a younger brother and we went from being a family to just the two of us. I felt a lot more alone then and I had to do more things by myself. Even though I had aunts and uncles, I did not see them much. I had to organize the laundry, pay the bills, take care of the house, make sure my brother went to school, and pay attention to him. I was doing these things on my own. This was something big that I took on without someone to back me up. For these reasons, walking the Camino does not feel as if I am taking something big on all by myself.

"There is this thing in Australia called 'going walkabout.'[4] When things were going bad with my family, there were times when I did just go walkabout. I just walked out the door. I did not have shoes on and did not know where I was going. In terms of the walking aspect, I was looking for that kind of experience on this pilgrimage. I didn't think that I would make a bunch of friends the way I did, or that some would even feel like my family. There is a German guy I met that I feel as close to as if he were a brother. I feel close to love with some of these people. I love it and am really glad that this happened, but I never honestly thought that I would find that love here. This was definitely a surprise for me.

"One night, because I wanted to be alone, I walked ahead

by myself to a town where there would not be anyone I knew. I wanted to do my own thing, which I have done since. I had an experience that I did not really enjoy, and which made me feel like I wanted to see my brother; we are really close and I wished he could give me a really big hug. The next day, in order to rejoin the people I knew, I only walked about a half a day's distance. Even though it was not the same as having my brother there, it was really good to be around people I was comfortable with. Even though I have been walking with them for only a few weeks, it feels as if I have known them for months and months.

"I just accepted the fact that, even though I feel as if I know them very well, I have to let go of them. I might think, yes, I will see them again and then something happens, and I don't. I might have hidden expectations that I will find a way to see them again, when I probably won't. In general, I can let people go; I value the experience that we have had, but I am ready to move on. Then there are those that I look forward to seeing again. Even if we think we won't see each other again, I really hope that we do. I guess the important ones I will.

"Now I walk alone most of the time. In the beginning I found people and we talked as we walked, but I am finding that I walk by myself more. At the end of the day, I find people and we talk. I LOVE to talk with people. Talking to people is one of the highlights of my day. Even though I like walking by myself, it is occasionally nice to have someone else join in, because I have a tendency to daydream and I am not here to do that. It is too easy to run away into your mind and hide there. Since I am physically doing the effort to walk on this pilgrimage, I need to put in the mental effort, get out of my mind, and appreciate what is going on around me."

One of the benefits of staying at an *albergue* or *refugio* is the socializing. People become gregarious. The supper meal is an opportunity to meet new pilgrims and reacquaint with others. People come and go in our lives and it is always a pleasure to see them farther down the Camino, with hugs and kisses, and then leave in the morning without goodbyes, never knowing if we will see them again.

Because of my tendinitis, the three-day recuperation, and then the short-distance days, I am traveling with a new wave of pilgrims and meeting new people. At supper, I sit with three men from Italy, one from Vancouver, a woman from Germany, and one from Denmark. We speak in French or English. After supper, one of the Italians sings opera *a capella* (unaccompanied) to us from the terrace. What an enchanting experience it is to sit beneath the Milky Way and listen to the *Marriage of Figaro*!

By evening Dennis is feeling better, just tired. Because the walls do not go to the ceiling, light is visible whenever someone turns on a lamp in an adjoining room, and every noise is amplified. Since there are several sick pilgrims in the *albergue*, I get very little sleep, once again.

Dennis and I share bread and jam with the feral cats before leaving the premises at 7:30 a.m. It is dark and we cannot find the yellow marker arrows and end up going around the block. As we try to decide which of the two paths to follow, a pilgrim comes up one of the paths to tell us that he walked several kilometers before realizing that he was not on the right one. Our decision is made by process of elimination. Once again, the Camino provides.

At 8:20, I am treated to another chromatic sunrise. It is as if the sun kisses the earth each morning and the earth blushes. As the morning sun rises over the mountains at our back, the earth appears red and the wheat-stubble, golden. Once again, our two friendly shadows accompany us as we trek westward to Santiago. We walk for six hours in a very poor and desolate area. People live in caves dug into the side of the hills. Many of the adobe homes are in disrepair; when the stucco finish is not maintained, rain dissolves the adobe and the house collapses.

The Meseta is not what I expected. It is not desert-like; the soil is hard, rocky and difficult to dig, and because of the drought, very dry. It is not drab and lifeless. There are birds and butterflies, thistle and blossoming flowers in yellow, red, blue, or white. The deep blue sky is a striking contrast with the deep green fields of alfalfa, asparagus, and cabbage-like plants; with golden corn tassels; and with the beige and browns of acres upon acres of dried bird-pecked sunflowers withering in the fields.

We crossed a medieval bridge over the Rio Cea and stop for a snack at San Nicolás del Real Camino, the last village in the province of Palencia. While we nosh at the base of the refurbished hermitage, Virgen del Puente, a Filipina named Vina joins us. She is a psychologist who walks with us until Sahagún. She talks nonstop in a short staccato rhythm; I doubt her patients can get a word in edgewise.

In Sahagún, we see the Moorish influences in the architecture, tile work, and art. We pass a huge arch with a belfry, which is all that remains of one of the largest and most powerful Benedictine monasteries of twelfth-century Spain. I remove my wide brim hat and use the umbrella against the sweltering October sun. I cannot imagine how oppressive the sun's rays are in July and August.

Once again, we come to a ill-marked crossroad. Our guidebook indicates two choices: the Real Camino Francés, suitable for walkers and mountain bikers; or the Calzada (roadway) de los Peregrinos, which is suitable for fit walkers who prefer the "more authentic, mainly Roman way." We want the easier route, but the signage is confusing. Ultimately, we make the correct choice, crunching our way down a two-meter-wide gravel path to the town of Bercianos de Real Camino. Dennis is spent from yesterday's bout with the twenty-four-hour virus, and the next opportunity for an *albergue* is 8 kilometers (about 5 miles) away.

The two-story adobe *albergue* in Bercianos is the most rustic one in which we have stayed. As we enter, the smiling *hospitaleros* welcome us. I sense genuine concern for our well-being, as if they are welcoming us into their home.

Linda Heiderer and Daniel De Kay are the first American hosts that we meet. They are volunteers from American Pilgrims on the Camino, an organization with the mission "to foster the enduring tradition of the Camino by supporting its infrastructure, by gathering pilgrims together, and by providing information and encouragement to past and future pilgrims." They in turn are delighted to see Americans come to the *albergue*.

On the registration table, there are water, melon, and hard

candies to refresh us. I note that the *hospitaleros* are kind and responsive to the pilgrims and do not rush anyone. When it is our turn, Daniel speaks to us in English; for the first time Dennis understands the registration discussion. As Daniel stamps our credentials, I notice that the *sello* is of a pilgrim watching the sunset.

After the usual *albergue* arrival routine, we visit a local café to use the Internet to call home, because there is no Wi-Fi at the ancient hostel. We deposit our euro, only to find out that the computer headphones are broken. I report this to the barkeeper, who tells me that she knows. When I asked her why she did not put up a sign to warn people, she looks at me as if that were a novel idea.

Signe Tøth from Denmark

Dennis and I help set the tables and prep for supper. Dennis meets the Danish woman, Signe Tøth, whom I met the previous night. She is a private person with a brilliant smile.

We have a delightful meal consisting of salad, couscous, and Apple Betty. What a refreshing change from the customary m*enu peregrino*! Between the salad and the main course we all go outside to see the sunset on the Meseta. For some, the simple beauty or the few minutes of reflection brings tears; others hug and dance. The joy of the moment follows us inside where, after finishing our meal, we group by nationality (Spanish, Italian, French, Brazilian, and American) and sing for each other. The American contingent is small and atonal. We change the lyrics to the Glen Campbell song "By the Time I Get to Phoenix" to "by the time I get to the *albergue*." It is all in fun, and the other pilgrims vote us the worst singers that evening. The number one choice is the Brazilian (Orlando) who precedes his song with heartfelt words about the Camino and, particularly, what this stay in Bercianos means to him. He vocalizes what many of us are feeling about the camaraderie and joy in sharing simple moments. Orlando then beats the table rhythmically, while singing a song in Portuguese. Though I do not understand the words, his voice and his passion move me to tears. At the end, he gets a standing ovation. This *alegria* (joy) makes this my favorite *albergue*.

After the songfest, everyone helps neaten the dining room, wash the dishes, and then prepare the tables for breakfast. Soon everyone is off to bed or to the pilgrim's blessing service that is offered daily in parochial *albergues*.

In the morning, Linda, the *hospitalera*, is too busy for an interview. The following conversation occurs after I returned from Spain.

Linda Heiderer

"To work as a *hospitalera*, one has to have walked the Camino. I walked the Camino last year (2010) in October, from Roncesvalles to Santiago, and it took me about a month. It was wonderful. However, my husband had died a year prior to that, so I was bereft when I walked. I needed to find a new path in life and I thought the Camino would provide me some quiet time and thinking time to help sort my life out. I had hoped to have a revelation about what I should do next. Even though I did not have a great revelation, I did get to know myself better and that was helpful in finding my path. The time for reflection also helped me let go of some things. I thought, 'I'm done with carrying around this excess baggage. I'm throwing it to the wind.' That was cleansing.

"Having the company of people who were on a similar journey and being able to share my thoughts with them was certainly helpful. I was sixty-two when I walked it last year. Though I came alone, I had steady companionship throughout the Camino. I walked the first week with a Finnish woman. When she left, I walked in tandem with a Dutch man. We would often walk on our own during the day, but meet up for tea along the way, and then again at the *albergue* at the end of the day. It was a comfort to have a companion for dinner and a chat at the end of a day.

"Last year I met Daniel on the Camino. He is a board member of the American Pilgrims [of the Camino]. He mentioned that there was training for becoming a *hospitalera* and asked if I was interested. Since it sounded intriguing, I kept in touch with him when I returned to the US. When I did take the training several months later, he was one of the trainers. At the end of the session, he asked if I wanted to join him to work at an *albergue*. We agreed on the dates and he took over from there, since he is very connected with the Camino people in Spain. He arranged for us to come to Bercianos. I was happy to come here because I had stayed at this *albergue* the year before and remembered it very fondly.

"As a volunteer, I only had to pay for my transportation to the *albergue*. Once there, room and board were provided. It was a labor of love. I absolutely enjoyed being a host. It was intensely fulfilling, joyful, and magnificent. Those were two of the greatest weeks in my life.

"It is difficult to chose which I enjoyed more, being a pilgrim or being a *hospitalera*. This year I walked just four days before coming to Bercianos and three days after. I still love the walking and the space it allows for reflection. However, staying in one place, having the pilgrims come to us and providing them with the basics—bed, shower, warm meal, and send-off breakfast—was also gratifying. With that said, Daniel and I wanted to add to the pilgrims' experience with more than the basics. To that end, we provided foot massage, blister repair, and often lent an ear to someone who was having a rough time.

"Another unique opportunity our pilgrims had was to cook the evening meal together. At about 5 p.m., I supervised the preparations for the meal. Since this was a *donativo albergue*, everyone helped in the preparation of the meal or in the cleanup. There were stations for the salad prep, chopping stations for the main course, and another station for making the salad dressing and cutting the bread. People also set the tables, and filled the wine bottles and water pitchers. I loved this part of the day. People came alive, talked with each other, and sang with the music, sometimes danced. It was a fun time. We needed one or two people to be the cooks, to stand by the stove and stir or sauté. Daniel or I knew what the meal would be, so we gave them instructions and they produced the final product. One night an Italian woman who we called 'Mama Italia' cooked such a delicious pasta Primavera we had her stand up to receive the applause of the group.

"The evenings at our *albergue* were full of delight. During dinner, we took time out to watch the sunset, a nightly event at this *albergue*. People went out to the patio to take a moment to appreciate the simple beauty of the sun going down. It was a lovely time. People gave each other hugs, took pictures, and marveled at the wonder of it all.

"Then after dinner we had what we dubbed songfest, or '*alegria* time.' For this, we had people group together by country, prepare a song and then sing it to everyone. The laughter and the smiles on people's faces were all we needed to know that music is universal and connects us. One night a young Frenchman, who had brought his violin, performed a solo that was just beautiful. On another night an Algerian played his flute, and an Irish guy played a tin whistle. Sometimes someone would sing a solo. It was usually someone with an amazing voice and they would sing something that had us near tears. The songfest was just great—for the participants and for Daniel and me. Every night we had a lovely concert to enjoy. Even when we had terrible singers, everyone applauded; the spirit of people on the Camino is so loving.

"After songfest and meal cleanup, we held a short prayer service, the pilgrim's blessing. Many people walk the Camino with heavy hearts; our prayer service gave our guests time to reflect or share what was in their hearts. For me, hearing these reflections from our pilgrims was the best part of being a *hospitalera*. Our priest had a routine, which we loosely followed. First, we read the St. Francis prayer in four languages. Next, we passed a candle around the circle of people who had gathered, and they took turns talking about what the Camino meant for them, or maybe they shared a burden they were carrying. The service concluded then with a beautiful recording of 'Amazing Grace,' sung by Judy Collins. Many times, as we joined hands to sing, people were moved to tears.

"After this service, we made sure that the pilgrims were off to bed, that the breakfast preparations were complete, and then we'd lock the gate. Our day usually did not end until 11 p.m. The following morning one of us got up at 6:15 to scald the milk for the coffee. After everyone departed, we'd tidy up the dining room and kitchen and then the entire *albergue,* which meant mopping, sweeping, changing pillowcases and sheets, and scrubbing toilets and showers.

"We usually completed the chores around 10:30 or 11:00

a.m. We then sat down for a nice leisurely breakfast. After discussing what we would have for dinner and planning the groceries, we'd take our showers and get ready for the 1:30 crowd. We'd try to take a nap during the day, because we got so exhausted with all the work and the long hours.

"Every three days we'd take the bus into Sahagún, load up three shopping carts with food and supplies, and then take a taxi back to the *albergue*. We didn't buy expensive groceries, mostly pasta, lentils, and rice were the main courses. We would rotate five basic meals that we learned from our predecessors. If we ran out of fixings for the salad, we would go to a local shop and buy them. Even though it was much more expensive to do this, the priest encouraged us to support the local businesses.

"One of the funny stories of being a *hospitalera* was my marriage proposal. One afternoon I was giving a foot massage to a Spanish man and he was enjoying it very much. He asked if I was married, and this made me laugh. He then said that if I were not married he would like to marry me to keep this foot massage going in his life. I laughed again. He then suggested that if I would not marry him, I should at least walk the rest of the Camino with him, so he could continue getting the foot massages. That night I had made an apple cobbler for dessert. This was very different from the Spanish dessert repertoire of yogurt and flan. That same Spaniard said, 'Linda, you made this? That's it, I am buying a ticket to Colorado; we have to be together.' This made me laugh even more. Since on that night there were two priests in the group, Jorge and a pilgrim, I said to the group, 'This has been such a special group of people today. Someone has made it extra special for me; I have had a marriage proposal.' I focused on the Spanish guy and said, 'Since there are two priests here tonight, let's just do it.' He shrunk down and turned beet red, but it was all in jest.

"There was another man one night who shared with me that his wife had died the year before and he just wept when he talked about his loss. I had so much compassion for him and I shared the loss of my husband with him. We had a good talk. The next day I wanted to say goodbye to him before he left and I wanted to put something tangible in his hand. I grabbed a granola bar and met him just as he was leaving. I told him, 'I am so glad I saw you. I wanted to give you this granola bar. Later today, when you are sitting down having a rest, have this for a snack and know that I am thinking about you and that my heart is with you.'

"Several days later, I was at the café in town that had Internet service when a man I did not know came in to use the computer. I told him I was the *hospitalera* in the *albergue* and asked if he were going to stay with us that night. He said that he was going to move on, but that he had had an email from a fellow pilgrim, who told him not to miss Bercianos, that it was one of the best *albergues* on the Camino. He was referring to the pilgrim who had lost his wife. It was very heartwarming to know that that pilgrim's stay in the *albergue* meant so much to him.

"The *albergue* had forty-eight beds and we usually had about forty guests. One night we had fifty-eight pilgrims staying as guests. If we had leftovers, we'd offer them to the pilgrims that arrived early the next day. We wanted to provide as much sustenance as we could for our guests.

"Being a host was a seventeen-hour workday. We opened the *albergue* at 1:30 p.m. and normally there already were a half a dozen people waiting to get in. We'd check the people in, making sure that there was a glass of water and a bowl of candy for them. We'd chat with them, find out where they were from and how they were doing and how far they had walked that day.

"Besides the priest, we had befriended the neighbors, Antonino and Tina, who were caretakers of the *albergue*. They have been doing this job for the priest for years. Each day we took money from the donation box, which we used for groceries and upkeep. When there was extra money, we gave it to Antonino to put in the bank. There was complete trust in us to handle the money.

"The Camino and the system that the Spanish have developed are wonderful. People come from all over the earth and are able to do the journey relatively cheaply; spending about €10 [$12.50] for an *albergue* is remarkable. One night at songfest, we had representation from the four corners of the earth: an Algerian, an Iranian, Koreans, Europeans, and North and South Americans, all experiencing the joy of one another's company. This joy is what we have to keep with us and take back with us. We don't have to fight one another. The Camino shows us what can be.

"Would I be a *hospitalera* again? Part of me would like to do it again, because it was such a wonderful experience. On the other hand, I feel that there are many things that I still want to do in my life and being a *hospitalera* again would be just repeating an experience and not expanding to something new. Though, there is a chance that I will do it again.

"One of the key reasons that Bercianos is so special is the priest, Jorge. He is a very holy man, emanating an incredible spirit. He graces that *albergue* with his love and warmth. Nevertheless, because I like to try new things, I would prefer to host in a different location if I decide to be a *hospitalera* again."

I am sleeping, facing the wall when someone crawls into bed with me. It is dark. I am confused and think, "Did someone returning from the bathroom mistake my bed for his?" I murmur, "You can't stay here, you must leave." I am grumpy about being awakened. Then Dennis says, "It's time to get up and I just want to cuddle for a few minutes." I relax. Nestled in his arms, we enjoy a few precious moments of togetherness. I wonder what the others in the room think as they rise to see the two of us snuggling together in the lower corner bunk. Envy perhaps? Though the pilgrims of old supposedly practiced celibacy while on the Camino, I do not think that practice is common nowadays. For those wanting privacy or a good night's sleep away from the dormitory noises, some private *albergues* offer single rooms for an additional fee; there are *casas rurales* (cottages), *hoteles* and *posadas* (inns), and *paradores* (luxury hotels). Also, there is camping.

The morning temperature is moderate; it should be a pleasant day. At midday, we picnic on sardines, olives, dark bread, and orange juice as we sit on a cement bench beneath shade trees. I hear a nearby stream bubble, songbirds, and in the distance, a farm truck driving through a field. The walk today is the best since the descent into St-Jean-Pied-de-Port; the air is crisp, cool, and autumn-like, just right for walking. I have found my stride and an inner peace. If, as Marianne Williamson, author of *A Woman's Worth*, said, "Joy is what happens when we allow ourselves to recognize how good things are," then I am joyous.

We stop for hot tea, and chuckle because it comes in a glass. Many customs such as this have me scratching my head. I speculate that the philosophy is "too hot to hold, too hot to drink." Even though the guidebook had suggested carrying extra supplies in this region, we did not need to; there are plenty of opportunities for food and drink.

Upon our arrival in Mansilla de las Molas, Dennis is the only man in the room at the *albergue* with me and five Korean women. With a wink, they joke that he will be very tired in the morning. We later cook dinner in the kitchen and eat in the geranium-filled central patio. As we finish our meal, a group of Spanish, Portuguese, Brazilian, and American pilgrims comes in with food to cook on a large gas cooker, specific for cooking paella. As they prepare the rice and meat dish, they drink beer and wine. Orlando, whom we met last night, plays the guitar and there is much *alegria*. I very much enjoy staying at the *albergues:* there is so much fun, and friendships develop.

Out on the patio, the Korean women we met earlier join with several other other Koreans to sing a national song, with arms waving and bodies swaying. Elodie and a friend join the festivities and we share hugs and kisses. She seems to be a favorite among the group and they cheer her into dancing under the limbo stick as Orlando plays a calypso. The *hospitalera* passes out the words to "Cancion del Peregrino Bamba" and everyone sings these words to the melody of "La Bamba." As we sing, we dance and create a conga line and march around the patio.

Yoori Ro arrives with her boyfriend. Whenever I see her on the Camino, she has a gorgeous smile and appears very happy and friendly. Her boyfriend wears a glittery gold top hat that allows us to recognize the two of them from the distance. I often see them walking hand in hand.

Yoori Ro

"I am a single, twenty-six-year-old Korean from Seoul. I speak Korean and a little English, nothing else.

"I like walking and I think a lot while I walk. This is the pilgrim's way.

"I am walking with my boyfriend and have been with him for three years. Because of the Camino, I know him a lot better. He is very good to me. We are very comfortable with each other; he is very funny and we laugh a lot.

"I was surprised by how long the Camino is and how many people are very kind to me. The walking has not been very difficult. My body is good to me. I am a little shy and it is difficult sometimes to meet so many foreign people.

"I am walking the Camino for cultural more than spiritual reasons. Though I have been going to church for twenty-one years, I have visited only a few churches along the Way. I like walking more. The walking is very peaceful and I like looking at the landscape that I cannot see in Korea because of the many mountains there. I like the sunshine and am enjoying the warm weather.

"I am really surprised by the number of people who are walking. They are very kind and friendly. There is nothing I do not like about the Camino. I do find the food in Spain to be very salty, but not very different from Korea."

The *albergue* has medieval-style pilgrim clothing and Dennis is the first that night to come to the patio in the garb. With his white beard and long hair, carrying a staff and gourd, and wearing a long woolen cloak secured at the waist with a hemp rope, a large brimmed traveling hat with the scallop shell attached to it, and sandals, he would have fit in with the pilgrims of old.

I see that Sonia has joined us. Though I had seen her in Grañón, this is our first opportunity to speak.

Sonia Sanchez

"I am Spanish from Spain and I am thirty-four years old. I live in Barcelona and am also Catalan. I speak Spanish, Catalan, English and *un petit peu du français* (a little French). I started my Camino in Roncesvalles.

"About five-and-a-half months ago I was totally broken. My life changed because of something that happened to me and I couldn't walk, couldn't talk, couldn't do anything. I cannot really explain how I was feeling. One day I decided that I would learn to walk. I said to myself, one step, then another.

"Then Maggie, my friend from the States whom I had not seen for seventeen years and with whom I have not had contact for about sixteen years, found me on Facebook. She sent me an email telling me that she was coming to Spain and would love to see me, but that she was coming to do the Camino de Santiago.

"This was a sign for me. Maggie is a super special person for me, someone that I thought I would see in my life again, but I did not know when. All of a sudden, she writes this email telling me that she was coming to Spain, and not only to Spain, but also to do the Camino. Doing the Camino was not an option I was even thinking about. All of a sudden there was this wide-open, not window, but door in front of me. I wrote her back telling her, 'Maggie I think this is a sign. I don't know if you are doing the Camino by yourself, but I would at least love to start the Camino with you'. I wasn't sure how she would respond. She said, 'I don't know how your life will change from now on with all that has happened to you. So no pressure, but if you decide to come, I would be very pleased, very happy, happy, happy. I am starting the Camino on September 18 and will be in Roncesvalles on September 17. If you decide you are not coming, feel free to do whatever you want, but I would be very happy if you were starting with me.'

"I have now been on the Camino for about three weeks and have found out many things. I would divide the Camino into four *etapas* (stages) of all the *etapas* we have walked. The first would be Me Meeting Maggie after all these years. Maggie and her way of being reminds me a lot of the person that I lost in an accident; someone who was a part of me. She reminds me in many ways about him. Even though it had been seventeen years since we saw each other, it felt like it was yesterday. We were like 'cling'— right back close to each other.

"We started the Camino together with another guy, Samuel, whom I met in Pamplona when I got on the bus to Roncesvalles, and he is still doing the Camino with us. The second stage was when the three of us became a huge group of people. We were like a family walking together.

Women of the Way

There was a seventy-year-old couple from Pais Vasco [Basque Country], someone from Murcia, three people from Barcelona, one from Estramadura, and then two more from Barcelona. With this family we walked all the way to Logroño, where more than half of the group left, since that was as far as they were going. It was very sad to leave them because it was the first encounter we had with the Camino and it was all very intense. We had gotten very close as we got to know each other. We may have walked alone or in small groups, knowing that at the village or town everyone would arrive and we would share dinner. This is a part of the Camino that I remember with love.

"Stage three. After Logroño we met other people, and they were as great as the group we had before. I think that is because we meet the best part of every person on the Camino. Everyone is with good energy, helping others, trying to find their way and walking with you, so you are never alone. We met other people and this group kept growing and changing. Then in Burgos, a lot of people left.

"Stage four. From Burgos on, it is back to the three of us— Samuel, Maggie, and me. We took it more easily because we have no time limit. The people in the first two groups were time-limited and we had been on their rhythm. But from Burgos on, we decided to take it more slowly because we wanted to enjoy ourselves. If we liked a town, we would spend more time there. We made the distances we walked each day shorter. We would walk on our own. Maggie, Samuel or I would leave earlier. We never got up at the same time and left together. Sometimes we would meet during the day, or not. We had the freedom of saying, 'I just want to be on my own' or 'I would like to walk with you.' I find this sense of freedom that I have with each of them great. I am doing the Camino by myself, but I am with them. Samuel stayed in Sahagún because he got tendinitis and the doctor told him to rest for three or four days. We will meet him in León. We will get there tomorrow and will wait there a few days until Samuel can catch up.

"I have met lots and lots of people. I love talking to people. It is very easy to talk with people on the Camino. I think that this is because everything comes from the inside. People look into your eyes when they talk with you. They are not in a rush, because all we have to do is walk. Also, when you get to a town you just relax and are open to anything that can possibly happen. I have met many people that I would otherwise not have met. Different ages, different cultures, different nationalities that I would not ordinarily have approached. But, I did, because I was walking.

"I love the spontaneous moments on the Camino. One day I was in a town that had only one street. I was sitting on a bench with my backpack on and drinking a Coke. A Korean, who was staying at a hostel that was in front of where I was sitting, saw me and came over with a tray with a large dish of Korean soup and a side dish of olives and peppers. I was amazed. I just love it.

"When I started, my objective was to learn to walk again. Things come, and things go, and I have to accept it. Nothing is forever. I had been attached to the idea that some things were forever. I think I got it. I can walk now.

"My next objective or achievement is to find the yellow arrows inside of me, just as there are the yellow arrows pointing to Santiago. I have to find the ability to listen to my body, my soul, my everything to be able to see the yellow arrows and where they point me. I have to learn to be open, because there is nothing to fear.

"On the Camino, I have nothing to fear, not even blisters, which is good because I have not had any blisters thus far. I have no fear. I always have the yellow arrows pointing the direction. For example, the other day I was walking in the dark because I awoke very early and decided to leave. My headlamp broke and I could not see anything. There was a turnabout with different ways. I tried to use my cell phone to illuminate enough to see an arrow, but I didn't find it. Therefore, I picked a way and kept on going. It was a long, long road with the divider for the cars and no arrows. I kept walking on the road because there wasn't a sidewalk. But, there were many stars above me. It was beautiful! I spotted Venus. I thought, 'What is the worst thing that can happen to me now?' I realized that the worst thing that could happen would be that I would have to walk more that day because maybe I was walking in the wrong direction. But, at that time, it was not a problem because I was walking and enjoying the moment. At one point, I stopped and said, 'Okay, please send me a sign so I know that I am on the good way.' I was not afraid, I just wanted a sign to tell me I was heading in the right direction. And then I saw a shooting star, just in front of me. Wow! It seemed to be the slowest shooting star that I had ever seen. I even made a wish. I continued walking for about 7 kilometers knowing I was on the right way."

That evening I journalize, "This has been a most wonderful day. I feel the engagement of the Camino, as if I am part of the community." After climbing into my bunk, I hear Elodie sing in French, her voice wafting up from the patio in the style of Edith Piaf, the French singer known as "The Sparrow." What a wonderful way to end a day!

When we leave in the morning, it is unexpectedly cold. About 3 kilometers (1.8 miles) later, I don my rain jacket over the fleece, dig out my gloves, and shiver forward. The walk into León, the largest municipality in the province and the fourth largest on the entire Camino, is not pleasant: traveling on paved streets, by car dealerships and industries. We cross the highway on a metal pedestrian bridge. There is a lot of traffic, lots of noise, and little beauty. I am not impressed. I find the immense stone buildings imposing and feel out of place in this large metropolitan city. Is my negativity the result of the overcast and cold clime or from feeling confined after the expanse of the Meseta? Or both!

The only thing I like about León is its international cuisine. We both are yearning for something spicy. At a Turkish café, I order Durum Kebob, a vegetarian gyro. After weeks of bland food, the intense flavors make my palate tingle with delight.

The municipal *albergue* is large, but the rooms have four bunk beds. When I go to wash up, the hook is on the outside of the door. I am peeved. Why is it that this shower, like most along the Camino, does not have shelves for toiletries or hooks situated to keep towels or clothing dry? Is the only solution to put the hook on the outside of the stall door? Why do I have to place my belongings in a plastic bag in hopes of protecting them from the water? I shower in cool water, which does nothing for my bad mood.

Women of the Way

I snuggle into my sleeping bag with my fleece clothing on. Once again, there is no pillow covering and I use my shirt as a pillowcase. As people arrive, the room gets warmer, but not enough for me to remove the extra clothing. Now that there are more Spaniards on the Camino, I practice my conversational Spanish. One Spaniard tells me the forecast is for cold for two days, and then it will warm up.

I have no interest in sightseeing. The cathedral, the Palacio, and the old quarter do not tempt me from my warm bed. Dennis goes out to scrounge supper and returns with more food than we can eat and we share it with others. The "kitchen" has two microwaves and a fridge—no running water, no utensils for cooking or eating. To get water for tea, we need to walk to the lavatory at the other end of the building. Not convenient.

It is 6°C (43°F) when we leave the next morning, but I am dressed for warmth. We walk 7 kilometers (4 miles) through parks and an industrial area before leaving the city. We pass a driver's training school for children that teaches with go-carts; a McDonald's with its genuine McIbéria, a one-hundred percent beefburger with Ibérian ham, manchego cheese (made from sheep's milk), oil and vinegar; and then past the Monastery of San Marco, which is a *parador* or state-run, five-star hotel located in an restored historical building. This *parador* is also a culinary school that teaches chefs ancient and local recipes and trains them in specialties such as fish and chocolate.

Once outside the city, there is a choice of two routes: the traditional route that follows the N-120 (road route) or the quieter, but longer, walker's route. We opt for the latter: twenty-four hours of city bustle and cars have me craving the countryside. Each time we have a choice of two routes I am reminded of Robert Frost's "Two roads diverged in a wood, and I,/ I took the one less traveled by,/ And that has made all the difference." For me, taking the alternate route has made a difference. My Camino is connected to nature more than if I had walked alongside the well-trafficked roads; I see more beauty in the rural settings than via the shorter, more direct routes. The less crowded Way offers fewer modern-day distractions and more time for introspection—and, more opportunity for getting lost.

Once again, we make a good choice. This way is spectacular; words fail to describe how stunning it is. I doubt that the best *National Geographic* photographer could capture the allure. The fields are red, gold, and white. There are tamaracks, chestnuts, and pine. Climbing out of Virgen del Camino, a small town that dates back to the tenth century, the mountains, all jagged and cloud covered, are eye-popping. In the foreground are fields of alfalfa, Swiss chard, and corn, adding color to the vast plains.

Villar de Mazarife is pilgrim-friendly. At the entrance to the village is a large monument featuring the town's belltower and medieval pilgrims. Passing the bell tower, I see that it is a stork "condo" with three huge nests on it. Each nest can weigh 60 to 250 kilograms (130 to 550 pounds) and are about 2 meters (6.6 feet) tall and 1.5 meters (4.0 feet) wide. I see smaller birds flying in and out of these large nests and wonder if they are feeding on the mites, stealing twigs, or making their own nests within the large ones.

At Albergue Mesón Tío Pepe in the center of the small town, Pepe and wife welcome us, their bright smiles dispelling any residual gloom from León. We enjoy the privacy of a "suite," even though it is the size of a closet and has bunk beds.

The next day we do not find our shadows until 8:32 a.m., when the sun rises. These late sunrises mean more time walking in the cold and dark.

Since my feet have grown, I start the day wearing my boots with thin cotton socks and then change into sandals when my toes cramp and hurt. I imagine these changes to my feet will be permanent; Dennis' feet never returned to his pre-Appalachian Trail size.

To reach Hospital de Órbigo we cross a twenty-arched, 204-meter (670-foot)-long Roman bridge, Puente de Órbigo, on which, in 1434, there was a month-long tournament known as El Paso Honroso (Honorable Pass). According to legend, Don Suero de Quiñones wanted to be absolved from a vow made to his lover, Leonor, to fast on Thursdays, and to wear an iron collar to symbolize that he was a prisoner of love. To be released from the vow, he proposed a jousting contest where he would break the lances of three hundred knights who wished to cross the bridge. After breaking one hundred and sixty-six lances, the judge absolved him. He then removed his collar and became a pilgrim. Since 1997, on the first weekend of June, the town celebrates the jousting. The festival attracts thousands of men and women dressed as medieval merchants, peasants, kings, witches, clowns, monks, and innkeepers. There are medieval dancers, games, and music. The celebration ends on Sunday afternoon with a grand, torch-lit procession.

Once again, we have a choice of routes: the one along the main road with its traffic and speeding motorists, or the more pastoral one. We choose the scenic route, which is not indicated on our map. This is where I meet Maggie, Sonia's friend.

Maggie Ervin

"My name is Maggie Ervin. Facing a physical challenge while surrounded by beauty in another culture is an exciting mix for me and is always very nourishing. For this reason, I knew the Camino would bring me many rewards. In my daily life, I don't give myself much time to reflect. I am constantly trying to keep myself busy, take in the news, and listen to podcasts. I don't give myself quiet reflective time and I think I need that. I feel that walking the Camino is a nice balance of being social and having time for contemplation.

"I heard about the Camino through a Spanish coworker in Colombia. After he mentioned it and I learned more about it, I knew that I had to do it eventually. It was just a matter of when.

"I decided to do the Camino this year because I am in the process of moving to Brazil, already uprooting myself. I put my stuff in storage, sold my bed. I thought to myself, 'Will there be another time when I will have one-and-a-half months free? Who knows? So I might as well do it now.' On a deeper level, I feel it is the perfect time. And, to be able to do it with my friend Sonia when she also finds it meaningful is great. I can't imagine having done the Camino without her. Sonia and I have known each other since we were seventeen, when she was an exchange student to Dover, New Hampshire, and we hadn't seen each other in seventeen years.

"There were days where the last few miles were grueling. One day I threw my backpack down, kicked it, told it off, and almost ripped it up with my pocketknife. I was exhausted and pissed off that the next town was eluding me. Some days are long like that, but I always feel great once I make it there. The practical lesson here is that I should have packed better and actually paid attention to suggestions to keep my backpack as light possible, as opposed to heeding my apparent delusions of grandeur. The Camino is humbling, and I guess we all need that sometimes.

"The last few days were a little stressful in terms of lodging. Suddenly there were throngs of pilgrims, and we all needed a place to sleep. I found a bed every night, but it was a bit of a headache those last few times."

Maggie's post-Camino comments:

"I would absolutely do the Camino again. It was one of the most meaningful experiences in my life. I am still only beginning to make sense of all the ways it reached me and unfolded in me.

"There were so many highlights that it's hard to convey them without sounding sappy. However, suffice it to say, connecting with other pilgrims was the most meaningful element of the Camino and then learning to let go of them. More than a few times I met a wonderful person with a much faster pace—always faster in my case. My slowness was yet another humbling element of the Camino. We'd get to hang out one evening, and then we'd never see each other again.

"The advice I would give is to do the Camino if you ever have the chance, and if you want to grow in ways you can't even conjure up. You'll be pushed, and you'll be glad you were. And you'll also eat great Spanish food."

After walking 31 kilometers (19 miles) we reach Astorga. I am tired. On the outskirts, we traverse the railroad tracks via a metal pedestrian bridge that adds about a kilometer to the daily distance. Just prior to that, we meet up with Orlando and his Spanish companions from the *albergue* in Mansilla de las Mulas. As we cross the bridge, the four of them rhythmically pound their walking poles: bang-bang-BANG, bang-bang-BANG; the din is almost unbearable.

Why is it that the historic quarters are always on the top of hills? After an arduous day of hiking, why do I have to make a Herculean effort to get to the *albergue*? I am tired and plod forward, each step an exertion. Once there, I must climb to the second floor before I can plop myself onto a top bunk, all of the lower ones having been taken. Luckily, we find side-by-side bunks in the corner of the room and then discover an electrical outlet. We upload pictures, and recharge phones and Kindles.

When registering at the *albergue*, we receive discount vouchers for a €12 ($15) pilgrim's menu at the Hotel Gaudi, a three-star hotel across from Gaudi's Episcopal Palace and the Santa Maria Cathedral. I tease Dennis about pressing the Armani before going out to eat. Dining at the hotel is luxurious with linens, silverware, and a delectable upscale menu selection. Even the wine is a better quality. What a treat!

Returning to the *albergue,* I check out the dining room. Tomorrow's breakfast will be a buffet. Even though I have just eaten an elegant meal, I look forward to oatmeal, fruit, and something other than pan-toasted bread with jam— that traditional morning repast is getting monotonous.

The Albergue San Javier is overcrowded; we squeeze between the bunk beds and navigate around baggage on the floor. I question if we could escape in a fire. Our bunks are under a skylight. Even though there is a cold breeze, I welcome the fresh air. In this crowded condition, I imagine the air must be stale on the other side of the room.

I spy Cheryl and Eric whom we met in Pamplona. They are resting on lower bunks in the corner of the room. Eric has added more than a hundred new bird species to his sighting journal while on the Camino. I spend some time speaking with his wife.

Cheryl Kinney Matheson

"I am ordained in the United Church of Canada, which is a liberal Protestant denomination. I am from Kenora, Ontario. I can't remember how I first learned about the Camino. I guess I have known about it for about five years. I took a spiritual directions training program to become a spiritual director. The metaphor that was used for that program was the pilgrimage. We read *The Art of Pilgrimage: The Seeker's Guide to Making Travel Sacred,* by Phil Cousineau. I became absorbed with that as a metaphor for life. Shortly afterward, I came upon the Camino and felt called to really experience this.

"I have been walking on the Camino for about thirty days. It is an amazing experience. I think some of the things that I thought about it when I started are not the things I will understand about it when I finish. I am now two-thirds of the way. It is hard and it is wonderful. I have been surprised by the community. That has been an amazing thing. I understand that the Camino is a metaphor for the spiritual journey and there is a sense of moving inward.

"There were some humorous but profound comments that I heard along the Way. I met a German couple, and we were each dealing with our foot issues. The man said 'How do they get thousands of people to do this every year?' I then asked him why he was doing it and he said, 'I don't know. I think I've forgotten.' I think the original reason for walking the Camino is blurred.

"Another time I was laughing with a woman from the Netherlands because we could not remember what day it was or where we started, and then she said, 'By the time we get to Santiago we will have even forgotten who we are.' For me, that was a profound comment in terms of the spiritual journey, that our illusions just get peeled away and that when we end this, we are not exactly who we were when we started it. We have moved more inward; I would call it to our soul. We discover something inside of us that is a new place of being. I have really felt this, especially when I went through the Meseta, which was hard for me because I had feet issues. I was in pain, day after day, and hobbled into *albergues*. I was amazed that I was in such physical pain and so aware of my body. I was tending to my body, which I don't normally do. At the same time, I was aware of a sense of joy. To me, this was a discovery of a different place within myself, a new place of soul.

"The huge challenge will be for me to take what I have learned from this experience and see how it will be in life. I don't want to go back to living just exactly as I did before.

"People say that you don't walk the Camino, the Camino walks you. I get that. I am a person who works in a very stressed job. I am a planner. I plan, plan, plan until it is coming out of my ears. And, I have just let all of that go. I don't know where I am going today. There is a wonderful freeness about that. It all works out.

"I am not sure if I would recommend the Camino for anyone else. I would say to them that you might think that you can do it, but you really have to want to do it, you really have to be called to do it. It is not a holiday. It is hard in ways that are hard to describe. It is not a fun pleasure trip. If you feel really, strongly called to it; yes, absolutely! But first, really discern why you are doing it. Do some serious thinking about it and just don't get on the bandwagon.

"I had shin splints, what the Spaniards call 'tendonitis.' I hobbled into Azofra. The next day I walked about 10 kilometers (6.2 miles), but very mindfully, leaning on my walking stick and careful with each step. I iced my legs. The pain lasted for about five days, during which time I had to be very careful, walk slowly, and elevate my feet whenever I stopped. I also had blisters that were excruciating. Now everything seems to be okay.

"My husband and I plan to walk about 20 kilometers (12.4 miles) per day, which would get us into Santiago around the October 23. But, one never knows. We are taking it one day at a time.

"I don't have a huge expectation about arriving in Santiago. I have refrained from reading other people's experiences. I read one book, but I refrained from reading too much because I did not want to have someone else's experience put on me. Of course, I hear the pilgrim talk along the Way, so I know that certain people have high experiences in different places. But, I am not setting myself up to have someone else's experience. Some of my high moments have been in inconsequential places. They would not be the same for anyone else. People just have to be open to the experiences. I am not expecting something to happen when I arrive in Santiago. It has been the whole thing, not just getting there. I am sure I will feel relief and joy. And the feet will feel great."

After completing the Camino, Cheryl wrote:

"The Camino was a wonderful experience, but coming home is a challenge. When my feet were in pain and it was hot beyond my ability to cope and I met someone who said they were doing it for the second or third time, I thought, 'You're kidding!' Now I understand the lure of this walk and would really like to do it again! I look at our pictures with a sense of disbelief and longing!"

After Astorga, the route becomes mountainous. The region from here to Cruz de Ferro (the Iron Cross) is the ancient historical region, La Maragatería. Its inhabitants, known as "Maragatos," are said to be descendants of the Phoenicians or the Berbers; its language is Leonese. The area has a unique way of building stone houses with large doors. The traditional cuisine is a soup called *Cocido Maragato,* which is composed of chickpeas, cabbage, potatoes, and seven different kinds of meat.

We climb steadily all day. There are evergreens and trees with changing colors, mostly browns and yellows, but are not as brilliant as they get in autumn in New England.

Throughout the farming areas there have been patches of flies. As we walk through the swarms, we swat at the winged insects with our hats, hiking poles, hands. They are pesky, but do not bite. One German woman has a unique solution. She wraps branches around her neck. As she walks, the branches bounce, keeping the flies away.

In Santa Catalina de Somoza, I enjoy sitting outdoors in the autumn sunshine, sipping on chamomile tea. I am relaxed. Life is good. I reflect on how much I enjoy talking with women and how eager they are to tell me their stories. Is it the Camino that makes this happen, or do women just want to be heard, too often silenced by society? I bond with each woman in a unique way. Is this bonding "sisterhood," or is it just what happens when two people acknowledge each other? Sisters are comfortable with each other and often share their innermost thoughts and feelings. In our conversations, women let down their defenses and speak openly with me. Certainly, this is sisterhood.

One of the great gifts that the Camino offers is the freedom to be yourself. People do not know your history; you have no reputation to maintain, no image of what or who you must be. One woman from Malaysia reveals to me that she feels like a little child again. Without the pressure to conform to others' expectations, she is laughing, singing, dancing, and having unanticipated fun. She and her walking companions play tricks on each other and laugh a lot. She tells me, "I am really grateful for this because it has been missing from my life in the past few years. Everything is so serious. I am supposed to be grown up and work hard. Now I have added a little joy to my life."

This freedom to simply be yourself is liberating, if you can accept who you are and your limitations. Some people are frustrated, especially at the beginning, because they cannot keep their self-imposed pace. As they accept the fact that they need to slow down, they become happier with themselves and with the Camino. It can be frustrating to have to take time off for illness or to heal; the people who learn to let go and give themselves permission to take the time or to alter their schedule, destination, or that day's activity become more accepting of themselves and, as a result, of other pilgrims' limitations. This acceptance teaches that there is no need to be judgmental of oneself or of others. Each person must make her own Way.

On our way to Rabanal del Camino, we spot the incongruous Mesón Cowboy with its forest-green doors and whitewashed walls. The banner says *De Lo Bueno Lo Mejor* (the best of the best). A huge antenna on the roof piques Dennis' curiosity. We stop for lunch and eat on the small *terraza* next to the café. Immediately to the left of the terrace is another café attracting pilgrims. The interior of Meson Cowboy is decorated with American cowboy memorabilia such as a saddle, cowboy hats, spurs, cowbells, pictures of cowboys on horseback, bullwhips, and even a stuffed horse's head; the fare is typical Spanish cuisine and offers natural cider.

Arriving at Rabanal del Camino, we camp in the fields across from the Posada El Tesin. This inn is a refurbished stone building. Pilgrim and local farming decorations hang on its yellow cantina walls. The innkeeper allows us to use the inn's bathroom facilities, kitchen, and Wi-Fi, and provides us with the *contrasena* (password). We set up our tent in a large field, then move the picnic table and lounge chairs near the tent.

This type of camping is pleasurable. We have all the amenities, the company of other pilgrims, and treasured privacy. Prior to coming on the Camino, we had heard that stealth camping (secretly setting up a tent and then leaving unnoticed) was prohibited in Spain. This is apparently a rumor, though some local prohibitions may exist. We have heard of pilgrims who camped under the stars without tents, others who camped in parks within towns or who asked a farmer for permission to camp in the fields. Camping in campgrounds can be more expensive than staying in a *albergue,* but camping at an *albergue* usually costs the same as sleeping within.

That day, instead of using liquid body soap to wash my clothes, I try a sliver of bar soap that is left at the washtub. For the first time, the red road dirt washes completely off my white socks; even the old embedded stains disappear. Spaniards use the bar soap *Legarto* for hair, skin, and laundry. It is available in most *supermercados*; the one sold in a brown wrapper is for personal use, while the one in the green wrapper is used for washing floors. I am not sure which I have, but I keep the sliver for future use.

Throughout the night, I hear large dogs walking through the field or baying in the distance. I am distracted by the noise, but manage to sleep well and awaken rested. By the time we take down the tent and have breakfast, it is warmer. We climb the Montes de León, stopping for a cold drink at Foncebadón, a once abandoned village that was rejuvenated because of the Camino. Many ruined buildings stand witness to the dire economics of the area.

Soon we are at the Cruz de Ferro (Iron Cross), the highest point on the Camino. This monument is an iron cross on the top of a long oak pole. It is believed that the twelfth-century bishop Gaucelmo Christianized this location by placing the cross over what was originally a pagan ritual site, either Celtic in origin or honoring the Roman god Mercury.

Traditionally, pilgrims bring an item from home to deposit at the base of the Iron Cross as a symbol of leaving their burdens behind. It is a very emotional time for many people. We see Elodie's husband's picture, but not her wedding ring. There are many personal objects left here, all meaningful to the person who carried and placed this "baggage" on the cairn. Among the rubble, I see hats, balloons, banners, an ear of corn, a helmet, a Rubik's Cube, stones with people's names and dates written on them, a pen, a toothbrush, letters, statues, photos, even a wrapped condom. I can only guess that someone left it in hopes of getting pregnant. Of course, there are tons of rocks from all over the world. The debris is piled 4 to 6 meters (13 to 20 feet) high. I guess the authorities must routinely clear away the stones and mementos. In 2011, more than 180,000 pilgrims passed this monument; most left an object. Without maintenance, the debris would quickly bury the cross.

Neither Dennis nor I carry a trinket with us from home to leave at Cruz de Fero; we did not know about the tradition before the journey. The only baggage I had taken with me concerned my losing my job, and I have already left that behind. As we descend the mound, Dennis comments that he is happy I did not leave him there.

Many mountain bicyclists ride off-road on the same arduous trails that we hike. Some of these bikers are female. Having ridden mountain bikes in New England, I appreciate the riders' skill and daringness. Many times, after a biker passed me on a steep rocky slope, I commented to Dennis about how thankful I was to be walking. Unlike these cyclists, I would have pushed the bike uphill and, if I did not push it down the other side, I would have screamed in fear on the downhill, which is often rutted, rocky and difficult to walk, never mind ride.

I have been looking forward to speaking with a female cyclist, but I have not had the opportunity to do so until Cruz de Fero, where two female mountain bikers, Laura and Maria, stop to visit the site. I am delighted to speak with them. Elena, a Spaniard, sees that I am struggling with the Spanish and translates for me.

Laura Fernandez Elvira and Maria Garcia Gamarra

Left to right: Laura and Maria in front of the
Cruz de Fero

"We are from Soria, Spain. We started our Camino in Burgos. We are doing the Camino not for religious reasons but for adventure. We like riding the bikes. We were planning on doing the Camino with more friends, but it ended up just the two of us. We are staying in the *albergues*. It should take us seven days to complete the trip. The most difficult things have been the poor road markings, especially in León. But, generally it is well marked. The Camino has been difficult with all the stones, but this was expected and normal for off-road cycling; and we really like it.

"We recommend the Camino for people who like to bike. We believe that in the entire world this is a reason to come to Spain and bike here. It is very exciting and the landscape is beautiful. And, our adrenaline keeps going up and up. There are many various terrains and good people. Even if you don't want to bike 100 kilometers (62 miles) a day, you can do it in different stages, depending on your morale and physical being. We are using mountain bikes and so far we have had no problems and no flat tires."

At the base of the Iron Cross is a huge sundial; I stand on it and my shadow indicates it is 11 a.m. Across the street is the Ermita de Santiago, built in 1982. The chapel, with its statue to St. James, is locked when we visit.

Elena Franganillo Ortiz

209

Women of the Way

"I am twenty-five years old and I am walking the Camino for adventure, to have fun, and meet new people. I met two Malaysian girls who are very funny and three Korean girls. I am from Barcelona and learned to speak English in London, where I have been living for about two years. I need to improve my English, but I can get along okay.

"On the Camino, I have learned to live day-to-day, not in the future. I am hoping to get to Santiago, but I may not be able to get there because I have problems with my knees and my foot. Now there are only nine more days of walking, so maybe I will.

"The most amazing thing to me about the Camino is meeting people from countries like Malaysia, New Zealand, and the US. It is interesting to me. I can ask them things about their countries and learn a lot.

"I started walking alone in Roncesvalles and met friends along the Way. I don't know if it is because of the Camino, but I am much happier now. I am not doing the Camino for religion, but I am in peace, happy, and very energetic.

"It is hard; sometimes it is painful. However, I recommend to everybody to do the Camino. I am really glad I did it. When you are in love, you go walking with a silly love smile on your face, and everything is brilliant and marvelous. That is how I feel now, but I am not in love with anyone!

"I have been a vegan for about one-and-a-half years and I am doing the Camino as a vegan. Every *albergue* has a kitchen. I buy vegetables and stuff and then cook for myself and for others, if they want.

"I hate the pilgrim's menu. It is not real Spanish food, just high-priced junk food for pilgrims. Everywhere I go it is bread and meat, meat, meat. Meat for breakfast, meat for lunch, and meat for dinner. It is hard for me to go to a restaurant, because they don't always have options for vegetarian people and yet I meet a lot of vegetarians on the Camino. Fortunately, I found a few places that have vegan food here and there along the Way. It is not so bad. I can always ask for toast with oil and salt and tea for breakfast. I carry some food, just in case there is no vegan choice or for when the shops are not open, especially on Sundays."

Elena's post-Camino comments:

"I am not sure if I would do the Camino again. I really, really enjoyed it. I met a lot of people and I had a lot of fun. But, you need plenty of time and money because it is not that cheap, especially if you are walking for a month. I don't like to repeat something I have done; I love doing different and new things. Now that I know I love hiking, I probably will do more, but not the Camino, something different.

"I had some difficult times, especially in Galicia. There were kitchens in every *albergue*, but no tools for cooking! I couldn't cook and pretty much all the restaurants didn't have vegan options. Even the salads had tuna. I found some rude waiters that didn't understand me. I was very angry and hungry! All I had to eat over those five days was chips and bread...not enough.

"When I got to Santiago, I saw an advertisement in a bus stop: free vegan food every Friday at 2.30 p.m. in Alameda Park. I was really surprised and excited to have vegan food and for free! It was Thursday, so the next day I had a feast. Later, I went to a vegetarian restaurant in Santiago and I met some vegan friends that I knew because they are members of the same vegetarian forum that I am. We all went to celebrate and had a lot of fun.

"The most meaningful moment for me occurred just after Logroño. All my friends ended their Camino there and I was alone, walking very slowly because my knee was painful. I walked alone for a few days, taking my time, doing just five or ten kilometers each day. I enjoyed the small towns in La Rioja, especially Azofra, where I had a chance to share wine and a traditional meal with a lovely family."

Elena walks with three other people who bonded together, laughing and having a good time. The three women choreographed a dance detailing the pilgrim's daily ritual. For our benefit, they dance and sing on the huge sundial at the base of Cruz de Ferro as onlookers laugh and cheer. The short skit includes waking, donning the pilgrims' attire, walking, scratching bedbug bites, squatting in the woods, laundering, and then going to bed. I love watching the performance of these younger people; they are obviously having fun.

One of the women who travels with Elena is Cecilia.

Ji Yeon Yoo (Cecilia)

"I am from Korea. I now live in Seoul, but my hometown is in the south part of Korea. Three years ago I saw a documentary on the Camino. From then, I really wanted to do the Camino. In April I quit my job and decided to come here, finally. I spent two-and-a-half months traveling in Europe before coming to the Camino because I had plenty of time. I am now running out of money. It is my last journey.

"I started at St-Jean-Pied-de-Port on September 15. I am twenty-eight years old and am curious about my next life in the thirties. I came here to think about my thirties. The problem is I keep thinking instead about which *albergue* will be good and what shall I eat today, just about the simple things and not about my future life. I am having a really simple life on the Camino.

"I met Jean, our other walking companion, and her sister

on the way to Orison on the first day and she and I have been walking together until now. Jean's sister walks ahead of us. She is the rabbit and we are turtles.

"This is an adventure for me. It is the first time that I go trekking. I bought all new gear. With this gear, I could go to Himalayas, if I so desired. With all the walking, I have lost some weight. I have seen many beautiful things and the weather has been good. I like it."

There is a slight breeze and the cooler weather makes it pleasant climbing. Along the crest from Cruz de Ferro to Manjarín are beautiful vistas of the mountain range. There is an old proverb that states that there are many paths to the top of the mountain, but the view is always the same. I think the view depends on where you look, on your frame of mind, and on the goal. If the goal is to get to the top, all you might see is the way down. If it is to experience the climb, the journey itself is the reward, not reaching the summit. I ponder this as I slowly do a 360° turn to admire the panorama. For me, there is joy in the climb, not just in reaching the top. I agree with the personal trainer Greg Anderson who says: "Focus on the journey, not the destination. Joy is found not in finishing an activity, but in doing it."

At a bend in the path is Manjarín, the most unique village I encounter on the Camino. The entrance and exit signs are a mere twenty feet apart. A low stone wall is decorated with colorful flags and signs marking distances to a dozen cities such as Jerusalem—5000 kilometers (3100 miles), and Santiago—222 kilometers (138 miles). Recorded Gregorian chants and incense invite the pilgrim to enter the simple refuge run by Tomás, a Knight Templar. The interior is crowded and dark, a solitary light bulb hangs from the ceiling by its electrical cord. Prayers, carvings, and notices cover the plank walls. A tattooed and pierced woman sells cold drinks, snacks, and beaded jewelry. At least twelve cats meow for attention. A bell, which Tomás rings to guide pilgrims to this refuge when there is fog or bad weather, hangs from a carved support beam. There is no plumbing; the outhouse is across the road. I am disappointed that Tomás is not here, because I would like to meet a modern-day Knight Templar.

During the Crusades, the Knights Templar was a monastic order comprised of skilled warriors and noncombatant members who managed financial transactions that were an early form of banking. The organization was disbanded in 1312. In the eighteenth century, there was a resurgence, though there is no historical connection between these "Neo-Templars" and the original order. Nowadays, the Knights Templar is an international philanthropic-chivalric order affiliated with Freemasonry. To be a Knight Templar, one must profess belief in a Christian God.

Autumn is evident. Gold, red, and brown treetops daub the slopes of the mountains; the greens are no longer very vibrant. The air is crisp and pure. A few cirrus clouds whip across the azure sky. From these heights, I see a ribbon of a road crossing the valley before us. We follow a stony path that descends and then rises, but overall we are going downhill towards Molinaseca, a small town in the valley, dropping about 1000 meters (3280 feet).

As we descend, we pass El Acebo, a village with very old, but inhabited houses; a cobbled street with a trench down the center; and a large stone with a bicycle sculpture honoring a pilgrim cyclist who was killed here in 1987. Someone has placed fresh roses on the memorial.

I continue to take small steps downhill, fearful of setting off my tendinitis. The slope is steep and I fall on my backside twice: better that way than careening forwards. I have been hiking in my boots and my feet ache. At Riego de Ambrós, a small village with flagstone houses and rural architecture, I change into my sandals, even though my boots are better suited for the terrain.

The trail to Molinaseca is very steep and lined with large old gnarly trees, reminding me of those in *The Hobbit*. Like the Tolkien trees, I can see facial characteristics in the bark, the limbs reaching out to me. What tales can these ancient trees tell?

On the advice of Marcie, a pilgrim from Seattle, Washington, we stay at the Albergue de Santa Marina. At dinner that night, I sit with two Finnish women, Paula and Sally, both dentists. They met in dental school and then went their separate ways. About seven years ago they renewed their friendship and have since enjoyed sharing adventures such as sailing the Atlantic from the Caribbean to Ireland. They started the Camino on September 20, ten days after I did; they have a quick pace, especially for women in my age group.

Tomorrow is Columbus Day, a national holiday, which means that the shops and cafés may be closed. I am hoping that we will have enough supplies and will be able to find a few open eateries.

In the morning, I hear bleating sheep before I see them inside a large concrete block barn. Hundreds of them are pressing to exit the barn, rushing forward like people trying to escape from a burning building. A solitary sheepdog keeps them in, the sheep in the front bracing to keep those behind in check.

In Ponferrada, we stop for a snack in a café that faces a Templar castle built in the twelfth century. I am warming up with hot chocolate when I spot Elodie and the gang from Cruz de Ferro. Everyone exchanges hugs and kisses. I tell Elodie that I saw the picture of her husband in the rubble at Cruz de Fero, but not the ring. She doesn't care if someone took it; she left the burden it represented behind. Leaving, I notice a mural of the Last Supper. This rendition has Mary Magdalene to Jesus' right, not the apostle John. I am pleased to see Mary Magdalene in this esteemed position, especially in a Templar town.

It is a quiet walk after leaving the café; there are only a few pilgrims and locals out walking. There are fewer Camino markers and we ask directions or guess which way to go. We leave the old picturesque part of the city and enter the modern and industrialized one. It takes about two hours to cross Ponferrada, as it is such a large city. At a busy intersection, there is a square dedicated to mothers. Unlike most squares, this one is grassy. Geraniums surround a statue of a mother holding a toddler, a younger child at her feet tugging on her dress for attention. Such public sculptures enrich the lives of the viewers and confirms the value of mothers and motherhood.

Spain has many statues dedicated to women. A little ways farther in Ponferrada there is a *glorieta* (circle) dedicated to *Las Pimenteras* (The Pepper Women). On this roundabout where four major roads intersect are four oversized bronze statues of women peeling peppers, honoring the housewives of the region who started the tradition of Bierzo roasted peppers. A popular nineteenth-century folksong tells of how four pimenteras of Ponferrada carried the statue of the Virgen de la Encina, patron saint of Ponferrada and the Bierzo region, on her feast day.

Las Pimenteras

We walk on a fieldstone path through a building, the only time the Camino Francés does so. How considerate of the planners not to make us walk around the building.

The next town we pass through is Columbrianos, where there is an elm tree carving of a peasant woman carrying a large basket of grain on her head and a daughter at her feet carrying a jug. The sculpture honors the rural women of Columbrianos.

It lifts my spirits to see the statues of mothers, working women, and female peasants. These respectful and well-maintained tributes to women make the day special for me; this art is a lasting reminder that women matter in these rural Spanish towns and that women's contributions are remembered.

Columbrianos Elm Tree Carving

At noon, after walking for four hours on paved roads, we stop for lunch at Fuentes Nuevas and then continue on to Villafranca del Bierzo, walking primarily through hilly vineyards This is the farthest I have traveled in one day 31 kilometers (19 miles).

Women of the Way

On the outskirts of town, a young man gives us a brochure about the upcoming Albergue Viña Fermita that features a spa-type shower. I look forward to removing the day's grime with a long hot shower and relieving my body's tension with the water jets.

Finally, we arrive at the *albergue*. As advertized, their shower is ultra-modern, with a seat, mirror, radio (which does not work), and pulsating water jets. I undress and then cannot figure out how to turn on the water—there are too many knobs and controls. After several frustrating moments, I dress and seek help. The *hospitalero*, proud of this space-age gadget, is more than glad to demonstrate how to operate it. As modern as this shower is, the doors leak and I need to mop the floor. It seems as if this nightly chore is the price for the luxury of being clean.

Albergue Viña Fermita does not have bunk beds or mats on the floor; instead, there are regular twin beds with linens and comforters. Beside each bed is a clothes rack and a dresser with a lamp, which makes it nice to read. I hope to get a good night's sleep. Tomorrow morning, I need to be strong as we tackle the mountains in Galicia.

Galicia

Galicia

"What you get by reaching your destination is not nearly as important as what you will become by reaching your destination." ~ Zig Ziglar

Galicia is mountainous. In the east, peaks rise to 2,000 meters (6,600 feet); in central Galicia the mountains are about half that height. Progressing westerly, the hills decrease, eventually ending at the Atlantic. Because of cattle on many farms and meadows, Galicia has earned the sobriquet "land of one million cows." In addition to farming, there is fishing and a canning industry.

I have been walking across northern Spain for thirty-five days. My body feels strong, fit. Since my clothes hang looser, I guess I have lost a few pounds, but not enough to affect my powerful stride and ability to hike long days. When I left the States, I was committed to completing the journey, but understood that circumstances might prevent me from doing so. Sore muscles, blisters, tendinitis, and food poisoning have not deterred me from my pursuit. I will be in Santiago in less than a week. As a goal-orientated person, I am surprised that getting there is not what matters to me now. What is important is the journey. I love the walking, seeing what is around the bend, making friends, and sampling different foods. Even though I have always been game to try things, meet people, and experience new sensations and challenges, I have not previously done so to the extent that I have on the Camino. For more than a month, I have been open to whatever awaits me; my only plan being to walk westward to Santiago. Can it be that the lessons I take from the Camino are simply to "slow down and smell the roses" and remain open to life's possibilities? I did not come on the Camino to have a life-altering experience, but these simple lessons, trite as they sound, seem to resonate within my heart. Can I retain this joy and happiness once I return to living in the "real" world? I must reconsider once again filling my life with plans and expectations without taking time to connect with nature, with people, and with whatever spontaneity awaits me. Katharine Hepburn said: "If you obey all the rules, you miss all the fun." Maybe what the Camino is revealing to me is to be more playful, to do something just because I feel like it, and to surprise myself with unscheduled pleasures that allow me to continually experience the world.

Not only has my body adapted to the constant walking, so, too, has my mind. I am never bored, as I thought I might be. I have not had "withdrawals" from the news or being connected; in fact, I purposely do not look at emails and no longer make time to read the Kindle. I use the Wi-Fi only to Skype my parents. I cherish the mental tranquility, too long missing from my life.

There are three ways to walk out of Villafranca del Bierzo. We choose the traditional route up over the mountains. A full moon lights our route through the city as we pass the castle and then cross the river via a Roman bridge. Not finding the arrows, we follow another pilgrim up a dark, narrow pathway and start a strenuous 500-meter (1640-foot) assent to the first lookout. Along this street that is too narrow for cars are doorways to people's homes. Occasionally light from a window illuminates the dark passage. I cannot imagine lugging a baby or groceries to a house on this street.

The cobblestones turn to dirt. We walk single file. I grab

plants and tree limbs to stabilize myself and help pull me forward. I pant and roll my sleeves up, heated from the exertion. It is predawn when I reach an overlook and see the city lights twinkling in the valley. Turning, I clamber up the looming dark mass in front of me; it is a long, hard climb.

At dawn, I crest the mountain and see the alternate route that follows the motorway far below. The valley is hazy. I gulp in fresh cool air. This is a special moment, with the sun rising behind us and the moon setting in the west, towards Santiago. The mountain I am on casts a shadow on the N6 tunnels more than a half kilometer below. We are in the Sierra del Caldeiron mountain range; the trees are turning colors and chestnuts hide under the fallen leaves. I am careful not to twist my ankle.

Up on these mountains, incongruous cell towers and power lines mar the pristine panorama. Extending far into the distance, power lines connect one valley to the other. Is there no longer a wilderness, a place unspoiled by humans? Am I too eager to accept the necessity of these blemishes on nature? Am I being haughty for not wanting this ugly reminder of society in this place of beauty? For over a month, pastoral settings have soothed my spirit, connecting me with nature. Yet, I enjoy a hot shower at night, lights, Wi-Fi, and other comforts provided by "technology" that, at this moment, affront my senses.

I keep musing until, at a crossroad, we follow the signs for a café. Dennis is looking forward to a cold drink and I want a hot tea. We walk about a kilometer when we encounter an old man and a donkey with saddlebags full of *castañas* (chestnuts). He tells us the café is closed; the owner is out gathering nuts. Everywhere there are nut gatherers. I ask a woman what it takes to prepare them. They can be roasted or boiled to remove the hard mahogany shell and then added to soups, eaten as a vegetable, or pureed. The chestnut seems quite versatile.

After a precipitous descent, we stop at a *tienda* (store) in Trabelelo for lunch. Three kilometers later, we are in las Herrerías. We do not realize that there are two towns by that name, only 10 kilometers (6 miles) apart, one spelled with a capital "L" and one not. That little difference makes a big difference. The guidebook explains our options: one for walkers and the other for cyclists. Since the way for the walkers doesn't make sense (because we are in the wrong town), we follow the Camino route for the cyclists, hoping to rejoin the walkers at a hamlet farther up the road.

Once again, we are climbing. After many kilometers, we see a town in the valley that we think is La Fabo on the walker's route. As on the second day of our Camino, we are on the wrong side of the river. To our left is an unmarked single-track footpath that might descend to the town, but we cannot tell if it crosses the river. We have three options: try the path, backtrack down the hill and then go back up the other side, or go forward. We decide to go forward.

We follow the N-VI, an auto road to Pedrafita de Cebrieto. From there we will cross the mountain pass to get back on the Camino. We marvel at the bridges more than 100 meters (330 feet) in the air crossing from one mountaintop to the other. From where we stand looking up, the tractor-trailers appear as miniature toys.

On our way to Pedrafita de Cebrieto we stop at a fountain and meet Angel, a blue-eyed cyclist who recommends the

Hostel Roballal, where he will be staying. We arrive in town at 5 p.m. It has taken us eleven hours to walk 40 kilometers (29 miles).

We drag ourselves to the hotel. There is a middle-aged woman working the bar. Since she is alone, we must wait for someone to come to show us the room. The wait seems interminable. At last, an elderly man arrives and takes us to the room on the third floor. Just what we need—more climbing.

After today's long hike, the hot shower is soothing, the warmth relaxes my muscles. I am appreciative that Dennis always lets me go first, so I can have hot water. Even though I try to conserve, he has only a mildly warm shower. It is the first time since Barcelona that we can cuddle in a downy queen size bed with real linens. We nap until suppertime.

There is a tour group of bicyclists at the hotel. The riders are discussing how grueling the 50-kilometer ride was, how difficult a day it has been, and how tired they are. I tell them how far we walked that day and how heavy our packs are. As we leave, I hear them toast our efforts.

Maria Elena Price is a bicycle tour guide with ExperiencePlus! Bicycle Tours.

Maria Elena Price

"I did a tour at the end of August this year. I had not been on the Camino for about three years and I found it different. It was cleaned up. There has been a lot of funding for numerous areas and sites. It was nice to see that many of the small towns have patched and repaved the town squares and fixed the fountains.

"Our tours are not on walking paths, but on roads that parallel the paths. The tour goes through ninety-five percent of the towns that a walking pilgrim goes through. From the road, we do not see the debris and human waste that the walkers see, especially in the last hundred kilometers, which is highly trafficked.

"To give the bicyclist a taste of what it is like to walk the Camino, we suggest that they hike from Las Herrerías to O

Cebreiro. About forty percent of the cyclists do hike that portion of the Camino, not only because it is an incredible walk but also because it is such a hard bike ride to the top of the mountain.

"Unlike many of the walking pilgrims, those on this tour stay in three- and four-star hotels. It is definitely a different experience. People come on our tours because they don't have the time or the planning capacity to do it themselves. I think they also do it for different reasons than many pilgrims do it. Most are looking for a supported tour through Spain. Soon, it becomes a personal pilgrimage. It is neat for me to see that change, even though we don't talk about it as a pilgrimage. In the end, everyone realizes that they are doing the Camino, just in another form than walking. Some look wistfully at the walkers who are staying in hostels or camping, but they are not realistically in a position to do it.

"Lodging is not the main difference between the hiking and cycling pilgrim on this tour. Any hiker with money can stay at the higher-end hotels. The main difference is that the cyclists do not carry their belongings; we have support vans that carry their luggage for them.

'Women comprise about fifty percent of the cyclists on our tours. In August, there were more women than men. I think the women are more affected by the Camino than the men are.

"Helmets are required on this tour. We tell people that it is a hard trip. On the Meseta we do 100 kilometers (62 miles) days, but we do not require a certain fitness level; we let the individuals determine if they are fit enough to do this tour.

"If people are interested in clipless pedals [pedals that 'clip' onto bicycle shoes that are fitted with a cleat, locking each foot in place], they need to bring their own. About fifty to sixty percent of the people bring their own pedals.

"The tour is fifteen days. There is no riding on the first and last days, which are arrival and departure days. There is one rest day, in León.

"My parents own the company and we started doing the Camino in 1996. Since then, lodging has improved. We revamped the route in 1999 and the tour has not changed much since then. It is a great trip. We make sure that all the parts—the route, the lodgings, and the equipment—works well. The tour guides are knowledgeable and culturally experienced. Being in a route with hundreds of people moving in one direction every year creates a special sense that many of our other itineraries do not have.

"I would tell women who are contemplating biking the Camino that it is an adventure that they will get a lot out of. They certainly cannot go wrong.

"For me, returning to the Camino this year made me realize how much I had missed it. I had done this ride two or three times a year for three or four years, then I went on break. It is so good to be back: it feels like home. I know the hotels, the restaurants, the folks who live there. Even though there may be new people working in these places, it feels very similar, very nice.

"There is no 'true' way to do the Camino. One can walk it or do it by bike, can stay at hostels or in better hotels. Whichever way is an important experience. One should not feel guilty for doing it one way or another.

"I enjoy the 'mini surprise' that the cyclists get on their own about the Camino. It is something that we cannot describe to them; it is something they must discover by themselves when they are on the Camino. It always changes. This last tour a couple got into collecting Pilgrim Passport stamps. By the end, they had four different passports because they realized how much fun it was to get the stamps. It was a way to go in and talk to the local people, a tool to enhance the Camino experience.

"Everyone takes the tour at a different pace. I enjoy seeing how everyone participates and appreciates what the Camino has to offer. That part of being a tour guide is really nice. The long days on the Meseta, even on a bike, which is much faster than walking, provide time to think. For some people, it is a great accomplishment just to finish."

Lindy Fergusson cycled on tour with Maria Elena. I interviewed her after she completed the pilgrimage.

Lindy Fergusson

"My husband and I landed in Madrid while the Pope was visiting there. That made it most interesting. We spent three days in Madrid and then two days in Pamplona, where we met with our ExperiencePlus! trip guides and then transferred by van, approximately a two-hour ride, to Roncesvalles. The next morning, August 27, we began our Camino cycling trip.

"We became acquainted with the tour group through a friend whom my husband and I met when we joined a cycling club in Calgary. Derek [the friend], had planned to do the Camino the year before with his wife. Since there had not been enough participants, his trip had been canceled. We asked him if he was planning to do it this year and if so, if we could come. There were eight of us in this spin class at the club and we all decided to go. None of us had known each other prior to joining this club, but we all got along and decided to do the Camino. The tour group consisted of the eight of us and another five people who came from various places in the US.

"I have done five other bike trips and this was the best one yet. I believe that this was because of the excellence of the tour company and that this trip had the added dimension of the Camino. The biking was excellent, as it had been on other trips; however, being on the Camino and the community experience with our own group and those we met along the route was something we had not come across before.

"This sense of community made this trip special. We would meet people at the hotels, in the towns, on the roads and then we would meet them again, and all were doing the same thing, traveling the Camino. Another thing that made this trip special was our Pilgrim Passport. In my journal the first night I wrote, 'This trip is more than just a bike trip. I went to the Mass in Roncesvalles. The church was full. There were about twenty-five different nationalities staying in Roncesvalles that night, all beginning their trip the next day.' It was a wonderful trip from the start.

"Even though I went to the Mass at the start and end of the trip, this was not a religious pilgrimage, per se. I think that most in the group felt some sense of spirituality or connectedness on the trip, whether they were denominationally religious or not. It was quite remarkable.

"The trip was physically challenging, but there wasn't

anything that I could not do. There were lots of days that I was very tired at the end. The hardest day was going to O Cebreiro. About two-thirds of the group biked the ascent while the other third hiked to the top; I biked it. One section was excessively steep; I had to stop and get off my bike to give my heart and lungs a chance to recover.

"I brought my own helmet, seat, and pedals. Since I was accustomed to these, I had no physical discomfort from riding the bike. I'm lucky; I tended to get stronger as the days went by, whereas some people got more tired. It depends how one's physique reacts to a challenge.

"We were traveling between 43 and 109 kilometers per day (27 to 68 miles). The eight of us would doodle all morning. We would stop for coffee, once or twice, and then lunch, and then pick up the pace in the afternoon. Most mornings we would leave the hotel by 9 a.m. The latest day getting in was about 4 p.m. On the longest distance day, we biked about five hours and had a couple of hours of stopping here and there.

"Cycling is a wonderful way to see a country, to see new things, and to meet people. I enjoyed the Spanish food. I like to try all the different things people eat in different countries. The local delicacies were interesting. The most unusual thing I tried was sheep's stomach in paprika sauce, which was quite different. I also tried other cuts of the meats that we don't tend to use at home. My favorite thing to eat to fuel up was the Spanish Ensalada Mixta. This was a very large pile of salad, usually with tuna on top. I had this for most lunches.

"The hotel breakfast normally consisted of a tortilla, which at home we would call a frittata. It was potatoes with egg cooked together like a pie. On the breakfast table there were usually sliced meat, fruit, bread, sweetbreads, boiled eggs, and coffee.

"The most memorable place for me was O Cebreiro. It was the hardest to get to and, once there, we had the afternoon free to hang around and enjoy the ambiance of the village. In our group, there was a woman who played guitar and she and her husband sang for us. He was an opera singer. We spent the afternoon relaxing and listening to music in the sunshine. After a hard ride, it doesn't get much better than that. It was just a wonderful afternoon!

"The Camino taught me to reach out more to people; the more you reach out, the more you receive back. We all went on this adventure to do the Camino, not just to have a bike ride. That changed the psyche of the group. We started and ended the Camino with the Pilgrim's Mass, we visited churches and hostels along the Way, and we thoroughly enjoyed collecting as many stamps as we could for our passports. As a whole, the Camino made a big difference in my life.

"Also, the group we were in worked well and we continue to be friends. The eight of us who went together are still doing Monday night training in Calgary. In fact, we got together a few weeks before Christmas for a Camino celebration, and to share photos. Some of our group have also stayed in contact with the other members that came from the US.

"Even though I did this with a group of friends, I would do the trip on my own. I absolutely felt secure, comfortable, and well taken care of. In fact, this coming August I am doing another trip with ExperiencePlus! All the other participants are unknown to me. In seven weeks, we will bicycle from St. Petersburg in Russia to Istanbul, a distance of approximately 4,000 kilometers (2485 miles).

"On the Camino, we met a man from Holland who was cycling to Santiago, meeting his wife there, and then planning to cycle back home to Holland with her. He was traveling with panniers on his bike, carrying all his gear and clothes, unlike us who had our belongings shuttled by van. He was a very interesting person and we enjoyed speaking with him. He was probably doing triple the mileage we were doing.

"At the end of the trip, in Santiago we were waiting in the stairwell [of the Pilgrim's Reception Office] with about fifty other people to have our Pilgrim Passport stamped and receive our Compostela. Spontaneous applause broke out as a fellow came down the stairs who was a double-leg amputee who had just completed walking the entire Camino on two prostheses. Everyone was speechless and awed by what this person had done. We all had our difficulties in our own ways doing the trail, but this person obviously had it much harder. It was amazing and humbling to see him and his accomplishment.

"I would advise anyone who is considering biking the Camino to do it. It is a most rewarding and wonderful trip."

In the morning, we snuggle in the down-filled comforter, grateful not to be awakened by people stuffing bags and preparing for the day's hike. We leave the hotel in Pedrafita at 8:30 a.m., against the advice of the proprietress who thinks we should wait until sunrise when the traffic will be able to see us. To make ourselves visible, we don our headlamps and climb 4.5 kilometers (2.75 miles) to O Cebriero, a small village of twenty houses that includes *pallazos* (typical Galician thatched buildings), a museum, hotel, *albergue*, church, and other tourist venues. We stop at a café and order hot chocolate. It is dark, thick and frothy, and served with sugar on the side; surely this is the best I have ever tasted.

From O Cebriero, the hike is supposed to be downhill, but it seems as if we are forever climbing. It is warm and we are low on water; the last several villages have not had potable water. As we enter another village, I look backwards and glimpse a fountain. Sometimes the solutions to our problems come from looking backwards, not forwards.

In Galicia, they speak Castilian and also Galician, a Romance language that mixes in Portuguese. There are Celtic influences and I hear bagpipes and jigs. The cuisine includes fish, shellfish, and octopus. I particularly enjoy the *empanada*, a meat- or fish-stuffed bread, and the *Caldo Galego*, a hearty potato, cabbage, and bean soup. The regional wine is Ribeiro, an aromatic white wine; the area is also developing red wines that I found fruity and easy to drink. *Quiemada* is a Galician alcoholic punch made from distilled wine and flavored with herbs or coffee, sugar, lemon and cinnamon. The punch is lit; as the alcohol burns off, brandy is added. Traditionally, the *quiemada* is prepared ritualistically, with incantations to ward off curses.

Women of the Way

There are markers in Galicia that count down the distance to Santiago; we have 135 kilometers (84 miles) to go. The *albergues* here have green doors and windows, and the municipal ones seldom have cooking utensils in the kitchens or doors on the shower stalls. Without the shower doors, it is even more difficult to hang my towel and clothes.

In Triacastela, we stay in a private refuge run by a woman named Lucita. The two-story *albergue* is meticulously kept, but very old, with stone walls, large wooden support beams, worn flooring, and a creaky staircase. The first floor has a beautiful thick-slab dark oak table and a desk with Internet access. There is a small kitchen as well as vending machines that provide coffee and soda. These machines and the modern bath seem incongruous in the old building, but this mixture of the old and new is representative of the Camino.

We dine outdoors at a local restaurant that has Wi-Fi and admire the sunset, with its rose-colored clouds dotting the pale aqua-blue sky. I sample Galician food and enjoy the cheese and honey dessert.

The next morning a German woman wakes everyone yelling that the *albergue* is infested by bedbugs. I am not bitten. Upset, she shows everybody the bugs she has squashed on her sheets. She exclaims that this is the third day that she has suffered from these pests. I conclude that she is porting them with her and hurry to leave her presence.

There are two routes to Sarria. We take the longer route because in the dark we cannot find the 3.5 kilometers

(2 miles) shorter one. We walk on shaded pathways with rustling beech trees, through small farming communities, and saunter by *hórreos* (aboveground stone granaries), and other old stone buildings. The roofs are now made of black slate, as opposed the red tile roofs seen till now. We stop twice to let herds of cows pass and then are careful not to step in the dung. I am glad we went this way because we go through Samos, with its imposing Benedictine monastery.

Reading about this huge monastery did not prepare me for its enormity. This massive, light-colored granite structure was built in the sixth century, and by the Middle Ages it was Spain's wealthiest and most powerful monastery. Surrounding the monastery is a cast-iron fence with a clamshell motif. The fifteen monks who currently live there follow the Benedictine rules of manual labor and intellectual pursuits. Though one can tour the church and cloisters, we do not.

As we leave Samos via a dirt road lined with stone walls, I imagine oxcarts rambling down the dusty path. I can see trout in a crystal clear stream. The air is cool and leaves crunch beneath our feet. Since leaving Samos, we do not know where we are. Several towns do not have names and those that do are not on the map. We trust that the yellow arrows will take us to Sarria and joke about how many times we have been lost since starting out on this adventure.

We stop for a cool drink in a nondescript town. Chickens clucking at our feet remind me of Key West, except that this is more rural. Dennis and I have not seen other pilgrims since leaving Samos. I enjoy his company. My Camino would be very different without him, with a lot less laughter; but, perhaps, with more reflection.

Tall ancient trees with large knotted limbs create a tunnel of leaves and shade. We picnic on the banks of the road, sitting on fallen leaves, sheltered from the sun. There are no other pilgrims on the road. This tranquil moment fills me with an overwhelming happiness, a deeply satisfying pleasure. I would like to sit here all day, my mind at peace and my soul jubilant, but I must move on.

Before we leave our picnic, we check to see how far it is to Sarria. According to the guidebook it is 25 kilometers, the Michelin map lists 21.5 kilometers, and the road sign has 20 kilometers. I can understand the road sign discrepancy; it does not follow the Camino. But, why is there such a difference between the two walking guides?

Sarria is the antique capitol of Galicia, trading in furniture and art. It is a modern city with a wonderful riverside promenade lined with eateries providing outdoor seating. Above the restaurants are residences. We order dinner and watch the townsfolk enjoy the early evening. In the pizza parlor, there is a child's birthday party and we listen to "Happy Birthday" in Spanish. People walk dogs, push baby strollers, or amble arm-in-arm. Groups of female teens strut by groups of male teens. One child rides his Big Wheel as if he were Evel Knievel.

Perched near the wall is a gray-haired septuagenarian who apparently reigns over this section of the boardwalk. She reprimands a man who is feeding the ducks, tells teens to quiet down, and advises me to move my bag of groceries from the chair to the ground near my feet. Though I have not seen signs of thievery throughout the journey, I figure she knows the area better than I do, so I move my bag, and thank her. Satisfied, she returns to her lookout.

The two-story Albergue Casa Peitre, located at the bottom of the stone steps that lead into the old quarter, is new, inviting, and comfortable. The chalet-style rooms are light and airy, immaculate, and designed for comfort. A large central desk accommodates four computers. The kitchen is well supplied with utensils, a rarity in Galicia. In the corner of the bathroom sits the mop and pail—ready for use. Later that day, two other Americans arrive, Jack and his mother Cathy Collins. I have seen them on several occasions, always surrounded by other pilgrims; they must be interesting and dynamic people. I do not get a chance to speak with them.

On the way out of Sarria we pass the Santa Marina church. On its walls is a wonderful mural of medieval pilgrims, which features women: women with children, women helping the elderly, women walking solo. This and the Galbete sculpture on Alto de Perdón are the only tributes to medieval female pilgrims that I have seen on the Camino.

Some of the cobblestones have an inlaid scallop shell marking, making it easy to follow the Camino through the city. Once outside of the city, I keep searching for the countdown markers indicating the distance left to Santiago. It becomes a game to see who will spot the next marker first. The norm is a marker every kilometer, but there are occasional half-kilometer markers. Sometimes the markers are easy to find, and other times they are hidden by foliage or are so old and worn that we miss them. At the 100 kilometer (62 mile) marker, I am overwhelmed with emotions: relief, a sense of accomplishment, sadness for the impending conclusion. This is a significant milestone; many people have inscribed messages and names on it, tied ribbons around it, or left mementos atop of it. If I am this emotional here, what will it be like to arrive at Santiago!

I see a group of pilgrims on horseback; all the horses are white. Unlike the pilgrims of old, modern-day equestrians on the Camino cannot expect free shelter and food and stabling for their horses. They need backup; someone with a trailer to take the horse, if necessary, and to carry farrier tools, horse feed, water, and other supplies. For the pilgrim on horseback, the Way may be solitary; they are faster than the walkers, but slower than the bicyclist. Those considering an equestrian pilgrimage may want to read *The Way of Saint James on Horseback Guide,* by Javier Pascual, which details what a rider needs to know to ride the Camino Francés from France to Santiago.

There are touring companies that cater to those wishing to ride the last hundred kilometers. For ten days, they provide and take care of the horses, arrange for first class housing in rural hotels or manor houses, for transit from the stable to the accommodations and back, and for entering Santiago. Though it seems glamorous, the excursion is expensive.

This last hundred-kilometer section is the most crowded part of the Camino; a pilgrim only needs to complete this final portion to receive the Compostela, the certificate of completion.

There is an influx of Spaniards in this section. I once heard that those with the Compostela are given preferences in employment similar to those in the US who have completed military duty. I have since learned that having the Compostela does look good on one's résumé for a person who lives or works in Spain, but that is not the reason why many Spaniards make the pilgrimage. Walking the Camino is part of the Spanish culture and consciousness. Many Spanish people make a vow or promise to walk the Camino in exchange for a favor, a special indulgence, or answer to a prayer. Walking as a fulfillment to a promise or a thank you to God is not limited to the Spanish culture. I met American pilgrims who too walked for such reasons. For example, Phil from Oregon promised to do the pilgrimage if his young son's eyesight were saved. Years later, his sighted son now an adult, Phil is completing his part of the bargain.

Whatever the reason Spaniards walk the Camino de Santiago, the outcome is a unification of the non-Portuguese Iberian Peninsula. It brings together the Basques, Catalans, Andalusians, Castilians and northern Iberian Celts, bonding them with a shared experience and accomplishment.

After the marker, the terrain keeps changing. A dirt path meanders through forests of massive old trees, all twisted and bent like a person with arthritis; gravel paths lead through green fields with stone walls, passing *hórreos* and barns; a puncheon (a large slab of timber) crosses a rocky riverbed; paved village streets are covered in sheep and cow dung. In one hamlet, a man tries to lead tethered animals into a field. On his leash are a donkey, two cows, and several goats, each going in different directions. A woman also has animals bound to her with a rope. They are patient with the animals and I wait several minutes before proceeding, hoping not to further distract the beasts, until the herders succeed in getting them off the road.

I hear bagpipes; the doleful sound resonates throughout the countryside. The "music" grates on my emotions as if someone were scrapping fingernails on the chalkboard of my soul. Deep inside, I feel a profound longing or sense of incompleteness. These feelings are so different from the joy I have been experiencing. While on the Camino I have become more sensitive to, or perhaps, more aware of my emotions. Possibly, that is why I react so strongly to the solemn, mournful dirge. In town, a violin teacher encourages a youngster; this melody pleases me and I no longer feel out of tune.

Once again, I am standing at a crossroad, trying to decide which way to go. A large cornerstone rock is marked with an arrow going in two directions and a question mark over the double-headed arrow. Does that mean we can go either way or that the person who marked the trail did not know which way to go? Is one direction longer than the other? More scenic? We make a choice and hope for the better.

The terrain today started hilly, but is now mostly downhill. Pastures alternate with small hamlets. Most of the buildings are made of stone with slate roofs. Large rocks and potholes make the walking treacherous. Dennis jumps from rock to rock in his descent, like a surefooted mountain goat; I am more gradual, carefully selecting my path and zigzagging on the steeper inclines, thankful that it is not raining, which would make these paths slippery and dangerous.

I come upon a cairn decorated with mementos, similar to Crux de Ferro. On it are a sleeping mat, hats, a pullover shirt, shoes, plastic flowers, several bicycle tire tubes, and two glycine envelopes—one with a newspaper photo of Pope Benedicto XVI, the other with a picture of the Virgin Mary. There is no indication why this colorful monument is here.

I cross a large, high bridge over the Rio Miño, the longest river in Galicia, to enter Portomarín. The current town of Portomarín was relocated to its present location in the 1960s when the river was dammed to create the reservoir. The Church of San Juan and other historical buildings were moved brick by brick from the valley and then reconstructed on the hill. If you look at the church from the outside, you can see the numbers on the stones indicating their positions from the time it was moved.

From the bridge, I climb forty-two narrow stone steps to a landing and then ten more to get into town. We stay at the Albergue O'Mirrador, where I meet Yoonjin Song.

Yoonjin Song (Yoon)

"Hi, my name is Yoonjin Song. It is a little hard to pronounce and to remember; everyone calls me Yoon. I will be twenty-two years old in two weeks. I am a college student taking time off from school to do this trip. I am majoring in management and Japanese literature. I speak Japanese, English, and Korean. I will be a senior next year and will need to get a job when I get out of school. I don't know what I want for my career. I needed time to think about it, so I decided to come to the Camino.

"One of my friends who is a Christian had told me about the Camino when I was a high school student. At that time, I did not have much interest in the Camino. I said, 'Okay, there is a Way.' Then last year I saw a documentary about the Camino; it was really nice. I thought I should be there and, consequently, I am here. I am very happy.

"I flew from Korea to Paris. It took seventeen hours. I spent three days in Paris. This is my first time to Europe. The scenery is totally different from Asia. I have not been to other continents. I lived in Japan as an exchange student for about a year. Going abroad was for me, at the time, going to Japan. This time, it is very far and very different.

"I started at St-Jean-Pied-de-Port on September 22. I am doing a fast trip. In the middle of the Meseta, I took a bus from Hontanas back to Burgos and from there to León.

"I had sent my stuff from St-Jean-Pied-de-Port to Logroño. I went to the post office in Logroño. The post office guy could not speak English at all. He tried to explain something to me, that I had visited the wrong post office and had to go to another. He was trying to explain how to get to the other post office, but I could not understand because I don't speak Spanish. I got the address, thinking I could ask other people how to get there. Then a Spanish lady came to me and said, 'I can take you by my car to the other post office.' I was very surprised. I did not want to interrupt her, so I said, 'Oh, no, thank you. You don't have to do that.' She said that when she visited other countries everyone was nice to her and now she wanted to be nice to a foreigner. She took me by car to the other post office. It just took five minutes, but it would have been very hard to find it if I had had to walk it. This was a nice experience for me.

"I have made a lot of friends. I stayed at Orison the first day. At dinnertime, we self-introduced. I met a Frenchman, a Canadian man, and a girl from Switzerland. I walked with them until Hontanas, where I had to say goodbye to them. That was sad.

"When I arrived at León, the weather was not that good. I had been on the bus for four hours and could not walk. León was too big a city for me. I was upset. I went to the cathedral and cried. At the *albergue*, I tried to sleep, but couldn't, so I went to the kitchen. There was a Malaysian woman there. She told me it was okay, that everyone has the kinds of feelings I was having. Her words were helpful. The next day I walked about 23 kilometers (14 miles) and I felt better.

"I have thought about my career. I still don't know what I want to do, but I feel less nervous about that. I realized that everyone has their own pace; you don't have to try to catch up with them. All you have do to is walk at your pace. If I go in the wrong direction, it is okay. You can come back, then go the right way.

"My flight is on October 23, from Santiago to Barcelona. After one night, I go back home to Korea."

When I meet Yoon several days later, I notice that she has two different poles. The red one is her father's and the other is her mother's. This way her mom and dad are walking the Camino with her.

Yoon's post-Camino comments:

"The Camino was the most special thirty days in my life. I'm very proud of myself. Everything on the Camino was meaningful and special: the Way, nature, friends, weather, and everything! I really miss walking on the Camino and want to go back someday to walk the Camino del Norte with my mother.

"I did have one difficulty. My phone was stolen on the last day before reaching Santiago. I put my cell phone on the charger and then went to bed. The next morning, the phone was gone. I was in a panic and didn't know what to do. Fortunately, two guys I met the day before were policemen of Spain. They barely spoke English, but they helped me. They took me to the police office and helped me write a police report. They were trying to make me laugh because I was obviously upset. You know what? One of the guys' name is Angel. He was literally an ANGEL to me! Such good friends. I still keep in touch with them.

"Bedbugs are the only thing that I hated on the Camino. I got bedbugs in Vega de Valcarce at the *albergue* municipal, and it was torture during my whole trip.

"I met up with one of my Camino friends last December. He flew from Paris to Seoul for a business meeting. It was a little bit weird because we both wore nice suits instead of hats, boots, and outdoor clothing; I put on makeup. We were totally back to normal life. Anyway, we had a great time and made a wonderful reunion.

"I tell people that if you are thinking about walking the Camino, do not hesitate. Just go. Every pilgrim gets his or her own philosophy after the Camino. I'm always talking about the Camino to my friends. At first, when I told them 'I'm gonna walk 800 kilometers in Spain,' they said 'You are crazy!' Now, however, all my friends want to go to the Camino because of me. 'Ha!' I tell them, 'Now, you too are the crazy ones.'

"Actually, one of my friends walked the Camino in January 2012. I'm looking forward to speaking with him when he comes back to Seoul."

We leave Portomarín in the dark and it is hard finding the arrows. Two German pilgrims signal that we are heading in the wrong direction, but they are wrong. I trip in a hole in the road and would have fallen down a steep cliff if Dennis had not caught me. I wonder why there is no indication or warning about this danger.

We climb the hill. The distances marked on the map are off and many small towns are not listed. This is a poor farming area with hamlets of one or two houses that have no electricity.

Robin Berry and Brenda Gaynor

Left to Right: Robin and Brenda

I walk with Robin and Brenda down lovely country lanes lined with stone walls and oak and chestnut trees. They are marine carpenters from Seattle, Washington. While taking a course in French, they heard about an inexpensive way to travel in Spain. They quit their jobs and left for their journey, starting their trek in Iceland, hopping over to England and then over to France. They started walking the Camino in Le Puy, then they walked about 320 kilometers (200 miles) before taking a train to St-Jean-Pied-de-Port. They have been walking since then. They carry heavy bags because they have camping equipment, including cookware.

They have both lost weight and look forward to more adventure. They are considering New Zealand and Tasmania, since pilgrims they met have invited them. They are planning to travel for about a year.

They are both free spirits and are thinking about not returning to the US. Since Robin's parents are both gone, she has no ties.

Brenda's post-Camino comments:

"We definitely finished the Camino at Santiago, but then took the bus close to Cape Finisterre and walked the last thirteen kilometers to Fisterra. For some reason, I had this fantasy in my head of what the atmosphere would be like in Santiago when we walked in. The fantasy was that there were people who would be waiting for all of the pilgrims to come into Santiago, and, when we came into sight there would be this cheer coming from the crowd. I imagined that as we walked toward the crowd they would pat us on the back and tell us: 'Congratulations! You made it. You

were brave.' That didn't happen in real life. There were
people, of course, at Santiago, mostly locals who see new
pilgrims coming through their city every day. I honestly
didn't know what to expect when we got to Santiago. At
that moment, while we were walking through the city to
the cathedral, I should have been telling myself that I was
brave. I didn't need confirmation from anyone else about
what I had just accomplished. I needed to believe in
myself.

"After our walking trek through Spain, we traveled for
another few months before going home, staying with a few
people we met on the Camino. We stayed with Thomas and
Ghyslaine in Paris, and they were absolutely the most
wonderful hosts. Then we flew to Tasmania and stayed
with Irene for a whole month. After that, we traveled
through New Zealand for a month. During our time in New
Zealand, we stayed with Jessye and Anthony. Anthony, we
discovered, is the two-time tango champion of New
Zealand! We felt very honored to have made international
friends who let us stay with them even though we only
knew each other briefly from the Camino. I was deeply
honored and moved by the kindness of these strangers we
met while walking, and who eventually became our friends.

"Right now, almost six months later, Robin and I have
moved to Portland, Oregon. We both decided not to return
to Seattle and that a change of scenery will do us good, so
to speak. We cut our year-long trip short because we were
running out of money and because my stepdad's mother
died and I wanted to be there for him. We flew from the
summer of New Zealand and landed six flights and forty-
eight hours later smack in the middle of an Iowa winter.
We stayed in a hotel for one week. We did a lot of reflecting
about the Camino during that week and missed our

Camino friends. Robin and I missed Spain and we missed the local people who encouraged us to keep going despite a language barrier. My heart still pangs with nostalgia about what Robin and I accomplished on the Camino. By 'accomplished,' I don't just mean the walking part. We conquered our doubts about whether we could finish, and we met amazing pilgrims on the Camino. We immersed ourselves into the Spanish culture by trying to speak the language. We worked ourselves through eating rock-hard bocadillos that scarred the roof of our mouths. As Cathy said one day when we sat ourselves down to eat at a Burgos restaurant, 'No mas patatas! [No more potatoes] I am sick of patatas!' Just like Cathy, I don't think I will ever forget the pilgrim's menu and the abundance of potatoes I ate along the Way.

"Every once in a while, my right knee will get a jolt of pain and it will remind me of the knee brace and the walking stick I had to use during the whole walk. Robin and I walked with thirty pounds on our backs for over seven hundred miles from Le Puy, France, to Finisterre, Spain. I am proud of the pain I feel in my knee because I know that it wasn't all in vain.

"We are working through our trip pictures right now and have made a slide show of our Camino walk. Every time we show this slide show to our friends, I begin to cry. I can't help it. This really changed my life and it has transformed me from a shy person into a more open person. We are excited to speak to anyone who wants to know about our experience. Still, we use caution not to give too much information about 'our' experience, because we don't want to taint their experience if they decide to do it. We began the Camino without preconceived notions, and that, I believe, is what helped us to keep going until the end."

I leave Robin and Brenda at a café and continue towards Palas de Rei. For a while, the trail parallels the one-lane road, which is flat and boring. With the increase of pilgrims, we all walk single file, about 4 meters (13 feet) apart. From a distance, we look like a line of ants returning to the nest. Later the trail passes through slender eucalyptus trees under which grow ferns. In these woods, I do not see pilgrims before me and I enjoy the illusion of solitude. In the twentieth century, the paper industry introduced this invasive species of eucalyptus from Australia. These trees are fast growing, sturdy, and drought resistant. The thick bark shields the tree from fire damage; the wind from fires blows the seeds to new areas.

There is the pungent odor of fire and smoke in the distant hills. The unusually warm weather, lack of rainfall, and prevailing easterly winds spread the blaze, burning over 4000 hectares (about 1000 acres) in Galicia. Two firefighters die attempting to contain the fire.

In Palas de Rei, a small but pretty town, we sit outside a café and try to determine whether to stay in town or go farther. The wonderful aromas from the café are tempting, but it is only midafternoon and Dennis thinks it would be fun to sleep in Casanova, which is only 4.8 kilometers (3 miles) away.

As we sit there, we speak with Claudia.

Claudia Sundman

"I'm doing [the Camino] in honor of my husband Roger, who died of cancer. The money I raise will help open The Cancer Support Community Eastern North Carolina, where people of all ages can gather to learn more about cancer, share their experiences with others, and find opportunities to laugh along the way. The program will be free.

"I first became interested in making this pilgrimage in 1994. That year, the February issue of the magazine *Smithsonian* ran an article about 'The long, sweet road to Santiago de Compostela,' by Simon Winchester. I was hooked! Mostly I saw it as a cheap way to travel across Spain on foot and sleeping in communal dormitories set up at convenient intervals to give rest to the weary pilgrim. It sounded like a great challenge and fun!

"Alas, life gets in the way of hopes and it wasn't until after my husband had succumbed to a brain tumor five years ago that the idea of making this pilgrimage resurfaced. I would make the trip, and I would make it in honor of my husband! More importantly, I would walk to raise awareness of (and perhaps some donations for) The Cancer Support Community Eastern North Carolina. This will be a place where anyone touched by cancer can go for support and hugs. It is a place that I desperately needed when my husband was sick. I needed the support of other caregivers going through the same ups and downs that I was experiencing. I needed support as I made the heart-wrenching journey from wife to widow to whole and happy life again. My husband needed support in a nontraditional way—by that I mean anything other than a support group. My husband would have NEVER gone to a 'support group,' but he was a man who would have walked through fire for a potluck dinner. Cancer Support Communities are big on shared meals that bring a community of supporters around a dinner table to eat, talk ,and sometimes laugh.

"Access to a cancer support community in eastern North Carolina would have made a world of difference to both my husband and me."

Claudia's post-Camino comments:

"I get asked often if I found any spiritual enlightenment along the path to Santiago de Compostela. My short answer is usually a frank, 'No.' There were no bolts of lightning or 'Ah ha!' moments that I can point to and say, 'There. That's a lesson I needed to learn.' But, I was grateful each day for the hundreds, if not thousands of people in my life and along my path that have made my journey easier.

"I remember one day I stopped in a little 'one church' town. The pilgrim's hostel I stayed in was attached to the very old church and was run [by] volunteers, love, prayer, and donations. As always, I took a shower first and then washed my clothes by hand, this time in the small space between the church's vaulted stone ceiling and the wooden roof. When asked, I was pointed in the direction of the clothesline, which, I assumed, would be in sight of the church, once I got out the door. It wasn't. It was a couple of blocks away. But, I didn't know this at the time, and, after walking one block, I decided that I must have gotten the directions wrong and was about to turn around and retrace my steps. Across the street there was an old man sitting on a bench who motioned to me and pointed farther up the street. I was SURE I was on the wrong path though, and didn't really think the old man knew what I needed— despite the obviousness of wet clothes in my hands. I waved to him and was still determined to retrace my steps. That's when this old man got up off of his bench and walked over to me using TWO canes. I met him halfway across the street and he then escorted me the next block to the clothesline. I had thought MY feet were sore.

"It was that kind of help from strangers that I cherished most. All along the path, I met people who pointed me in the right direction or walked me to a destination or helped in either subtle or obvious ways. It was an amazing experience!

"Life is a trip."

We cannot find the *albergue* in Casanova, so we continue

forward from town to town, ending up in Melide. This section of the Camino is abandoned, everything is closed and without eateries. It is a long day, starting and ending in the dark. We arrive at the municipal *albergue* at 7:30 p.m., having walked 34 kilometers (21 miles). The *albergue* is not very full and we have a choice of cots. Even though Melide is renowned for spiced octopus served in wine on wooden platters, we are both hungry and too tired to walk to a restaurant; we have *raciones* (servings) at a nearby pub. Though *raciones* are usually shared with several people, Dennis and I order them as a main course. As we wait for the food, we watch televised reports about the sixteen raging forest fires in northern Spain.

Except for seeing the news in a few bars, I have not seen television, read the papers, or followed blogs for almost two months. I am no longer in the loop, unaware of politics or world happenings. I do not miss it nor did I have withdrawals. This hiatus makes me question what is important in my life. If I can leave what I thought is important without regrets, is it that important? Is it all just a distraction, something to do? When I get back, will I see the Camino as a momentary respite, a chance to breathe deeply before jumping back into my activism, or will I not get as involved? Will I have the fortitude to keep a quiet mind? I do not want to return to my previous habit of overfilling my life with activities, schedules, and concerns, especially those about which I can do nothing. I must find the strength to say no and not overcommit. Doing so will be a challenge, but I am determined: I want to keep this sense of peace and well-being in my life.

Dennis and I both use ibuprofen cream and take an ibuprofen tablet before going to bed to prevent cramping. Dennis moans a lot in his sleep, so I think he has sore legs.

My feet are thicker, the muscles having developed. I never considered this a possibility, but I guess it makes sense with all the pounding over different terrain and with the added weight of the pack. My feet have also grown in length and width. Since I have been walking in sandals, my feet are tired at night, but recover by the morning; my blisters no longer hurt and my right big toe, which was tender from pushing against the shoe, is now more comfortable.

I am losing weight or at least toning up. I can pull my skirt down without unzipping it, even though I eat high carbohydrate foods that I rarely eat back home: SAS lemon soda, beer, wine, bread, croissants, French fries, pastries, and Principe cookies, not to mention the large pilgrim's menu portions with the two entries and *postres* (desserts). The pilgrim's menu does not contain many seasonings and the desserts are not very sweet. For this reason, I am looking forward to eating spicy and seasoned home cooking after we return home. Once at home, I will need to eat well-balanced meals and forgo the carbs to stay as fit and trim as I am now—one more benefit from all the walking.

I awake early and let Dennis sleep; while hiking he has not been having his customary naps, prescribed by the doctor after his six-artery bypass in 2007, and we have not had a day off since Azofra, twenty-four days ago. We are about two days from Santiago, where we will decide if we will walk to Cape Finisterre or take the bus. If we walk, we have bragging rights to walking across Spain from the Pyrenees to the Atlantic, but it would also be nice to get there and relax by the seaside for a few days.

As we leave the *albergue*, a pilgrim asks us to hold the door for him. He is hiking with a dog and slept outside with his canine companion, who is not allowed in the building. This is only the second person I see walking with a dog. If you are thinking about walking with your canine friend, consider the following. You cannot stay in *albergues* with the dog nor enter churches, cathedrals, museums, and other public places. If the animal is not extremely fit, you may need to slow your pace or lower the distance walked for each day. You will need to carry water for both you and your dog and be mindful that your pet does not drink contaminated water. If he becomes sick, it may be difficult to find a vet when you are out in the countryside. Consider your dog's paws. Are the pads of the animal's feet prepared for the sharp rocks and hot pavement? As a precaution, you might consider purchasing leather boots for your pet. You must also consider the logistics of taking an animal to another country and home again.[5]

We arrive in Arzúa around 1 p.m. We stop to eat and I order a hamburger with ham and bacon. Since I am hungry, I eat it all, which surprises Dennis because he usually gets a portion of my meal. We encounter Harry, whom we met in Azofra, and he gives me a woven bracelet from O Cebreiro as a thank-you for helping him at the doctor's office. He has completely recovered from his fall; the scar on his forehead is a souvenir of the Camino.

After pushing for three days, we decide to stay in Arzúa and rest. There is no hot water in the *albergue*; I re-dress and go to tell the host. The *hospitalera* tells me to run the water a while longer until it heats up, which I do without success. This time, when I complain, she only shrugs her shoulders. Until a Spanish pilgrim bickers, she does nothing. I do not think it is a linguistic problem, but a cultural one, with the Spaniard knowing how to manipulate the *hospitalera* to provide the hot water. By the time the water is hot, I no longer need it, having taken a cold shower.

In this last hundred kilometers, there are many new faces on the trail, in the restaurants and *albergues*. These pilgrims have new clothes, heavy packs, and unsullied boots. They walk fast and end up with blisters. They sit on the floor to tend to the sores and leak blood and pus all over. The hosteler makes them wash the floor, but they leave it wet and soapy. One pilgrim who is wearing jeans complains about chaffing. Another complains about her tender shoulders, but she is carrying a hair dryer and enough cosmetics to open a perfumery. I feel sorry for them; their four- or five-day Camino is a penance to be endured instead of a blessing; it seems that they are missing the whole point of the Camino. In their haste to "get it done" they are not experiencing the camaraderie, the inner peace, or the joy of the Camino.

The newcomers are making this last 100 kilometers ugly by not respecting the other pilgrims and the ways of the *albergues*. Not having developed a sense of camaraderie, many of the recent starters leave the kitchen and bathrooms dirty, monopolize the aisles and the outlets, don't mop up after themselves in the showers, and are very noisy. They also litter more on the trails, not carrying their trash to dispose of properly. If only there were guidelines on pilgrim etiquette! At a minimum, my list would include:

- Be quiet.

- Respect other pilgrim's space and property.

- Follow the *albergue* rules and do not demand

special treatment.

- Leave the *albergue*, kitchen, and bathroom clean. Ask yourself if you would like to eat off the plate you washed or brush your teeth in the sink you used.

- Be hygienic. Do not lance blisters while sitting on the bed or where body fluids can contaminate an area.

- Do not carry bedbugs with you. If you get them, have your belongings professionally fumigated.

- Do not put your backpack on the bed, because it could infect or get infected with bedbugs.

- Do not litter.

- Do not shine your headlamp at people.

- Do not take toilet paper from the *albergues* or bars. Buy your own—biodegradable is best.

- Do not be judgmental.

This pilgrim etiquette is appropriate for all those who walk the Camino, not just those doing the last 100 kilometers. I only mention it here, because in this last section with its concentration of new pilgrims, there are many who have not had time to learn the "rules" or have not yet embraced the spirit of the Camino.

The next morning, it is cold and cloudy. For the first time on this trip, I use my umbrella for rain and Dennis puts on his backpack cover. It only drizzles for about twenty minutes, but it remains overcast all day.

We travel up and down mostly dirt paths and dirt roads

through several small river valleys. We pass by a memorial to Guillermo Watt, a sixty-nine-year-old Italian pilgrim who died here, just one day before reaching Santiago.

In the little town of A Rúa we stop at a modern stone building, which fails to blend in with the ancient rural setting. It is a tourism office and I inquire about places to stay in Santiago. The college-age attendant suggests making reservations at a hotel. Instead, I ask about *albergues*. Am I stuck in a pilgrim's mentality or just not ready to return to "normal" life?

The end of this journey is near; tomorrow we will be in Santiago. What will it mean to me to actually arrive? For the last month and a half, my goal each day was simply to walk towards Santiago. Once I make it, what is next? Most likely, we will go to Cape Finisterre before heading to Madrid and then back home. I have not given any thought to what comes after that, nor do I want to spend my last few days on the Camino doing so; I am having too much fun.

Near O Pedrouzo/Arco, we emerge from the eucalyptus forest at a busy street. To the left is the town, but the arrows lead us across the road and back into the forest. My instinct is to go left, but, unsure of the best way, we follow the arrows. The path forks and there is no marker indicating which way to go. We follow the trail on the left and eventually end up in the far western end of town near a school. From there, there are few markers to direct us, and we end up walking in a roundabout way to the town center.

We arrive in O Pedrouzo in the early afternoon. For dessert after lunch, Dennis orders an ice cream sundae and the waitress brings it to the table with sparklers. It is a lot of fun and seems an appropriate celebration, one day from Santiago. I order a hot chocolate. It has the consistency of hot, dark chocolate pudding. I delight in each yummy spoonful.

The Albergue Porta de Santiago is located in the center of town and resembles a storefront more than a hostel. This is the first *albergue* that has lockers. They are stacked four high, eight wide, and are painted in a patchwork of blue, white, yellow, and red. It costs €3 ($4.00) to use the locker. The walls are yellow and the support beams are fluorescent green; the place reminds me more of a kindergarten than an *albergue*. In the center of the building is a glassed-wall garden, letting light into the building. It is cold in the *albergue* until the doors close at 11 p.m. Once again, I cannot sleep; the caffeine in the chocolate is keeping me awake. I get up and walk around the *albergue*, reading the signs and trying to tire myself. Since there is no morning curfew, the lights come on at 4:30 a.m. People who want to make the noon Mass in Santiago are leaving early.

Yoorjin is in the bunk next to me. During the night, someone stole her phone, which she had left on the charger in the hall. She is very upset; not only was it her form of communication, but also her camera and she lost the photos of her journey. This is disconcerting to all of us. For 800 kilometers (500 miles), there has been honor among the pilgrims. That this should happen the day before arriving in Santiago riles me.

In spite of this disappointment, there is excitement in the air. Today we arrive at our destination. I have mixed feelings: glad and sad that the journey is ending. My feet are definitely glad! We leave the *albergue* at 7:30 a.m., go for breakfast, and then head out.

Signage is almost nonexistent and, after a few wrong starts, we backtrack to the woods via the school. As we pass the airport, I think that it won't be long until we are in Santiago, but the airport is 12.5 kilometers (7.7 miles) from the cathedral, and it will take us about three hours to walk the rest of the way.

This morning's walk is hilly, sometimes steep, but paved. The last hill before reaching Santiago is *Monte do Gozo* (Mount Joy), so named because in the past pilgrims could glimpse the towers of the cathedral from this grassy mountaintop and were joyous that the journey was ending. Today, treetops conceal the view. Oddly, I feel no emotion, no sense of joy, nor urgency to finish.

There is a chilly autumn wind and I don my jacket. I see Sonia running up to a modern sculpture that commemorates Pope John Paul II's visit to the site. She says it is a tradition to run up this hill and look for the spires. Whoever sees them first yells *Mon Joie* (My Joy) and becomes king of the group.

The Albergue San Marcos, on the top of the hill, accommodates five hundred pilgrims who can stay free for one night. It was built in 1993 to alleviate overcrowding in the city *albergues* and hotels.

We continue forward, walking on a hard-pack track that parallels the road. We stop for pictures at the Santiago marker, which is about 2 meters (6.5 feet) tall. It is made of concrete and inscribed with a staff, gourd, and scallop shell. We follow the scallop shell markers inlaid in the sidewalk through an industrial area, past the bus station and large commercial buildings, and across many busy intersections. Santiago is a large metropolitan area and it takes us about forty-five minutes to reach the Old Quarter. As we enter the well-preserved old section, we walk along narrow cobblestone streets, which make the number of pilgrims seem multitudinous. Everywhere there are people with backpacks and maps in hand. I am amazed that I do not recognize any of them. At the crowded Plaza de Cervantes, we bump into the Finnish dentists, Paula and Sally, whom we have not seen since Molinaseca—about two weeks ago. They too are searching for the cathedral; none of us can see this huge edifice with towering spires nor can we locate the markers. How can we be this close and not see the cathedral? We continue down a flight of steps, into the main Plaza de Obradoiro and there it is, at last.

Reaching the cathedral is anticlimactic; I felt more emotion at the one hundred kilometer marker. I am not sure what I expected, but surely it was not this lack of response, no excitement for completing the longest walk in my life, no sadness at its coming to an end—nothing. I am happy, though, to see many pilgrims in the plaza that we have met along the Way. There is much hugging and congratulating. Some people dance in the streets; some cry, overwhelmed; others smile, overjoyed. Our friend Pablo lies on the granite pavement to photograph us in front of the cathedral. All of the English-speaking pilgrims agree to meet in the square that evening and then go out for a celebratory drink.

From here, we proceed to the Oficina de Acogida del Peregrino (Pilgrim's Reception Office) to get the final stamp in our Pilgrim Passport and one of the two certificates. Pilgrims who trek the Camino for religious or spiritual reasons get the *Compostela*; those who undertake the journey for recreation, culture, or tourism receive a simple *certificado* or certificate.

Written in Latin, the Compostela translates as follows:

"The Chapter of this Holy Apostolic Metropolitan Cathedral of St. James, custodian of the seal of St. James' Altar, to all faithful and pilgrims who come from everywhere over the world as an act of devotion, under vow or promise to the Apostle's Tomb, our Patron and Protector of Spain, witnesses in the sight of all who read this document, that (name) has visited devoutly this Sacred Church in a religious sense. Witness whereof I hand this document over to him/her, authenticated by the seal of this Sacred Church. Given in Compostela on the (day) (month) AD (year)."

The receptionist writes my name in Latin: Iaonnam. Dennis' name is Dionysium.

The simpler Spanish certificate reads:

"The Holy Apostolic Metropolitan Cathedral of Santiago de Compostela expresses its warm welcome to the Tomb of the Apostle St. James the Greater; and wishes that the holy Apostle may grant you, in abundance, the graces of the Pilgrimage."

Below, Catherine, a pilgrim from Canada, proudly shows her Compostela. I interviewed Catherine after she returned home.

Catherine McCoy

"I am a mother of five children. If I were to pick a single defining phrase, that is it. I became a mother twenty-eight years ago and I will always be a mother, but I am at the point of redefining who I am in this journey of life. If someone were to say, 'Tell me about yourself,' what would I say? Am I my job? I love my job, but no. What am I other than the mother of five children? I am very grateful to have had that honor, but the thing is those children are now young adults and need to follow their own paths and to experience their own successes, hardships, challenges and adventures. They don't need me hovering over them and trying to fix things. It is time for adventures of my own. It is time to broaden my focus, learn new things, and have new life experiences: it is time to walk.

"From September 3 to October 12, 2011, I walked 700 kilometers (435 miles) across Spain. As I walked between six and eight hours per day, I had a lot of time to think. I've been asked, 'What did you learn?' My first few days home I didn't know how to answer that question. I now realize that my number one lesson on the Camino de Santiago is about the value of time.

"A few weeks ago, we gained an hour when switching back from Daylight Savings Time and there probably is not a person who wasn't happy about that. We all know that time is a commodity, a precious thing to have more of. It is so important that there are university courses offered in Time Management. We have calendars, organizers, watches, alarms, and most importantly, smartphones that provide all of the above.

"With all this focus on time and schedules, you would think we all understand the value of time. But, do we really? It's not hard to imagine that a person who has been given a couple of months to live really understands the value of time. So how did walking the Camino help me to learn this? Those who have walked before have said, 'There are three stages of suffering to overcome while on the Camino. These stages are physical, mental, and spiritual suffering.'

"When I began walking from St-Jean-Pied-de-Port on September 5, I was heading up the Pyrenees mountains. My body was in no way conditioned to be walking up a mountain and especially not for 25 kilometers (15.5 miles). I was carrying 8 kilos (18 pounds) on my back and was struggling with a preexisting lung condition. I would see a very long, steep hill ahead of me and, one step at a time, I would focus on making it to the top. As I approached the top it was never the top at all; it would just be a curve and I kept going up, up and up for hours! My legs were hurting, my shoulders were aching, and my heart and lungs were saying, 'Are you trying to kill me?' I was consumed with my physical discomfort and the effort that I was expending; I missed most of the beauty of the Pyrenees. Every so often I would stop, sit, and look about me, and it was only at those moments that I was blown away by the amazing sight before me. Then I would start to walk again and focus on nothing but my own discomfort. This period of overcoming my physical suffering lasted approximately ten days.

"The second stage was one of overcoming mental suffering. The walking was almost effortless and I could no longer feel the weight on my back. The heat of the sun continued to drain my energy and threatened to burn through my skin as I walked for about eight hours a day across the flat plains of the Meseta region. When boredom began to threaten my sanity, I started to make rhythms with my walking poles. I began to count as my poles touched the ground, '1, 2, 3, 4, 5, 6, 7, 8; 1, 2, 3, 4, 5, 6, 7, 8.' Over and over again. At one point I became angry. Angry that these Spanish people couldn't speak English; angry when I couldn't get Wi-Fi; angry that there was never any toilet paper or soap! There were moments when I could see the beauty and was in awe as I walked through the quaint little towns that had been there for hundreds of years. But for much of the time, I was wrapped up in my annoyance and my judgments and the incredible heat!

"Then came the last phase of the Camino—overcoming spiritual suffering. I cannot say what day it was that I realized my mind had become empty. I simply didn't have a thought left in it. I didn't know what time it was, or where I'd even end up each day. Several times, I didn't even know what day it was. As I walked, I began to see many beautiful things. In fact, almost every little thing I saw was beautiful! I saw every wildflower along the dusty paths; I enjoyed the sheep and cows that I shared the roads with. As the days were getting shorter, I almost always started walking in the dark. I was amazed by every single sunrise.

"During this time, I met a man who had been walking for five months. He was sitting at a café in a little village and had other pilgrims gathered around him. One person asked him, 'What is one thing you've learned on your walk?' He answered, 'I've learned the value of time. I am a rich man because I have time to be here and to be sitting in this village in Spain talking to you today. Most people will tell you that time is money, but they are wrong: time is life.'

"As I was approaching the end of my journey, I thought about this. I thought about the ways I had spent time in my life, but even more about how I had allowed my time or my life to be taken over by the demands of others.

"Now that I am home, my Camino continues and I have a new challenge: to live in the world with its demands and its schedules and its technology, while at the same time appreciating each minute and opening my mind and my eyes to the beauty around me. It is only when I do this that I truly understand the value of time."

Having completed our pilgrimage registration, we proceed to the Office of Tourism to inquire about a place to stay. I just want to take my backpack off; the last several hours on pavement have been hard on my lower back. We stay at *Mundoalbergue* because this hostel has a double bunk on the bottom with a single bunk above. It is not exactly private, but it offers us the luxury of sleeping together. I am happy to see Diane Rodrigue and Sylvain Cyr from Canada; they are returning from Finisterre and are leaving for home in the morning.

At 7 p.m., we return to the plaza in front of the cathedral. There are about forty of us gathered and we kiss and hug each other in congratulations. Some pilgrims I have not seen since the first weeks of walking. It is a joyous reunion, all of us having shared the Camino experience.

There is only outdoor seating at the restaurant; a youth group of a hundred Spanish pilgrims arrived in the city today and they have indoor reservations. Because it is cold, seven of us find an indoor eatery. Dennis and I order a seafood platter and share it with everyone. On it are squid, king prawns, clams, octopus, mussels, and something else in the squid family. It is served with *pimentos de Padrón*, small peppers pan fried in olive oil and then sprinkled with coarse salt.

The next day, Dennis and I go to the Pilgrim's Mass at the cathedral. We arrive at 11:45 a.m. and it is standing room only. I am surprised at how small the interior is in comparison to the exterior. A nun teaches us the refrains that we will sing during Mass. There are many pilgrims lined up for the confessional. To satisfy the canonical conditions for the indulgence, pilgrims must confess their sins, receive communion, and do a good deed. Donating money is considered a good deed.

Pilgrims still observe many medieval rituals and traditions at the cathedral. At the entrance is the Portica de la Gloria, a carved and sculpted gateway leading into the church. On it are 185 statues making up religious scenes. The central pillar is the Tree of Jesse, the earliest remaining visualization of Christ's genealogy carved around a cylindrical pillar, and on which sits St. James carrying a pilgrim's staff and a scroll with the inscription, "The Lord Sent Me."

For a millennium, pilgrims perform rituals at this gateway. They place their right hand on St. James' left foot and say a prayer of thanks and pay homage to him. As a result, there are five indentations worn in the marble, an indication of the quantity of people who have completed the pilgrimage. Behind the portico is a statue of Mateo the Master, who sculptured the gateway. This statue is nicknamed "The Saint of the Bumps" because pilgrims kneel before it, then knock foreheads with Mateo's three times in hopes of gaining some of his genius, and perhaps to enhance memory.

There is a huge bejeweled and golden statue of St. James behind the High Altar. Pilgrims climb a stairway behind the statue to "hug" him. Kissing the hem of his jeweled cloak, once part of the tradition, is now discouraged to prevent disease transmission.

During the Mass, the priest announces the country of origin and the number of pilgrims from each country of those who received the Compostela the preceding day. The sermon is in Spanish, but I understand enough. He talks about the distance in kilometers as well as the distance in spirituality. The priest tells the pilgrims to open their hearts as if opening a window and then to let the light of love, peace, and compassion enter. My eyes water and I cannot sing the refrain to the song that follows his speech. I am overwhelmed by emotion, and this reaction surprises me.

Women of the Way

I recall all the "trail angels" who helped me, all the kindnesses and encouragements I received, all the laughs I have shared, and all the friends I made along the Way and give thanks. Without them, my Camino would have been very different.

The cathedral has the world's largest *botafumeiro*, a large metal thurible (incense burner). On certain days, eight monks pull ropes to raise and then swing the *botafumeiro* over the crowd from one end of the church to the other, arching high to the ceiling, and scenting the church with aromatic incense. Today, they use a smaller version from the altar and the air smells pungent.

After the Mass, Dennis and I, like ten centuries of pilgrims before us, queue up to climb the narrow, worn steps behind the altar to hug the statue and then descend to the crypt where the remains of St. James are kept in a silver casket. Afterwards, we walk around the church looking at the stained glass and various side chapels.

We lunch with Sonia, Claire, Natalia, and others at Casa Manolo, having heard about its excellent traditional Galician cuisine through the pilgrim grapevine. The restaurant does not take reservations and we have to wait for a seating—that youth group again. This is goodbye for many of us, but one done with smiles, not tears; Natalia decides to join Dennis and me on the morning bus to Finisterre.

In the streets, we are happy to see Trish from Canada, our first roommate in St-Jean-Pied-de-Port; we have not seen each other since France. She is staying at the Monastery of San Pelayo Antealtares, which accommodates women pilgrims. On her Camino, she did not have difficulties with her feet or legs, but did have problems with bedbugs. When she arrived in Santiago, she brought everything to a professional cleaner that specialized in getting rid of the pests. She is still traveling with her friend and they both took a few days off when her friend had tendinitis. As for many of us, what she loves best about the Camino is the camaraderie.

Musicians, artists, living statues, mimes, and beggars fill the streets of Santiago. In the plaza, I see a statue of Gandhi that I do not recall seeing earlier. I walk around the statue very slowly before I see the staff move almost imperceptibly. I sit on a low wall and watch this amazing street entertainer who keeps a pose for such a long time. Dennis drops a few coins in the vase before the "statue" and "Gandhi" hands him a scroll with the message "Earth provides enough to satisfy everyone man's need, but not every man's greed." ~ Mahatma Gandhi. It is an appropriate saying for a pilgrim.

I see Cathy Collins with her son, Jack. Cathy and I have spoken several times on the Camino, but this is the first time we sit and chat, sharing a plate of pimientos de Padrón and drinking lemon sodas.

Cathy Collins is a seventy-two-year-old from San Francisco, California. She is traveling with her son Jack, who is forty-seven years old.

Cathy Collins

"The idea to go on the Camino started with a childhood memory. I was about ten years old and in Catholic school when one of the sisters talked about the Camino de Santiago. She said that it was about a four hundred and fifty mile journey of prayer and devotion, not so much as devotion to Saint James, but more for love of the Lord. In my childlike understanding, I thought to myself, 'Oh, I love the Lord, but I couldn't do that. I couldn't walk four hundred and fifty miles,' and the idea of doing this receded into my memory. Then I started hearing about people who were doing this pilgrimage, people who were older, not just youngsters, and I thought that if they could do it, I could do it.

"I thought about it a lot and decided to do it in the fall of last year, because the weather is cooler and more favorable at that time of the year. Then Jack said that if I waited one year he would do it with me. He needed time to set some money aside for the trip. I agreed.

"Last summer I spent a month in Jerusalem at the Tantur Ecumenical Institute. On the very last day that I was there, I injured my foot. My foot rolled over a loose rock creating the most horrible pain in my heel. It took months for that to mend. By February, it was better and Jack and I started doing training hikes. We walked in the many open spaces near San Francisco.

"We started in Roncesvalles. The first two days were exceedingly difficult. People had told me that it was hard, but no one had said how hard it really is. Those first two days were so arduous that if I had not had Jack with me I might have quit. We took the third day off to rest. We only walked from one end of Pamplona to the other and stopped.

"Walking with Jack was the trip of a lifetime; I will never forget it. It was wonderful. Jack and I were already close, but now there is a different quality to our closeness. Jack was exceptionally patient with me. I am so slow. I am not the oldest on the trail, not the plumpest, but I am the slowest. Jack would walk ahead of me. Every now and then, he would turn around to make sure I was okay. We joked and teased each other a lot. Twice we misread the way to go. We did not get seriously lost, but did go the wrong way. We doubled back and it was fine. Now, I can tease him about leading me astray.

"Jack read me in a different way. He could tell when I had to stop. He would suggest that we stop to eat; he knew before I did that I needed fuel. We would stop and eat and then I was fine to go again.

"On the day we were coming into Santiago, I had this

childlike image of coming out from the forest that we had been walking through for about twenty miles, with its soft forest ground and all the beauty, and then walking right into the cathedral. Instead, we had to walk for miles from the outskirts through the industrial part of the city. It was disappointing. Throughout the Camino, as we were approaching the villages and small cities, the first things we would see were the spires of the church. In the walk through Santiago, you cannot see the church. I thought that it was childish of me to imagine coming from the forest directly to the cathedral because Santiago is a modern city.

"Now that I have finished the pilgrimage, I don't know if I have been changed by it. I think that I will know that sometime in the future. I prayed a lot. There was a lot of quiet and alone time. Even though Jack and I walked together, we did not walk side-by-side every step of the way. What I have learned and how I have changed is something that I will discover as I reflect on the trip.

"One of the best things about the Camino is the people I have met. Oh my goodness! Absolutely wonderful people. We were walking into Carrión and I was feeling sick, very nauseous. I knew that I could not walk much farther. Some of the people we met had been sick with a twenty-four-hour flu that was going around, and I had caught it. We stopped at a bar-café at a crossroads about 15 kilometers (9.3 miles) from Carrión. Jack asked the woman to call a taxi because I was not feeling well. She did, but the taxi would not come that far to pick me up. Since she spoke only Spanish, it took us a few minutes to understand. She was saying, '*Yo, Yo,*' (I, I,) patting her chest, '*Mi coche*' (my car). She then closed up her shop and drove me to Carrión, where she showed me where the medical office was. I have often thought of that woman. This would never have happened in the United States. As we were leaving the café, another couple was arriving. She told them, '*Veinte minutos*' (twenty minutes), and indicated a seat for them to sit on and wait until she returned in twenty minutes. That kind of generosity inspires me to be more generous.

"I will come back to Spain, though I don't intend to walk the Camino again. I will study Spanish, so I know more than just words. I felt badly that I could not communicate with her. 'Muchas gracias' did not really convey to her how grateful I was.

"For me, walking the Camino has always been a spiritual journey. I am not sure if it has been for Jack. I went to Mass several times along the Camino, both on Sundays and during the week, depending on where we were. The Mass today at the Cathedral de Santiago was the first time that Jack joined me, and I know that it touched him.

"We stayed mostly in *albergues*. I enjoyed the ones that were run by the various country associations the most. The *hospitaleros* were people who had walked the Camino and they were really, really hospitable. The ones that provided food put out just a little bit more effort to make it delicious and welcoming.

"The pilgrim's menu got old. It was very repetitious. I found that if you went off the Camino just a little bit, you could find a restaurant that did a better pilgrim's menu. It might cost a bit more, instead of €9 to €10 ($11.30 to $12.50) it would cost €12 to €13 ($15 to $16.30). But, it was creative and delicious. There is good food available. It is just that what is available in the tiny stops along the

Women of the Way

Camino is very much the same.

"There is a saying, 'The Camino provides,' like when that woman took care of me. There is another saying, 'That's a Camino moment,' which is when you reach out to someone else. At one point, Jack was off doing something and I was just sitting on a bench in the square. A couple came in with their backpacks and I wished them a 'Buen Camino.' This couple was from England. They were doing the Camino in one-week segments; every year they take a week. They were beginning their third week the next day. I invited this couple to join Jack, me, and some other pilgrims for dinner. We were from many countries, but we were able to speak in English. The next morning this couple thanked me for inviting them. It had been a wonderful beginning for their Camino. It was natural to ask them to join us for dinner, but it was special for them."

I am disappointed at the Museo de las Perigrinaciones by the lack of information about female pilgrims. There was only one small statue of a woman in pilgrim's dress. At the exit desk, I ask about the obvious lack of information. The receptionist is bewildered by my "astute observation." Since women are more than forty percent of the pilgrims, not having information about them in a museum in Santiago dedicated to pilgrimages is an affront. I manage to find two postcards showing French female apparel from between 1530 and 1550. I assume that this must have been how the French pilgrims dressed during that time, though there is no scallop shell, staff, or gourd—the symbols of the pilgrim.

I begin a quest to find a souvenir statue of a female pilgrim. I inquire at all the stores and tourist kiosks without success. There are statues of the Virgen del Camino, the patron saint of León, of female witches and comic figures, but nothing serious; in all of Santiago, there is not one female pilgrim statue! I am met with questioning eyes when I ask about a statue of "*la perigrina*." Several enterprising storekeepers, seeing the potential for sales, say they will commission some for next year, but that is too late for me.

It is overcast and chilly. Instead of a statue for my souvenir, I buy myself a fleece jacket with the yellow marker arrow on it. Though it is warm and practical, I would have preferred the statue, which would last longer.

On the streets, marketers tempt us with samples of Galician cuisine. The Tarta de Santiago is an almond cake decorated with powdered sugar and imprinted with the Cross of St. James. The Tetilla cheese is a dessert cheese shaped like a small breast with a nipple. Bakeries offer samples of their pastries, as do the candy stores. Though they do not offer samples, the fish and meat stores display their best and freshest wares. There are octopus, crustaceans, mollusk, and large fish at the fishmongers; ham and roast tempt the meat lovers. Everything is pricey.

At this last *albergue*, I am not surprised to find the pail and bucket in the unisex shower room. What I do not expect is having to shower in the dark; the overhead lights are not working. Dennis ties my headlamp to the shower head and this provides enough lighting for me to wash up.

I get very little sleep. There are many goings-on in the

dormitory. The woman across from us keeps "tsk-ing" at all the snoring. She awakens her husband, who gets up, walks over to the snorer, and then nudges him to turn over. They repeat this scenario several times throughout the night. Since the Camino is over, the hostel does not impose a curfew. People come in at all hours of the night. The man bunking above us comes in around 1:30 a.m. He uses a lighter with a two-inch flame to illuminate the way to the bed and then to search his bag for his headlamp. I worry about a fire. He has a woman with him and the two climb into the single bunk. I hope it will not collapse with the weight; I imagine being impaled by a bed slat. The folks above us turn on a light under the covers every ten or fifteen minutes like a long-timed beacon from a lighthouse; I cannot imagine what they are doing. Finally I doze until the predawn activity in the *albergue* awakens me as people set off for the airport or train station.

Dennis and I meet up with Natalia (whom I first met more than two weeks ago in Terradillos de los Templarios) to walk to the bus station, and then head to Cape Finisterre, the most western area in Spain. Many pilgrims walk three or four days to visit Fisterra or Muxia. Fisterra is a seaside town with a wonderful lighthouse, 143 meters (470 feet) above the Atlantic. In Muxia, there is the "Pedra de Barca," a stone balanced on one point that wiggles in the wind. At one time, the stone was used to determine if a person was guilty or innocent of a serious crime. This is where Tom Avery brought the ashes of his son in the movie, *The Way*.

Along the route to Fisterra, I see bays filled with islands, fishing and sailing boats; steep cliffs, upon which wind generators stand like sentinels guarding the coast; beaches of coarse sand; and buoys bobbing in the waves. It is a tortuous route and Dennis gets motion sickness. He tries to nap, hoping to escape his discomfort. I chat with Natalia. She is self-assured, with a quiet demeanor. Her interjections and comments in our conversations indicate a unique outlook on life and a quick wit.

She loves photography and carries a camera with heavy lenses. One day at a café, I noticed that she was particularly cheerful, humming a song. Her good mood resulted from having danced the salsa on the Camino that morning. Earlier that day, someone commented on how heavy her camera was and she replied, "*Se vale la pena*" (It is worth the trouble), which is also the name of a song. Everyone then started to sing in Spanish and she and another danced along. She apparently has a passion for dance as well as photography.

Natalia has been involved in the travel industry for over ten years, visiting destinations such as Nepal, India, Egypt, South America, and Asia. Prior to the Camino, she worked a season on the boats in the Balearic Islands.

I have no regrets for riding the bus several hours to Fisterra instead of walking the distance. This way, I have a wonderful conversation with Natalia.

Natalia Cohen

"My name is Natalia Cohen. I was born in South Africa and grew up in the UK.

"I did not have a specific reason for doing the Camino. Basically, a year ago in August I terminated my contract. I was working in Peru. I moved to Buenos Aires and spent four months there. Then I went to Cape Town and spent four months with my family. That made eight months of no work. I was thinking that this was not going to look too well on my CV (résumé), and that maybe I should turn it into a year's sabbatical or maybe that I should do a little bit of work on boats, which is something I always wanted to do. At the end of my time in Cape Town, I took some courses and then went to Palma, Mallorca.

"I heard about the Camino quite a few years ago, but

nothing had grabbed m
interesting experience.
Camino about three yea
recommended it. My life
a wandering lifestyle, a n
of travel and have been ve
was another short adventu
plan was to do the Camino
and looking for work. At th
me that if I wanted to look
earlier. So, I decided to wo
boats, and then do the Can   ⸺ ᴊpent four
months in Mallorca, and the   ⸺ᴛarted my journey on
September 20 in Roncesvalles; I finished on October 20. It
took me one month. I did not feel as if I was hurrying; I
was comfortable with the pace. It was an incredible
experience.

"I think many people do the Camino because they are
looking for something specific. Perhaps they have had
experiences in their lives where they want to leave
something behind. Or maybe their routine grind in life has
gotten them to such an extent where they feel that they
need to do something completely different to get away
from that lifestyle and put themselves in a completely new
environment. I have met incredibly inspirational people on
this walk, of all ages and all cultures. I think most people
do the Camino for spiritual reasons. I think most people
deep down inside would love to have a life-altering
experience on the Camino, something that touches them
profoundly. Many people that I have traveled with have
those types of experiences, and that has been really
beautiful to observe.

"However, I did not come on this Camino, this journey, for

n. To be honest, there was nothing I
ponder upon and nothing I felt that I
ork through. Everyone has issues and
part from what am I to do with the rest of my
ch is a normal issue for me because I move so
, I often ask myself if I am on the right journey, if I
on the right path.

"In fact, yesterday I was sitting in a café in Santiago watching the other pilgrims come in. I was thinking that the Camino has given different things to different people, and I considered what has it given me. I am going to read what I wrote, because it was a nice revelation, actually. 'We have made our way into the city of Santiago, which is a city like every other. There is nothing specifically pilgrim-welcoming about it and the Way is not so beautiful. I am not sure that anticlimactic is the word I would use to describe it, but more of a realization of something I already knew, that the Camino is the end of an incredible accomplishment and the beginning of other moments and paths that will and have opened up for all who walk it. The city could perhaps have given us more of a welcome, but the Camino teaches and the Camino gives us the confidence to know and believe in ourselves and to appreciate that the Way is within as well as without. If the people maintain their alertness and openness that they felt while walking, they will live richer moments.'

"I think that people become different people when they walk the Camino. Even though they are the same people, they allow themselves to open up a lot quicker and a lot easier than they would in their normal lives. People just walk up next to you and—boom!—you have their story. I wonder if that is the energy of the Camino and if that is what the Camino wants the people who walk it to do. Why

286

don't they live like that normally? Why are they not open, alert and observant of what is going around them at every moment? Why only on the Camino?

"I very much wanted to walk the Camino on my own. It was something that I started on my own and did not have any plans to meet up with anyone and walk it with anyone. For most of my Camino, it was a solo journey while meeting people during the walking and in the evenings. Ten or eleven days ago I met Sonia. For whatever reason our paths crossed and we connected instantly and the rest of the Camino was with her. We became sort of one doing the Camino together. We are very different people, from very different backgrounds, and looking for very different things, so this was very interesting. I had thought that I wanted to do my own thing. Meeting her—it was okay to go with someone because our journeys were exactly the same at that point of the Camino. She has become a sort of a soul mate.

"A lot of things have happened while I was walking with her. I would ask for certain things, and it would happen. It was very bizarre. Once I was saying I wanted rainbows. I did not want it to rain, but I really wanted rainbows because I love rainbows. Later that day we arrived at a village somewhere before O Cebreiro that had a restaurant with rainbow flags everywhere. I thought, 'That is strange.' Another time I wanted to find an *albergue* with a terrace and a laptop so I could download some photos, and then we came across the *albergue* in the middle of nowhere that had everything that I had asked for. We decided not to stay there, but it did have everything that I had asked for. Just strange things like that.

"This year I spoke to the universe and said, 'I'd like to find my soul mate. This is my year of love and I am ready.' Now I am spending my time with Sonia, who is a form of soul mate, because I connected instantly with her. I would not have walked the Camino with just anyone. So maybe I have to become more specific with the universe: 'I want a male soul mate.' But, Sonia is definitely one of my soul mates.

"I also wrote, 'The Camino for me has been a representation of my life so far: the varied and ever-changing stages, and the transience of wonderful people, culture and landscapes coming and going from my life. My attempt to always live every moment to its fullest, always observing and remaining present, a constant uncertainty of exactly where the path or the Way will take me, but always a constant certainty that if I follow my heart—or the yellow arrow—I will always be guided in the right direction. The journey is what is important, not the destination.'

"People, places, and lessons that you learn along the Way will shape who you are and enrich your life. One of the phrases that I love is 'Yesterday is history. Tomorrow is a mystery. Today is a gift. That is why it is called the present.' Everything changes, that is the law of nature, with no cravings, nor aversions, the whole Vipassana philosophy.[6] I love life. Special moments and special people keep moving forward and the energy carries me.

"There was no life-changing realization for me. There was a realization that the path that I have chosen for my life has been a beautiful path. Some people do the Camino and get only a glimpse of a beautiful path in life. If they could take everything that they learned on the Camino and implant it into their own lives, however mundane or routine they think that life is, they would have an incredible life. Everyone writes their own story. Most people are blocked by fear alone. If they can open and not fear anything, and let themselves shine through, then the Camino that they begin here will be their Camino for the rest of their lives.

"We all need love and compassion. On the Camino, people automatically have this love and compassion for everyone that they come across. There is an understanding that we are all doing this incredible thing together. It is an incredibly bonding experience; the blisters, the pains, and the aches all bind us.

"In normal life, you don't have those hours and hours to relax and look around to see and understand what is happening. The Camino provides that time.

"I think the Camino is something that everyone should experience. I don't know how it compares to the other big walks that people do, but for a short walk—a month!—I think it is such a unique experience. I am definitely putting this on my résumé; it says so much. It shows commitment."

At the bus terminus in Fisterra, there are several women offering a private accommodation in their home. We have been approached in other towns by such enterprising women; this is the first time we consider the offer. A short middle-aged woman shows us pictures of her available rooms and we negotiate a price. We are unhappy with the first choice, because it does not meet Dennis' ham radio needs. We explain these needs to her and she shows us another place across town with a nice quiet room, large kitchen, on a hill and with a garden. Dennis is happy and we move in to what will be our home for the next two days.

Our room is at the back of the apartment. From our window, we see a chicken coop and several chickens scratching the soil. I hope that there is no rooster to crow at dawn. There are three other bedrooms in the apartment; at the moment, we are the only people here. The communal bathroom is dark marble with a real tub, but the shower has no curtains and in the corner are the mop and bucket. The kitchen is spacious and fully equipped.

We buy food for a picnic and walk about 3 kilometers (2 miles) to the lighthouse. We pass the 0.00-kilometer Camino marker, the hotel *O Semáforo,* and sit on the rocky cliff behind the lighthouse. Light shimmers on the water far below us, gulls dive for food, a light breeze musses our hair and whips our jackets, and huge waves crash on the rocks near us. In the past, pilgrims would bathe in the ocean and burn their clothes or shoes on the rocks. Now there are signs prohibiting burning. It is the third week in October; I have no desire to swim in the cold frothy water. I am content to sit on the rocks and bask in the warm autumn sun. We eat our sandwiches and sip on a beer. I am at peace, holding hands with Dennis. We are both reflective; neither of us is very talkative. One result of the Camino is a deeper bond between us, which, after thirty-seven years, I would not have thought possible.

We stay on the crags until the clouds roll in and the wind gets chilly. On our descent, we meet Sue (Hammock Hanger) and Ann (Aloha Ann), friends of Dennis' who walked the Appalachian Trail, as he did. Sue has been following me on my trail journal. They were ahead of us, but walking more slowly than we were. It is fortuitous to meet, even if only at the end.

Sue Turner

"I was an outdoor instructor for Girl Scouts in Palm Glades, south Florida for twenty-odd years, and then an Adirondack backpack instructor for eight years. I started long-distance hiking in 2001 with the Appalachian Trial (AT). I did it in two sessions: 1000 miles (1609 kilometers) in the first and then the remainder in the second. I had terrible foot pains in 2001; it turned out I had a sewing needle in my foot. In 2002, I spent five days in the hospital with Lyme Disease. Though hiking has had its difficult moments, they have not been a deterrent; each time I rebound. It's all part of the adventure.

"Over the years, hiking has stressed my knees and caused them to degenerate. People used to ask me, 'What do you do to prepare?' I would tell them I just get out there and walk, and eventually I get in shape, which is true, but I never realized how important the quad muscles are. Now I know that exercising my quads could have saved my knees a couple of years' of damage, but I didn't know that then. I also hiked in sandals. People say this is great, and it was, but, again, I did not give my knees the protection that they needed and this caused them to degenerate earlier.

"On November 1 last year, I had my left knee operated on, and on April 1 this year, I had my right knee done. I started walking the Camino five months after the last surgery. I had my doctor's blessing as long as I promised to be a good girl and stop walking if the knee hurt or swelled. Although I had an occasional swelling, it never was major. On the whole, I was never any more sore than other hikers who walked all day. If needed, I took an ibuprofen in the morning and was fine. Just because one has knee surgery does not mean one has to stop doing the things one likes. I am thrilled with the results and I can't wait to get back and hug my doctor. For the past five years, the hiking had been painful. Friends and family would ask me why I go hiking when I am in pain and I would reply, 'Because I love doing it.' Now, I can hike without pain, and that is fabulous. Every day I say, 'Oh my God, thank you, thank you, thank you!' This is my passion. I don't drink, smoke, or ride a bike. Hiking is what I do. To have my knees go was really terrible. Now they are brand new. They're babies!

"The Camino is easier than the other long-distance hikes. I don't have to cook or carry the food or the tent. Just those things make it easier than a wilderness trail. There were times when I enjoyed this ease, other times I craved my hammock and solitude. But, the international culture I got by interacting with all sorts of people made it all worthwhile.

"A lot of people come to the Camino for the spiritual experience. I did not come here for that experience, I came here to hike and to see how my knees would work. I had a much more spiritual hike when I was alone on the AT than I did on the Camino, even though I did talk to my God whenever I entered a church.

"It was a lovely trail. I am glad I did it. Since I don't like to repeat trails, I most likely will not come back to the Camino Francés, unless my husband wants to do it. There are other Caminos, however, and my walking partner and I are already discussing the Portugal one.

"This was a lovely trip, very diversified, totally different from any of my wilderness trips. I have developed a plan that I will do a wilderness trail in the US one year and alternate it with a European adventure the following year. Hopefully, I will have the money and the time.

"I turned fifty-five years old the day before I flew to Spain and my partner turned fifty-five last week. This is our "double nickel" hike. My partner Ann and I found each on an AT women's hiker forum the year before we did the 2001 hike. We met on the 2001 AT hike, though we did not hike together. We have become long-term friends and have since hiked together."

For the first time in forty-four days it rains and the temperature plummets. I sit curled up in the *albergue* with a cup of tea and a good book while Dennis attempts to make amateur radio contacts on his portable ham radio. It is nice to relax and not walk. I luxuriate in the quiet atmosphere and am disappointed when other guests arrive.

As I sit, I try to digest the Camino experience. I am proud

to have withstood the heat, the weight of my pack, the pounding of my steps, and other physical challenges. At the moment, I am happy to stop. If I were to do it again, I would change only a few things. I would get better maps and guidebook. I would not be so regimented in my daily schedule; I had a sense of needing to constantly move forward, and, consequently, I did not take time to visit places that were of interest, such as the monastery in Samos. I would be more adventuresome in sampling the Spanish cuisine, and look for places that offered good and reasonably priced food. Getting the pilgrim's menu was economical and easy—most every town had a version—but it did become monotonous.

Once the rain eases, we go to a pizzeria that offers free Wi-Fi and I Skype my parents. They are happy that the trip is coming to its conclusion and that we will be home in about a week. We are close-knit and the separation has been hard on all of us. We are looking forward to seeing each other.

This restaurant is one of the only affordable ones in town. As in many coastal vacation destinations, the prices in the shops and dining facilities are exorbitant: €100 ($125) for lobster, €65 ($82) for fish with potatoes, €1 ($1.25) for a slice of bread—such a difference from the pilgrim's menu. We buy groceries for breakfast and lunch and return to the pizzeria for supper the next night.

We leave Fisterra at 11:45 a.m. Once in Santiago, we walk from the bus station to the Renfe depot to buy our tickets to Madrid. There are no sleepers available and we will have to sit in the tourist coach all night. Since the train does not leave until 10:30 p.m., we decide to spend time in the city. To my delight, we bump into Phil from Oregon as he exits the Pilgrim's Reception Office. Our visit is brief; he must get to the bank before it closes.

That night, I leave Santiago and end my pilgrimage. In one sense, I am no longer a pilgrim; I am once again a tourist. In another sense, I will always be a pilgrim. The last forty-four days have changed me intrinsically. I now look at life differently. I am more mindful of the present. Having experienced joy, I choose to live a joyous life by living deeply and fully. I choose to be happy.

To continue that sense of peacefulness and joy, I must learn to hold the endless chatter of modern life at bay, to deal with what is important to me, and to let the rest go. As my friend Judy Helgager says, "Learning new things is not for cowards." What is important is connecting with others, with the earth, with nature, and with whatever journey I am on.

Over these days as a pilgrim, I have become reacquainted with Dennis and have a deeper appreciation for his humor, honesty, and sincerity. I am returning home, not to sit in my rocking chair recalling this or that adventure but to continue holding hands, sharing laughter, and launching forth on the next leg of our journey together.

As I reached out to the women of the Way, I realized that women need "sisters" to travel life's journey. We cannot do it alone. We need to incorporate into our lives that camaraderie that many of the women cherished on the Camino. As in this allegory for life, one just needs to be open to others, to acknowledge them from the heart, and to be willing to spend time together.

In sisterhood, this is my challenge to you: "Don't walk in

front of me and be my leader, don't walk behind me and be my follower, but walk beside me and be my sister." ~ Unknown

My post-Camino comments:

In November, still high from our trip, Dennis and I throw a Pilgrim's Menu Party at our home in Florida. With our friends, we share foods typical of the Camino, drink sangria, and end the meal with a *Tarta de Santiago*, a wheatless cake made from almonds. Afterward, we show them a photo essay of our journey. Preparing for this party was so much fun.

Peregrino Menu

Primer Plato
- Ensalada Mixta (Mixed salad)
- Ensalada Rusa (Potato salad)
- Pasta con tomate (Pasta with tomato)
- Caldo Gallego (Galician Broth)

Secundo Plato
- Pollo asado (Roast Chicken)
- Carne asada (Pot roast)
- Tortilla Española (Spanish omelet)
- Empanada (Galician meat pie)

Pan, Postre, Vino, Agua
(Bread, Dessert, Wine, Water)

Menu for our post-Camino Party

For eight months following our return, I prolong my pilgrimage by writing this book, *Women of the Way*, reliving the experiences by looking at photos, listening to recordings of each conversation, and exchanging emails with the women in the book. Often as I write I become overwhelmed, my psyche in tune with emotions and feelings awakened on the Camino.

As many women have expressed, the camaraderie on the Camino is what made the pilgrimage special, uplifting and inspiring. What a pleasure it was to be accepted so openly and completely! The women who shared their stories with me were genuinely happy to see me again farther along on the road to Santiago; their warm smiles and embraces made me feel accepted and cherished, liked a much-loved family member. I have never had such warm and endearing receptions by so many people. I believe that the Camino is unparalleled in hiking excursions for developing this sense of community and belonging. This camaraderie is what makes the Camino unique. Being accepted for who you are in the moment is satisfying, perhaps addicting. Everyone wants to be validated; being on the Camino does so. No wonder many people want to return.

As for many pilgrims on the Camino, the adventure changed me in many lasting ways—all for the better. I am more relaxed. Each day, I try to walk in the early morning, listening to songbirds and woodpeckers, watching the squirrels, feeling alive. Though it may only be a half-hour walk, this time keeps me connected to the earth and to nature. It is easy to lose this connection, and I am mindful not to do so.

I try to remain spontaneous, open to whatever may come my way. Sticking to the same routine—day in, day out— may be comforting for some; for me adding a little fun to the mix makes life more palatable, the unexpected adding flavor to my existence.

I try not to "over plan." On the Camino, I found that even with planning, things happen. Being able to adjust to the changes makes life much easier.

The kindness of other pilgrims taught me the importance of my being kind to me. From this lesson, I learned to say no, such a simple but empowering word.

Having been accepted, while on the Camino, for who I am was liberating. I no longer feel a need to live up to the expectations of others.

I always find time for family, but, since the Camino, I spend more time with friends doing fun stuff. I fully appreciate these outings with friends. I never regret these moments, and look forward to more.

My priorities have changed. What was important before the Camino is no longer important. I am spending my energy on different things, strangely without regret or remorse.

Walking the Camino, my first long walk, is a feat I am proud of completing. But really, this end is just the beginning. With all these changes that happened to me as a result of this journey, I now need to figure out who I am becoming and how my life can still make a difference; perhaps figuring that out is part of my next journey.

Afterword

Thank you for purchasing and reading this book. I hope you enjoyed reading it as much as I enjoyed writing it for you. As I wrote the book, I was once again on the Camino, prolonging the experience, feeling connected to the universe, and recharging a sense of well-being and happiness. I hope reading this book encouraged you to hug old friends, make new ones, and journey into joy.

Please consider leaving feedback about the book either on the site where you purchased it, if you bought it online, or on my website WomenoftheWay2011.com. Your review makes a difference to those considering buying the book.

If you have comments or suggestions, please contact me, jane@janevblanchard.com

This is the first book in the "Woman On Her Way Series." To see other book in the series, please visit janevblanchard.com

Jane V. Blanchard

June 25, 2012

Women of the Way

Acknowledgments

Thank you, dear husband, for your vital encouragement, support, and technical expertise as I wrote this book. Most important, thank you for your company, humor, and conversations along the Way.

Áine, thank you for clarifying what was important and what to let go. I could not have asked for a more supportive daughter.

A special thanks to my editors, who helped make the book more insightful, more accurate, and more appealing. Elizabeth, I appreciate your editorial help, especially in pointing out what needed clarification and expansion. Gina, thanks for your guidance and suggestions in keeping my focus, adding more substance, and making it more interesting for the reader. Bunny, thank you for affirming the book's value. Sonia, thank you for taking meticulous notes as you read the book, and then making the effort to contact me with comments and suggestions. Liz, I am most grateful for your attention to detail and high professional standards.

Lastly, thanks to all my family and friends for their moral support.

Women of the Way

Appendix

Appendix A: The Women

Appendix B: Spanish Terms Used in this Book.

Spanish	English
Albergue	Hostel
Alegria	Joy
Bomberos	Firefighters
Buen Camino	Have a good Camino
Caixa Electronica	ATM
Comedor	Dining rooms
Contrasena	Password
Credencial del Peregrino	Pilgrim Passport
Donativos	Hostels that run on donations
Etapas	Stages
Hospitalero, Hospitalera	Volunteers working in the *albergues*
Hospitals	Hostels
Paseo	Stroll
Pensiones	Guest rooms
Peregrino, Peregrina	Pilgrim, a hiker on the Camino
Panadería	Bakery
Postres	Desserts
Propina	Tip

Spanish	English
Ración/Raciones (media-ración)	A serving of food eaten in a bar or café, often shared with friends. *Raciones* are larger and more elaborate than tapas. *Media-raciones* are half servings
Refugios	Pilgrim's shelter
Sello	Stamp
Supermercado	Supermarket
Tapa	small, appetizer size portions of almost anything —olives, small sandwiches, ham and cheese, pickled vegetables, seafood, etc.
Tienda	Store
Vino tinto	Red wine

Appendix C: Handy Spanish Words

The following are words I learned on the Camino.

English	Spanish
ATM	Cajeros automáticos
Backpack	Mochila
Bakery	Panadería
Bathroom	Aseos (public toilet) Baño (with bath)
Blister	Ampolla
Bedbugs	Chinches
Boots	Botas
Border	Frontera
Breakfast	Desayuno
Coffee	Café
Contribution	Donativo
Decaf coffee	• Descaffeinado or café sin caffein (usually instant) • Descafeinado de cafetera, a decaf made in a Italian style machine
Dinner	Cena
Hiking pole	Polo or Báculo (crook)
How much does it cost?	¿Cuánto cuesta?

Ice cream	Helado
Lunch	Almuerzo
Onward	¡Ultreïa! (Galician) the traditional pilgrim greeting (instead of Buen Camino). The response is ¡Et suseïa!
Password	Contrasena
Pilgrim	Perigrino, perigina
Pilgrim stamp	Sello
Plateau	Meseta
Post office	La oficina de correos
Sandwich	Bocadillo
Shin splint	Tendinitis
Supermarket	Supermercado
Tab	La ficha
Tent	Tienda
Tip	Propina
Toilet	Aseos or Servicios

Appendix D: Regional Foods

Ordering food in another language can lead to interesting meals. Use this list of regional foods to help demystify the Spanish menu.

Spanish	English
Aguardente	An alcoholic beverage made from the distillation of the pomace of grapes
Bacalao a la riojana	Cod with tomato sauce
Bacalao al ajoarriero	Salted cod cooked with tomato and garlic
Bacalao al pil-pil	Breaded cod
Bacalao con ajo	Baked cod with garlic
Bacalao en salsa verde	Cod in green sauce
Bacalao picante	Spicy cod
Caldo Gallego	A hearty soup of potatoes, cabbage and beans. Sometimes has ham, sausage, or pork added
Chuletas de cordero a la guipuzco	Basque-style lamb chops rubbed with garlic and salt
Cochinillo asado	Roasted suckling pig
Cocido maragato	Stew composed of chickpeas, cabbage (which can be changed for any

	other vegetable), potatoes and seven different kinds of meat
Codero asado	Roast lamb
Empanada	Meat- or tuna-filled pastry
Filloas	Custard-filled crepes
Infusion	Herbal tea
La tripotcha	Beef sausage, sliced and fried flat
La zurrugutina	Basque cod
Lacón con grelos	Pork shoulder of with parsnip tops
Langostinos	King prawns
Morcilla	Spanish blood sausage
Perdices con chocolate	Partridge with chocolate
Perdices ederra	Partridge with apples and cream
Pinchos	Small snacks "spiked" with a skewer or toothpick, usually served in bars, popular in the Basque country and northern Spain
Pulpo a la gallega or in Galician "Polbo á Feira"	Boiled octopus cut into small pieces and laced with olive oil, sea salt, and paprika
Sopa de ajo	Garlic soup
Tapa	Hot or cold appetizer

	served in bars
Tarta de Santiago	A wheatless cake made from almonds
Tetilla	Galician cheese shaped like a breast
Truchas a la navarra	Trout stuffed with Serrano ham
Vieiras	Sea scallop baked with onion, parsley and breadcrumbs and served in its own shell
Zumo naranja	Orange juice

Tarta de Santiago

Women of the Way

Appendix E: Camino Books and Guides

Alcorn, Suzan *Camino Chronicle: Walking to Santiago* gives interesting historical background and cultural references that provide insights to what is involved in walking the Camino, 2006.

Blanchard, Dennis *A Few More Zeroes, Lost with the Wind and the Stars on the Camino de Santiago,* is a hilarious account of his 2011 journey, 2010.

Brierley, John *A Pilgrim's Guide to the Camino de Santiago: St. Jean * Roncesvalles * Santiago (Camino Guides)*, is one of the best guide book on the Camino, 2011.

Coelho, Paulo *The Pilgrimage, A Contemporary Quest for Ancient Wisdom*, a parable about self-discovery. 2008

Confraternity of Saint James, *Pilgrim Guides to Spain: 1 Comino Francés,* 2011.

MacLaine, Shirley *The Camino: A Journey of the Spirit*, a personal story more about the spiritual adventure than the physical one, 2000.

Michelin *Maps and Guides: Camino de Santiago* 2010.

Walker, Bill "Skywalker" *The Best Way, El Camino de Santiago*, a unique and humorous perspective of the Camino, 2011.

Women of the Way

The following books on horseback are available from the Confraternity of St. James (CSJ) Bookshop.

Confraternity of St. James *The Riding Pilgrim* London 2008.

Gallard, Babbet *Riding the Milky Way: A Journey of Discovery to Santiago.* Pilgrimage Publications 2006.

Pascual, Javier *The Way of Saint James on Horseback* Guide Madrid, 2002.

Phillips, Mefo *Horseshoes and Holy Water: On the Hoof from Canterbury to Santiago de Compostela* London, 2005.

Books on Bicycling the Camino available at the CSJ bookstop are:

Curtin, John *The Cycling Pilgrim on the Camino Francés* CSJ, London 2007.

Dedman, Greg and Nilsen Sylvia *Your Camino: on foot, bicycle or horseback in France and Spain* Lightfoot Guide, 2011.

Appendix F: Women's Hiking Clubs, Groups, and Organizations

There are many organizations and clubs to join, some of which have divisions for women hikers. The following clubs, groups, and organizations are primarily for women. This list is also available with links on WomenoftheWay2011.com/links/

Adventures for Women
Midland Park, NJ
http://www.adventuresforwomen.org/

Adventures in Good Company
http://www.adventuresingoodcompany.com/
(Provides guided tours for women with destinations around the world)

Becoming an Outdoors Woman (BOW)
Stevens Point, WI
http://www4.uwsp.edu/CNR/bow/
http://www.facebook.com/pages/Becoming-an-Outdoors-Woman/42311557536
(Provides weekend long, multi-course workshops held all across North America and in New Zealand.)

Boise Women's Hiking Network
Boise, ID
http://groups.yahoo.com/group/BoiseWHN/

Call of the Wild
http://www.callwild.com/
(Provides adventure travel for women)

Charlotte Lady Hikers
Charlotte, NC
http://www.charlotteladyhikers.com/

FLAB: Fun-Loving Advensuresome Broads
Los Angeles, CA
http://www.hikingwomen.typepad.com/

Hardass Hikers
http://www.hiking-for-her.com/index.html

Hiking in Heels
Seattle, WA
http://www.meetup.com/Hiking-in-Heels/

North Bay Wanderwomen
North Bay, CA
http://www.wanderwomen.org/

Oahu Women's Hiking Club
Oahu, HI
http://www.facebook.com/pages/Oahu-Womens-Hiking-Club/238162890071

Portland Women's Hiking/Wilderness Community
Portland, OR
http://www.meetup.com/Portland-Women-Outdoor-Group/

Roam the Woods
http://www.roamthewoods.com
https://www.facebook.com/pages/Roam-The-Woods/178757132202102

San Diego Women's Hiking Club
San Diego, CA
http://www.meetup.com/women-561/

Trail Dames
chapters in various states
http://www.traildames.com/

Trail Wanderers
Elkton, MD
http://www.meetup.com/Trailwanderers-com/

Washington Women Outdoors (WWO)
Washington, D.C.
http://www.washingtonwomenoutdoors.org/

Women Outdoors
http://womenoutdoors.org/

Women's Exercise Network
http://www.womensexercisenetwork.com/hiking/index.ht ml

Women's Outdoor Network
Atlanta, GE
http://www.wonatlanta.com/

Women of the Way

Whidbey Women's Hiking Club
Oak Harbor, WA
http://www.facebook.com/pages/Whidbey-Womens-Hiking-Club/126366419815

Wildside Adventures for Women
http://www.wildsideadventures.com/

Women Hikers
http://groups.yahoo.com/group/WomenHikers/

University Women's Club Hiking Group
Boulder, Colorado
http://boulderuwc.org/index.php/interest-groups/all-interest-groups/hiking-group/

Untamed Adventures
Jacksonville, FL
http://www.untamedadventures.org/

Endnotes

1. "According to an article published in November, 1998 in *Textile Chemist and Colorist*, an industry journal, 'repeated home launderings (regardless of whether or not the detergent contains an OBA [optical brightening agent, the compound commonly found in household detergents, mainly to 'keep whites white']) does not reduce the UPF rating of a woven or knitted fabric of cotton, polyester, or nylon. On the contrary, UPF ratings are enhanced or remain unchanged by repeated launderings up to 20 times.'" *FAQ* Sun Protection Store.Com. http://sunprotectionstore.com/?page_id=33

2. Craig, Leigh Ann. *Wandering Women and Holy Matrons, Women as Pilgrims in the Later-Middle Ages.* [Leiden, Netherlands: Brill,], 2009 p. 114.

3. Craig,Leigh Ann. (2003) "Stronger than Men and Braver than Knights: Women and the Pilgrimages to Jerusalem and Rome in the Later Middle Ages ." *Journal of Medieval History*, Vol.29 p. 166

4. "The term 'walkabout' comes from the Australian Aboriginal. The idea is that a person can get so caught up in one's work, obligations, and duties that the truly important parts of one's self become lost. From there it is a downward spiral as one gets farther and farther from one's true self. A crisis situation usually develops that awakens the wayward to the absent true self. It is at this time

that one must go on walkabout. All possessions are left behind (except for essential items) and one starts walking. Metaphorically speaking, the journey goes on until you meet yourself. Once you find yourself, you sit down and have a long talk about what one has learned, felt and done in each other's absence. One talks until there is nothing left to say -- the truly important things cannot be said. If one is lucky, after everything has been said and unsaid, one looks up and sees only one person instead of the previous two. Source Unknown." Keturah Weathers. *Going on a Walkabout!* worldrace blog. Web. November 21, 2009. http://keturahweathers.theworldrace.org/?filename=going-on-a-walkabout

5.   A pet leaving and returning to the US must comply with the same requirements as one entering for the first time. For more information, contact the Customs and Border Protection, Center for Disease Control, and the U.S. Department of Agriculture's Animal and Plant Health Inspection Service.

6.   Vipassana is a meditation practice, characteristically Buddhist. The philosophy behind it is of mindfulness and an awareness of what is. It focuses on the interconnection of body and mind.

Made in the USA
Las Vegas, NV
22 March 2022

46142657R00187